THE

# HEROINE

*with*

# 1,001
# FACES

# Also by Maria Tatar

*Enchanted Hunters: The Power of Stories in Childhood*

*Off With Their Heads! Fairy Tales and the Culture of Childhood*

*The Hard Facts of the Grimms' Fairy Tales*

*Beauty and the Beast: Classic Tales About Animal Brides and Grooms from Around the World*

*The Annotated African American Folktales,* with Henry Louis Gates Jr.

*The Annotated Brothers Grimm*

*The Grimm Reader: The Classic Tales of the Brothers Grimm*

*The Annotated Hans Christian Andersen*

*The Annotated Classic Fairy Tales*

Dante Gabriel Rossetti, *Proserpine*, 1874

THE

# HEROINE

*with*

# 1,001
# FACES

## MARIA TATAR

LIVERIGHT PUBLISHING CORPORATION

A Division of W. W. Norton & Company

*Independent Publishers Since 1923*

For information about permission to reproduce selections from this book,
write to Permissions, Liveright Publishing Corporation, a division of
W. W. Norton & Company, Inc., 500 Fifth Avenue, New York, NY 10110

For information about special discounts for bulk purchases, please contact
W. W. Norton Special Sales at specialsales@wwnorton.com or 800-233-4830

Manufacturing by Lake Book Manufacturing
Book design by Marysarah Quinn
Production manager: Lauren Abbate

ISBN 978-1-63149-881-7

Liveright Publishing Corporation, 500 Fifth Avenue, New York, N.Y. 10110
www.wwnorton.com

W. W. Norton & Company Ltd., 15 Carlisle Street, London W1D 3BS

1  2  3  4  5  6  7  8  9  0

For some of the 1,001 heroes
and heroines in my life—

Elizabeth Demeter Tatar
Joseph Tatar
Julius Martinez
Nick Tatar
Liza Tatar
Laura T. Courtney
Rebecca Tatar
Steven Tatar
Lauren Blum
Daniel Schuker
Jason Blum
Giselle Barcia
Roxy Blum
Booker T. Blum
Isabel Barcia-Schuker
Bette Sue Blum
Lucas Adrian Barcia-Schuker
Anna, John, and Steve

*Unhappy the land that is in need of heroes.*

BERTOLT BRECHT, *Life of Galileo*

*Pity the land that thinks it needs a hero, or doesn't know it has lots and what they look like.*

REBECCA SOLNIT, *Whose Story Is This?*

*But the effect of her being on those around her was incalculably diffusive: for the growing good of the world is partly dependent on unhistoric acts; and that things are not so ill with you and me as they might have been, is half owing to the number who lived faithfully a hidden life, and rest in unvisited tombs.*

GEORGE ELIOT, *Middlemarch*

# CONTENTS

# INTRODUCTION

*Begin this journey with caring and patience*
*and love and laughter and passionate curiosity.*

—*Madam Secretary*

*Power is actualized . . . where words are not*
*empty and deeds not brutal, where words are not*
*used to veil intentions but to disclose realities, and*
*deeds are not used to violate and destroy but to*
*establish relations and create new realities.*

—HANNAH ARENDT, *The Human Condition*

JOSEPH CAMPBELL wrote *The Hero with a Thousand Faces* while teaching at Sarah Lawrence College in New York. His classes on comparative mythology at the then all-women's school were in such high demand that he was soon obliged to limit enrollment to seniors. During his last year of teaching there, one of those seniors walked into his office, sat down, and said: "Well, Mr. Campbell, you've been talking about the hero. But what about the women?" The startled professor raised his eyebrows and replied, "The woman's the mother of the hero; she's the goal of the hero's achieving; she's the protectress of the hero; she is this, she is that. What more do you want?" "I want to be the hero," she announced.[1]

"What about the women?" This book tries to answer the question posed by Campbell's student in a different way, by showing that the women in the mythological and literary imagination have been more than mothers and protectors. They too have been on quests, but they have also flown under the radar, performing stealth operations and quietly seeking justice, righting wrongs, repairing the fraying edges of the social fabric, or simply struggling to survive rather than returning back home with what Campbell calls boons and elixirs. They wear curiosity as a badge of honor rather than a mark of shame, and we shall see how women's connection to knowledge, linked to sin and transgression and often censured as prying, is in fact often symptomatic of empathy, care, and concern. Ever since Eve and Pandora, our culture has positioned curious women as wayward curiosities, investing their desire to know more with dark, forbidden cravings.

Even before Bill Moyers introduced Joseph Campbell to a broader public through the PBS series *Joseph Campbell and the Power of Myth* in 1988, catapulting the professor to celebrity status, *The Hero with a Thousand Faces* was making the rounds in Hollywood and soon became required reading among studio executives. They did not have to work their way through the entire hefty volume with its excursions into sacred writings from East and West. Instead they could refer to a conveniently abbreviated version of the book: a seven-page memo, widely distributed as "A Practical Guide to *The Hero with a Thousand Faces.*" Drafted by Christopher Vogler, who went on to teach Campbell's work at film schools and to publish the bestselling *The Writer's Journey: Mythic Structure for Writers* (1992), the practical guide became an important cheat sheet for those in the film industry. Here at last was the secret sauce that had led to the blockbuster success of films ranging from *Spartacus* to *Star Wars*. Joseph Campbell became not just an erudite guide to the mythological universe, but also a serious adviser to the managers of the Hollywood Dream Factory. Never mind that he had also become, through the display of avuncular charm and broad learning, the guru to whom Americans looked for personal and spiritual growth.

Campbell was never more than mildly irritated by the fact that the academic world failed to take his writings seriously. In my many years on the faculty of the Program in Folklore and Mythology at Harvard University, I never saw Campbell's name on a syllabus. It was clear that Campbell was persona non grata, not just because "Follow your bliss"

Joseph Campbell
*Courtesy of Photofest*

seemed corny and banal, a remnant of 1970s hippie culture with its faith in flower power, but because the Jungian philosophy and study of archetypes to which Campbell subscribed had long been derided and dismissed. Gone were the timeless universals, and the academic world scrapped eternal truths in favor of cultural constructs and post-structural indeterminacy.

Nowhere does the rigidity of archetypal thinking emerge more clearly than in the binary model of the male and female principle as it surfaced in Campbell's study of world mythologies. The biological function of women is "to bring forth life and nourishment," Campbell intoned in one work after another. What do women represent in mythology? The answer is simple: the "nature principle," for "we are born from her physically." The male, on the other hand, represents "the social principle and social roles," we are told in Campbell's meditation on goddesses. "The father is the initiator into society and the meaning of life, whereas the mother represents the principle of life itself." In other words, anatomy is destiny. But all the talk about women as the source of life and nourishment is quickly taken back, for Woman is also the "mother of death" and the "night sleep" to which we return.[2]

Reading about Campbell's goddesses and women was revelatory, for lurking beneath their fruitful beneficence was nothing more than the face of death. Suddenly, in the dark nights of a global pandemic, I understood the rage of one of my undergraduate students, who described her journey into the world of folklore and mythology as a crusade against Campbell, for whom the role of women in every culture was grounded in cults of fertility and death. At the time of the student's outburst, it had seemed to me that Campbell was doing little more than capturing the symbolic worlds of our ancestors and revealing their gendered divisions of labor rather than solidifying outworn cultural beliefs.

It was only when I noticed that Campbell considered goddesses (and women) not just as fertility deities but also as muses that I began to wonder about his reading of mythologies far and near. "She's the inspirer of poetry," Campbell observed about women. This muse has three functions: "one, to give us life; two, to be the one who receives us in death; and three, to inspire our spiritual, poetic realization."[3] *Our*: when I read that word, I knew exactly what was meant by it. Self-actualization through language is reserved for men. Women, like the muses of Homer, Dante, and Yeats, were there to do little but inspire. Why could women not raise their voices as well or share the creative impulse so revered by Campbell? These concerns about Campbell's messaging coincided with my reading of "The Laugh of the Medusa," an essay by the French critic Hélène Cixous about how women must begin to free themselves from the trap of silence and resist accepting a place at the margins, or "in the harem," as she put it. Writing, and creativity in general, had been the domain of "great men" and would stay there until women stormed the arena, using words as their weapons.[4]

Madeline Miller is one of many contemporary authors who responded belatedly to Cixous's manifesto and to the call of other women writers, not just by writing, but also by endowing women from times past with voices. In *Circe*, a novel narrated by the Greek enchantress who famously turned men into swine, we hear the voice of the goddess and listen to her side of a familiar story, discovering that she had good reason to resort to magic.[5] We also learn about how Circe processes the tales told to her by Odysseus—vivid first-person accounts of what Homer had described in *The Odyssey*. Something strange happens when she retells those stories to her son Telegonus: "Their brutalities shone through," and "what I had thought of as adventure now seemed blood-soaked and ugly."[6] Even Odysseus is transformed in her accounts of his adventures, turning from a man of courage and cunning into someone "callous" and less than admirable. Suddenly we are given a different perspective, and we discover that stories operate with kaleidoscopic dynamism, changing dramatically when given one small twist. What we will see in the pages that follow is that, when women begin to write, the story changes.

In this volume, I will look at how stories, particularly those set in times of war, conflict, crisis, and suffering, shift in meaning over time, depending on who tells them. And I will also look at new narratives that have emerged over the past centuries, listening first to the voices of the old wives who told nursery tales, then to what Nathaniel Hawthorne called "the damned mob of scribbling women" and what V. S. Naipaul more recently referred to as "feminine tosh."[7] Once women took up the pen, how did they redefine the archetypes Joseph Campbell identified in world mythology? How did they reinvent heroism and what new forms of heroism emerged as they sat at their desks and scribbled?

There is a clear arc that takes us from the #MeToo movement back to ancient times and even to the old wives' tales that we now dismiss as fairy tales. What did Philomela do after being brutally raped and having her tongue cut out but weave a tapestry revealing the crimes of her brother-in-law, Tereus? Arachne bravely worked the sexual assaults of

Zeus and other gods into the tapestry she wove in competition with Athena. And in the old wives' tales from times past, women in witness stories—the British "Mr. Fox," the Armenian "Nourie Hadig," and the German "The Robber Bridegroom" come to mind—rescue themselves by exposing, often at a wedding feast, misdeeds and injuries. They escape domestic abuse and violence through storytelling. Rarely wielding the sword and often deprived of the pen, women have relied on the domestic crafts and their verbal analogues—spinning tales, weaving plots, and telling yarns—to make things right, not just getting even but also securing social justice.

Nearly two decades ago, Clarissa Pinkola Estés encouraged readers of *Women Who Run with the Wolves: Myths and Stories of the Wild Woman Archetype* to embrace the archetype in her subtitle and discover the hidden depths of the female soul.[8] This study, too, explores a range of heroic possibilities, but it is less invested in finding therapeutic tools in lore from times past than in understanding how those who were socially marginalized, economically exploited, and sexually subjugated found ways not just to survive but also to endow their lives with meaning.

Today we are reframing many stories and histories from times past, recognizing that women were also able to carry out superhuman deeds, often without ever leaving (or being able to leave) the house. Their quests may not have taken the form of journeys, but they required acts of courage and defiance. Like Penelope in *The Odyssey* or Scheherazade in *The Thousand and One Nights*, they used their homespun storytelling craft or drew on arts related to textile production to mend things, offer instructions, and broadcast offenses, all in the service of changing the culture in which they lived. They are rising up now to take their places in a new pantheon that is reshaping our notion of what constitutes heroism. It requires not just intelligence and courage, but also care and compassion: all the things it takes to be a true heroine.

We live in what the evolutionary psychologist Steven Pinker has called an age of empathy, with dozens of books on why empathy matters, on the neuroscience of empathy, on the empathy gap, and so on. Search Amazon's website and you will discover hundreds of books—among them psychological studies, self-help guides, and parenting manuals—with "empathy" in their titles or subtitles. Curiously, "empathy" was not part of our shared lexicon until the early twentieth century, and the frequency of its usage did not spike until the first two decades of the twenty-first century, when it turned into one of our most cherished cultural values. The sharp rise in the use of the word coincides, not surprisingly, with the rapid entry of women into the labor force over the past decades, and some psychologists, most notably the British Simon Baron-Cohen, tell us that empathy is tuned especially high in women's brains, while hyper-systemizing, the trait that drives invention, is more likely to be found in the male brain. But Baron-Cohen concedes (condescendingly, perhaps) that "empathy itself is the *most valuable resource* in our world," and he worries that empathy is "rarely, if ever" on the agenda in education, politics, business, or the courts. Since 2011, the date when Baron-Cohen published *The Science of Evil: On Empathy and the Origins of Cruelty*, empathy has become something of a national obsession, figuring importantly in all the domains enumerated.

Barack Obama famously taught us about a major failing in our social world, and what is it but an "empathy deficit"? Economist Jeremy Rifkin urged us, in a book called *The Empathic Civilization*, to make the leap to "global empathetic consciousness." In a book called *Far from the Tree*, psychologist Andrew Solomon wrote about children who are dramatically different from their parents and about how they manage during times marked by a "crisis of empathy." To be sure, there has been some pushback. In a psychological study with the provocative title *Against Empathy*, Paul Bloom validates "cognitive empathy" (by which he means the ability to understand the pain of others) even as he worries about "emotional empathy," an instinct that spotlights one injury at the expense of many and often leads us to focus on those who are like us.

"I do not ask the wounded person how he feels. I myself become the wounded person," Walt Whitman famously wrote in *Leaves of Grass*. Pondering those words leads us to wonder if there is not something inherently problematic at the root of "emotional empathy," or what I prefer to call empathetic identification. What will emerge in the pages that follow is an understanding of heroism that is driven less by empathy than by attentive care, an affect that is triggered by openness to the world, followed by curiosity and concern about those who inhabit it. Lack of curiosity becomes, then, the greatest sin, a failure to acknowledge the presence of others and to care about the circumstances and conditions of their lives. Is it possible that our new attentiveness to the value of empathy has been fueled by the heroism of women from times past, women who had themselves been marginalized and disenfranchised but still cared deeply about those who had been crushed and enslaved, beaten down and brought to heel?

How do we define heroes today and why are heroines in such short supply? The first chapter of this work will explore the association of heroic figures with military conflict and action and interrogate our cultural understanding of what it means to be a hero. Heroes are often warriors, but they can also be saints and saviors, men who draw on reserves of spiritual strength to defeat monsters.[9] Joseph Campbell observed that women had "too damn much to do" to waste their time on story (an extraordinary statement from someone with the deepest reverence for the culture-building power of storytelling). He acknowledged the existence of "female heroes" and a "different perspective" in fairy tales, the old wives' tales that circulated in times past. Those tales featured intrepid women who rose to countless challenges. But during the great migration of fairy tales from the fireside to the nursery, they were for the most part lost, in large part because they took up taboo subjects about family dynamics, courtship rituals, and marriage customs. When those tales vanished from the repertoire, many models of heroic behavior went missing.

Few will doubt that the hero with a thousand faces has dominated the Western imagination, and my first chapter will explore Campbell's work and its implications for reading epics like *The Odyssey*. Women may appear in the triumphant stories of a hero's deeds and accomplishments, but all too often they are strangely invisible, lacking agency, voices, and a presence in public life. We see Odysseus in action, revel in his victories, feel his sorrow, and rejoice when he finds his way back home. Penelope, by contrast, like her many cousins in epic and myth, is confined to the domestic arena, with little to say for herself. But she too, like her mythical cousins, is on a mission, and today we are finally paying attention to more than just her patience and fidelity.

Chapter 2 will explore tales of "abduction," beginning with Persephone and Europa, and will consider how weavers like Philomela and Arachne become artisans and artists on a social mission. It will also investigate mutilation—the cutting out of tongues—and examine how that form of torture was used in fiction and in real life to silence women, to make examples of them, and to deprive them of the one weapon they possessed. A related set of stories, tales about the Persian Stone of Patience, is revealing in its emphasis on the value of testimony, of telling your story (sometimes in the form of complaints against backstabbing rivals) even when your interlocutor is nothing but an inanimate object. That Stone, which can be found in fairy tales from many cultures, becomes a patient listener, so moved by an account of abuse that, unable to burst into tears, it explodes in an act of empathetic identification.

Over the centuries, fairy tale and myth have shown remarkable resilience, surviving censorship, expulsion, bans, and myriad forms of colonization to enter a cultural archive that is constantly renewed and reinvigorated even as it preserves stories from the past. Chapter 3 will explore how fairy tales, associated with women's speech—chitchat, gossip, and rumor—were discredited even as the mythology of the Greeks and Romans was enshrined as "sacred" and seen as the repository of timeless and universal truths. Rebecca Solnit reminds us of the stakes in disparaging fairy tales. What we have done, as a culture, is enshrine stories about heroes and power (which often translates into the power to injure) and dismiss stories about ordeals that require resilience, persistence, and the forging of alliances. "Underneath all the trappings of talking animals and magical objects and fairy godmothers," Solnit writes, "are tough stories about people who are marginal, neglected, impoverished, undervalued, and isolated, and their struggle to find their place and their people."[10] Stories that come to us through oral traditions reveal how silenced women carried out impossible tasks or recruited helpers as they climbed glass mountains, sorted piles of grain, or turned straw into gold. What strategies did women use to talk back, create solidarity, survive, and triumph? A look at some of the fairy tales that did not make it into the contemporary canon will be revealing. As always, it is paradoxically the iconoclasts who preserve our cultural stories, destroying them yet also reinventing them for the next generation. The chapter concludes by considering how Anne Sexton, Angela Carter, Margaret Atwood, and Toni Morrison reclaimed the fairy-tale canon, demystifying, demythifying, and repurposing the stories in it.

The history of the English word "curiosity" is full of surprises, with unexpected shifts in meaning over the centuries. Curiosity has attached itself to a certain type of female character (not necessarily a heroine in the traditional sense of the term). Chapter 4 will explore the multiple meanings of curiosity, especially since they bifurcate into two channels, the one, now obsolete, signifying "bestowing care or pains," the other, as used today, defined as "desirous of seeing or knowing; eager to learn; inquisitive." Women's curiosity and the spirit of passionate inquiry found shelter at many sites, but with two that are deeply symptomatic of gender trouble. First there was the novel of adultery (usually written by men), for infidelity was one of the few forms of freedom available to women in earlier centuries. Second, there was the genre invented by Louisa May Alcott, which showed girls—and girls alone—as bold, daring, and adventurous, at least in their imaginative worlds, if not always in real life.

All the desires, passions, and appetites that turn grown women into monsters can safely be experienced and expressed in childhood. The protective cloak of childhood innocence enabled women to self-actualize by writing about girls and also to develop forms of care and concern through their writing. Louisa May Alcott's Jo March set the stage for a host of other aspiring artists and writers, a cast of characters stretching from Anne of Green Gables all the way to Carrie Bradshaw in HBO's *Sex and the City* and Hannah Horvath in HBO's *Girls*. The cult of the girl as author leads almost directly from *Little Women* through fiction for girls to screen fantasies about writing as professional work.

Chapter 5 moves from curious writers to girl detectives and sleuthing spinsters to show how these figures, driven by investigative energy, also become agents of social justice, taking on all the allegorical qualities of Nemesis. Carolyn Keene's Nancy Drew, driving her blue roadster; Agatha Christie's Miss Marple, knitting in her rocking chair. These seem to be the two dominant types of the female detective, one brash, eager, well funded, and attractive, the other marginalized, isolated, superfluous, and almost invisible. A look at William Moulton Marston's Wonder Woman will show how—Praise Aphrodite!—women are forever to double duty bound, managing to survive assaults on their identity as women yet also protecting the innocent from evil.

A final chapter takes us to Hollywood to see how films today recycle mythical tropes and stories of heroism from times past. Are we watching nothing but nostalgic re-creations of the old (Disney's *Snow White and the Seven Dwarfs* and *Cinderella*) or are critical adaptations (David Slade's *Hard Candy* and Joe Wright's *Hanna*, to cite just two examples) part of the new cinematic calculus? Hollywood has worked hard to invent a new heroine, a female version of the mythical trickster. She is carrying out her own surreptitious operations, functioning in furtive ways as an antisocial hacker or a crazed undercover operative, and covering her tracks to ensure that her powers remain undetected. From Lisbeth Salander in *The Girl with the Dragon Tattoo* to Mildred Hayes in *Three Billboards outside Ebbing, Missouri*, these female tricksters do more than flex muscles and outmaneuver the authorities. They also function as part of an extrajudicial system designed to counteract and repair the flaws in the legal system. They form a sharp contrast to the threatening new Eves and duplicitous schemers featured in cinematic culture today, with films like Alex Garland's *Ex Machina* and Jordan Peele's *Get Out*. As heroines emerge with new faces and features, and as they begin to put themselves on display, they inevitably provoke a backlash in the form of antiheroines, specters that haunt us and become a palpable and present feature of the cultural landscape, reminding us that fashioning new heroines is always shadowed by the project of inventing new villains.

IT HAS BECOME something of a commonplace for authors to claim that they have been writing a book all their life. This volume is one that takes stock of a reading experience spanning many decades, from the 1950s to the present. It took a global pandemic, a vow to limit streaming to one hour a day, and the folly of the so-called golden years to summon the courage to take up a subject that required me to reinstate the voraciousness with which I read as a child. The project began as a reckoning with what disturbed me when I started reading my first chapter books (Anne Frank's *The Diary of a Young Girl* and Charlotte Brontë's *Jane Eyre*), unsettled me as a teenager (William March's *The Bad Seed* and William Golding's *Lord of the Flies*), rattled me as a student (Nathaniel Hawthorne's *The Scarlet Letter* and Erich Maria Remarque's *All Quiet on the Western Front*), and inspired me in my years of teaching at Harvard University (too much there to tally).

I started teaching in the 1970s, a time when, as Campbell himself conceded, women were moving into arenas once dominated almost completely by men and for which there are "no female mythological models."[11] "Unsex me here!"—that's what Campbell believed to be the rallying cry of many a new combatant in the "masculine jungle," something that was, to my mind, nothing more than a repulsive projection uttered in a fraught era of social change. Still, I was observant of how, at faculty meetings, my colleagues spoke about "the best man for the job" and how, for years, invitations to Harvard's faculty meetings, coming straight from the President's Office, began with the words "Dear Sir." It was then that I began to pay attention, not just to women authors, but to how women were represented in the texts I was teaching. And my students kept after me, year after year, urging me to think more and think harder about gender, whether reading Henry James's "The Turn of the Screw," watching Fritz Lang's film *Metropolis*, or turning the pages of Vladimir Nabokov's *Lolita*.

As graduate students studying literature at Princeton University, we were all aware that the wife of a faculty member had a study space near the seminar room where our classes were held. She was working on a book about women writers, and her name was Elaine Showalter. How odd, we all thought, and wondered whether she was a real academic or just a "faculty wife" (that was the common designation in those days for the spouses of our all-male professors). She was, after all, working on a topic that was not of any real interest to the rest of us, knee deep as we were in Nietzsche, Tolstoy, and Kafka. We read *The Genealogy of Morals* without considering how our own perspectives were limited and biased, pondered *Anna Karenina* without worrying about women and suicide, and entered the labyrinth of *The Metamorphosis* without noticing the odd way in which women were marginalized yet also symbolically central.

My most vivid memory of graduate school, however, remains my dissertation defense, that final sprint in a four-year marathon to the PhD. Some time ago, the actress Natalie Portman described just how much she had taken for granted in interactions with powerful men in Hollywood. "I went from thinking I don't have a story to thinking, 'Oh wait, I have a hundred stories.'"[12] And she began rattling off incidents, not so much of sexual assault but of predatory behaviors. Her words led me to realize that we all had stockpiles of stories, stories that had not, at the time they happened, cried out to be told. Like many others, I silenced myself.

When my dissertation defense was delayed by an hour while faculty members conferred in our seminar room, I began to get nervous, but not excessively so. Still I grew increasingly wary during the defense, sensing that something was not quite right. Only after the event, when my adviser, Theodore Ziolkowski, forever a hero in my book, asked to meet with me after the dissertation had been provisionally accepted did I learn about the determined efforts of a faculty member in the department to block my degree. A year earlier, I had fled his office when he tried to cor-

ner me, and I can still hear him declaring his passion for red-headed eastern European women as I grabbed the handle of his office door, relieved
to discover that it was not locked.

I cite these two incidents—disregarding the work done by a woman
and suppressing a story of predatory behavior—because they might have
ended differently had I fully understood the value of curiosity and care
as well as the importance of speaking up and telling your story. That is
the takeaway of this book. There I was, sharing research space with a
woman who was working on a dissertation that would become *A Literature of Their Own: British Women Novelists from Brontë to Lessing* (1977).
Elaine Showalter's book would go on to transform the field of literary
studies by opening up an entirely new line of inquiry, but her work, not
to mention her persona, was marginalized back then in ways that mystify
me now. Why didn't I take more interest in her work and her presence?
And, then too, why did I not have the words to talk about what had happened to me in the professor's office? When my dissertation adviser asked
whether there was some history between the faculty member and me,
all I could blurt out was: "Wouldn't it be unethical and unprofessional
to talk about personal relationships?" Unethical? Unprofessional? Why
did I find it impossible to speak up and tell the story of the embarrassing
encounter ("traumatic" was not part of our vocabulary in those days) in
his office? As an immigrant to the United States and the recipient of a
scholarship from an institution I revered, the thought of challenging and
standing up to authority was unthinkable.

*The Heroine with 1,001 Faces* is a deeply personal look at a lifetime of
reading, misreading, and rereading myths, epics, fairy tales, fiction, and
film. At a time when we are moving beyond gendered divisions of heroism, our past continues to weigh on us, haunt us, and invite us to reflect
on the evolution of values embedded in the stories we tell, write, and reenvision. What has it taken to be a hero or a heroine, and what does it take
to make one today? This volume may not be exactly the right resource
for that student of Joseph Campbell's who insisted that she wanted to be
the heroine, but my hope is that it will serve as a point of orientation and

mark the beginning of journeys toward self-understanding and empowerment through the stories that we tell and that our ancestors once told.

At times, I felt as if I was flying blind over territory that I had thought to be utterly familiar. Didn't I practically know *The Odyssey* by heart, after reading it in high school, in college classes, during graduate school, and with my children? And didn't I understand exactly what was at stake in fairy tales after teaching them for decades? Hadn't I fallen asleep as a child with *The Diary of a Young Girl* under my pillow, revered Thomas Mann and James Joyce as a college student, overdosed on Proust and Camus in graduate school, and reveled in the pleasures of teaching great books to my students? Familiarity never bred contempt, but it closed my eyes to much that became self-evident when I started tracking women with the hero's journey in mind. My hope is that *The Heroine with 1,001 Faces* will reveal the value of remaining open and curious about who inhabits our world and also standing up and using our voices even when those who came before us were silenced. With women now better represented in the workplace—as doctors, pilots, firefighters, preachers, and judges—it is almost impossible to mourn the world we have lost. Women now provide models (imaginary and real) in abundance, changing the myths we live by, and remaking the human world in ways that promise to make the world more humane.

CHAPTER 1

# "SING, O MUSE"

## The Hero's Journey and
## the Heroine's Mission

*I do not want to alter one hierarchy in order to institute
another. . . . More interesting is what makes intellectual
domination possible; how knowledge is transformed
from invasion and conquest to revelation and choice.*

—TONI MORRISON, *Playing in the Dark*

*There are no heroes of action, only heroes
of renunciation and suffering.*

—ALBERT SCHWEITZER,
*Out of My Life and Thought*

THE CONCEPT of a heroine with a thousand and one faces risks sounding less like an answer to Joseph Campbell's *Hero with a Thousand Faces* (1949) than an effort to do him one better. But the thousand and one heroines of this volume are, in their various guises, not at all in competition with Campbell's thousand heroes. The Arabic 1,001 designates a vast measure, and the final digit of "one" in that number goes beyond a thousand to suggest a swerve into something without limits. The number in my title is meant to capture the boundless possibilities as well as the bravura magnitude of heroic behavior.

In many ways, heroes and heroines gleefully resist definition and classification, and it has not been easy to avoid falling into the trap of reducing heroines to a model that does little more than mimic Campbell's archetype with its twelve stages of the hero's journey. Both critiques and sequels run the risk of repeating and reinforcing the models they seek to challenge. But as Campbell emphasizes, heroes are forever surprising us with their spirited unpredictability and unnerving defiance of rules, norms, and regulations. Never mind the actual grotesqueries of heroic behavior. The Winnebago figure Wakdjunkaga eats his own intestines; the Greek warrior Achilles defiles Hector's corpse by dragging it around the city of Troy; the Irish Cú Chulainn is subject to seizures that turn him into a vicious monster.

Some heroes may act like thugs, but that does not keep them from becoming our cultural role models, and we continue to revere them by emphasizing their courage, valor, and wisdom. They return from battle, as well as from solitary quests, covered with "glory." They keep us in thrall, when we are young and as we age. We continue to hold them in awe, celebrating their "journeys" and "quests," as Campbell puts it, and overlooking their flaws, tragic and comic.

Joseph Campbell set out to tell one "marvelously constant" story about heroes. To his credit, he cast a wide net, exploring many corners of our symbolic universes, from Native American lore to Greek myths, and boldly venturing into religious traditions from both East and West. His manifest goal was to identify the distinguishing features of the hero archetype and to chart the stations of a journey that takes the hero from what is often a humble abode across a threshold into adventures writ large, followed by a triumphant return home with a healing elixir. Campbell's confidence about what it takes to be a hero is daunting, matched only by his conviction that women have no place in his pantheon of heroes.

In the grammar of mythology, Campbell argued, women represent "the totality of what can be known." He correctly intuited that the mythical imagination links women with knowledge, often in insidious ways. The hero, he added, somewhat craftily and cryptically, is "the one who comes to know." In other words, women never need to leave the house. They are "paragons of beauty" and "the reply to all desire." As "mother, sister, mistress, bride," they are the "bliss-bestowing goal" of the hero's quest. And to drive home the point that women are at their best when lifeless and inert, Campbell enshrined Sleeping Beauty as the fairest of them all. She is the "incarnation of the promise of perfection."[1]

Why does Campbell introduce *The Hero with a Thousand Faces* with a fairy tale, with a story about a rebel princess? An analysis of "The Frog King," the first entry in the Grimms' *Children's Stories and Household Tales* (1812), takes up a good part of Campbell's first chapter. The title of that chapter? "Departure," and it is there to signify the first steps in the hero's adventure. Campbell retells the Grimms' story about a princess who loses her golden ball in the deep waters of a well and then makes a grudging

Mrs. Percy Dearmer, *The Frog Princess*, 1897

bargain with a frog, who is willing to retrieve her plaything in exchange for a set of demands that turn on providing him with companionship. One small blunder—failing to catch a ball after tossing it in the air—and an entire universe opens up, bringing with it the illuminating power of adventure, transformation, and redemption. In this case, both lowly frog and high-born princess are implicated in the golden myth of rebirth.

If the hero's journey maps a quest narrative, marked by a fearless adventurer who goes out into the world, the heroine's mission is something very different. In the case of "The Frog King," the amphibian is transformed (and it is his journey that interests Campbell), but the princess (who never leaves home) dashes the erotically ambitious frog against the wall, and, splat! he turns into a prince. Suddenly we see that the behavior of girls is spring-loaded with unexpected forms of insubordination and opposition. But that detail is of no interest to Campbell. Instead he draws attention to the contrast between fairy-tale girls, who can aspire to little more than crossing the threshold between childhood and adult life, and real heroes, who battle their way to glory and some kind of transcendent meaning. As for me, I needed to know more about the princess's act of defiance and its liberating effect. That was also the part of the story that my students fretted about. What? No redemptive kiss? That was not how they had heard the story.

Campbell concedes that there are in fact some heroines who undertake quests and carry out difficult tasks, and he cites the case of Psyche, only to dismiss her story as one in which the "principal roles are reversed." For him, the tale is an anomaly. But the second-century Latin prose narrative of "Cupid and Psyche," written down by Apuleius of Madauros (modern-day M'Daourouch, in Algeria), reveals that a woman on a quest is driven in ways that radically diverge from what motivates heroes on their journeys. Psyche displays all the traits that define the heroic behavior of mythical women: curiosity, care, and determination. On a mission to rescue Cupid after curiosity about the creature who climbs into bed with her under the cover of night gets the better of her—rumor has it that he is a monster—she carries out a series of impossible tasks. Psyche sorts grains, collects wool from malicious sheep, and retrieves water from the source of the rivers Styx and Cocytus. In the end she succumbs once again to curiosity (as do Pandora, Eve, and a host of other knowledge-seeking heroines) on a mission that demonstrates a commitment to caring for others.

Campbell famously placed the hero's journey at the center of his analysis and emphasized a crusading drive that required audacity and determination, strength and mobility. If heroines possess the first two attributes in abundance, they often fall down on the job when it comes to the last two, for they are depicted as lacking the muscle and agility of heroes.

For many months, I imagined that the title of this book would be something along the lines of "The Hero's Journey and the Heroine's Ordeal." Stuck at home, enslaved, exiled, or imprisoned, heroines are handicapped in ways that point to trials rather than journeys. But there is something troubling about the gendered bifurcation of heroism into action on the one hand and suffering on the other. Were women from times past destined to suffer silently and simply endure? And what about heroes like Achilles, Theseus, or Hercules? Don't they sustain injuries and endure pain, and are their lives also not one long ordeal?

It was then that I came across the Romanian story "The Enchanted Pig," a variant of Apuleius's "Cupid and Psyche." In it and in all the variants of the story I later explored, the princess heroine makes the mistake of trying to break the magic spell that turned her husband into an animal by day. When she fails, her husband is obliged to abandon her. "We shall not meet again," he tells her, "until you have worn out three pairs of iron shoes and blunted a steel staff in your search for me."[2] The young woman walks on and on until her last pair of shoes falls apart and her staff is blunted. No wonder Kelly Link observes in a short story inspired by Hans Christian Andersen's "The Snow Queen": "Ladies, has it ever occurred to you that fairy tales aren't easy on the feet?"[3] One final act of sacrifice, and the soon-to-be princess is reunited with her husband in his human form. The worn-out iron shoes are a feature of many fairy tales and a powerful reminder that treks up glass mountains and across frozen expanses can form an important response to the challenges facing heroines. More than that, the impulse motivating the princess is an altruistic one, and, when she travels, she is on a mission, determined to find a happily-ever-after but focused more on rescuing and transforming her beloved than on simply reuniting with him.

The heroines found in the tale type folklorists call "The Search for the Lost Husband" rarely seek to extend their power. Instead they rise to challenges imposed on them by superior forces, sewing shirts with star-shaped flowers on them or cooking and cleaning for stepmothers, witches, and dwarfs. And they form alliances with creatures who become helpers: foxes and doves, fish with golden eyes, and swarms of ants and bees.

Heroines share a crusading spirit, and the goals of their missions (often marital rather than martial) pale by comparison with the shining glory bestowed on heroes. Still, the rebel and her cause are often right there, in plain sight, though not necessarily where the heroic action has traditionally been located. As I was writing this book, it only gradually dawned on me that heroines were habitually bent on social missions, trying to rescue, restore, or fix things, with words as their only weapons. Heroes, by contrast, are armed and ready for battle. They embark on quests and journeys that have as their goal more than a return home. Seeking glory in conflict, often military and martial, they chase down immortality more than anything else. And they secure enduring fame through a process that can be described, plain and simple, as self-aggrandizement and self-mythologization. No wonder that, when asked to list examples of heroes, we quickly rattle off the names of men and gods. It takes a bit longer to come up with the names of heroines.

## Words and Deeds

What is a hero? That is a question put to us again and again. It absorbs us from school days onward, when we are asked to define our cultural values and aspirations by sizing up the lives of figures from times past: shining Achilles, cunning Odysseus, brazen Anansi, or the indomitable Sun Wukong. Our collective storytelling archive—rich with histories, myths, parables, legends, and much else—provides countless examples of heroic behavior, and we turn to those well-stocked reservoirs for models of conduct. The academic world has supplied us with abundant definitions, and, as a student, I dutifully took notes on Herculean heroes, figures whose greatness had less to do with goodness than with what was referred to as "the transforming energy of the divine spark." One of those authorities on the hero described exploits that were an unnerving combination of "beneficence and crime," "fabulous quests and shameful betrayals," and "triumph over wicked enemies and insensate slaughter of the innocent."[4] I recall that the phrase about slaughtering the innocent gave me pause, but I continued taking notes.

With studied intensity, we ask ourselves that same question—what is a hero?—when we read headlines or ponder stories from the here and now about those who have acted in ways that inspire admiration, wonder, and appreciation. "New York City Firefighter Pulls Nurse from Burning Building." "Park Ranger Carries Dehydrated Hiker to Safety Down Treacherous Trail." "Man Rushes to Pull Driver from Car after Fuel Explosion." I have plucked these headlines at random from the news, but I could also just say the name "Sully," and who would not remember the pilot who saved the lives of passengers after a bird strike disabled both engines of US Airways Flight 1549? Heroes are not just role models, they are also protectors. They reassure us, with soothing authority, that the world can become less fragile, safer, and more generous because of their acts of kindness. With help from strong, fearless men, it will evolve into a better place.

Our word "hero" derives from the Greek ἥρως, and it was first printed in the English language in 1522. The *Oxford English Dictionary* (*OED*), our authoritative source on language usage, offers several definitions, the first of which reads as follows: "A man (or occasionally a woman) of superhuman strength, courage, or ability, favored by the gods." Some sixty years later, the word "heroine" makes its first appearance in a church document, and by 1609 the British playwright Ben Jonson is using the term to describe women of "a most invincible and unbroken fortitude."[5] The *OED* defines "heroine" as "a woman distinguished by the performance of courageous or noble actions; a woman generally admired or acclaimed for her great qualities or achievements." It is impossible to imagine the insertion of "or occasionally a man" in that definition.

Heroes are superhuman, while heroines are distinguished and admired. These definitions suggest that we might be wise to let go of the term "heroine" and turn "hero" into a gender-neutral term for us all. But perhaps not. As *The Heroine with 1,001 Faces* will show, there are important differences between heroes and heroines, and the features that make them commendable or laudable change over time. Heroes and heroines have deployed different strategies for earning merit—the one rousingly percussive in most cases; the other, stereotypically veiled and still, yet also quietly creative and deeply inspiring. Today we may be expanding our understanding of gender with new nonbinary, gender-fluid identities, but that fact makes it all the more important to understand the culturally scripted performances and inflexible binary codes enacted in the myths, legends, and fairy tales from times past.

In *Heroes*, originally published in 2018, the actor and writer Stephen Fry retells stories from what he calls the "Age of Heroes." By that he means ancient times. He reminds us that his subjects are "men and women who grasp their destinies, use their human qualities of courage, cunning, ambition, speed and strength to perform astonishing deeds, vanquish terrible monsters and establish great cultures and lineages that change the world."[6] (He could have added the gloss "and occasionally some women," for most of his stories feature men and male gods.) Reading through Fry's volume led me to wonder what the women were doing while the men were out slaying monsters. The relentless emphasis on conquest through brute strength threw a switch and led me to ask whether there were other forms of heroism in our myths and lore.

I want to highlight here Fry's use of the term "astonishing deeds," in part because women were for so long excluded from spheres of public action, staying at home while men went to work and to war, to the places where daring feats could be performed, with those deeds later commemorated through a collective heritage. The German-Jewish philosopher Hannah Arendt tells us that deeds in particular—fragile and ephemeral—are subject to forgetfulness, existing only at the moment of performance. Through stories, however, deeds come to be preserved in cultural memory and become sources of encouragement for future generations, examples to which we all aspire. Remembrance venerates as it preserves. For this reason the Greeks valued poetry and history, because these conferred immortality on heroes and rescued heroic deeds from oblivion.[7] After all, it was Homer who ensured that we would know the names of Achilles, Hector, and Patroclus.

Words and deeds: Arendt's linkage of language and action sets us thinking, in large part because heroes, in their redemptive vocation, are remembered for performing "astonishing deeds" far more often than they are for making great speeches. Enthralling words seem to matter less than epic deeds when it comes to heroes. Is it possible, then, that in the gendered division of heroic labor, men acquire glory and are remembered for what they *do*, and women for what they say, tell, or report? The yoking of words and deeds paradoxically calls our attention to the disconcerting bifurcation of speaking and acting when it comes to heroic behavior, with heroes all action and heroines limited often to language alone, words spoken less in public spaces than in the privacy of the home.

Who better to make the case for the sorcery of words (and how women make use of that magic) than Scheherazade, the heroine of *The Thousand and One Nights* (*Alf Laylah wa-Laylah*), a collection of folktales from many sources—Arabic, Persian, Indian, and Turkish, to name a few—collected in the Islamic Golden Age. The stories in what is sometimes called *The Arabian Nights* or *The Arabian Nights' Entertainments* were translated many centuries later into English, with the first British compilation appearing in 1706. I will have much more to say about Scheherazade later in this volume, but for now I want to parse the heroic declaration she makes to her sister Dunyazad. Scheherazade has volunteered to marry Shahriyar, a tyrant so maddened by his wife's infidelity that he murders her, along with her entire libidinous retinue. To ease his humiliation, Shahriyar crafts a plan of spectacular excess, one that requires cruelty taken to an extreme. Each day he will take a new wife, and, on every morning after, he will ritually behead her. Scheherazade has her own plan for survival. "I will begin with a story," she tells her sister confederate, "and it will cause the king to stop his practice, save myself, and deliver the people."[8] Words are her weapon, and she plans to craft narratives (it will take 1,001—in this case, not an endless number) that will enable her to escape death and transform the culture in which she lives. Shahriyar, as it turns out, takes the bait, ends his reign of violence, and the two marry, living "happily ever after" with the three sons born to them. As both creative storyteller and procreative partner, Scheherazade remakes the world and ensures the possibility of redemption, transformation, and orderly succession.

Scheherazade smuggles storytelling into the bedroom and uses narrative to win over the king. She persuades him that beheadings will not assuage his rage or sate his appetite for revenge. Women today have deployed storytelling in other ways as well, relying less on imaginative fictions that divert and instruct than on real-life accounts that are compelling in their inventory of grievances and offenses. As headlines from the past years reveal and as the #MeToo movement has shown, stories are a powerful weapon for combating forms of social injustice, righting the kinds of wrongs that Scheherazade sought to eliminate. There is no denying the power of narrative as testimony to accuse, indict, and sentence in the courtroom of public opinion, and the extrajudicial arena can operate in influential ways, inflicting punishments that can exceed what is in the penal code of a culture. Telling your story—revealing injuries

Edmund Dulac, illustration for
*The Thousand and One Nights*, 1907

inflicted and harm done—has come to be invested with unprecedented weight, and it carries with it the same sense of a social mission that drove Scheherazade to risk her neck to save the lives of other women. Women in fairy tales repeatedly made use of that strategy in denunciation narratives that can be found not just in Anglo-American and European folklore but in storytelling repertoires from around the world. These are the old wives' tales that have been dismissed and discredited as nothing but fairy tales.

When asked about the woman's hero journey and whether it was the same "as for a man," Joseph Campbell paused to reflect. "All of the great mythologies and much of the mythic storytelling of the world are from the male point of view," he acknowledged. While writing *The Hero with a Thousand Faces*, he wanted to include "female heroes," but discovered that he had to go to fairy tales to find them. "These were told by women to children, you know, and you get a different perspective."[9] In fairy tales, we have not just the perspective of women but also their voices. Women may have been silenced in the myths told and retold by bards, but they spoke up in narratives that were told by women not just to children but also to all those who made up sewing circles, congregated in spinning rooms, prepared meals at the hearth, washed clothing, and engaged in what has traditionally been known as women's work.

Fairy tales often focus on the power of words and stories. Talk can get you in trouble, but there are also times when it can get you out of a bad fix. In the British fairy tale "Mr. Fox," a woman named Lady Mary draws on the revelatory power of narrative and uses storytelling as a form of exposé. Built into the story is a tutorial about stories as instruments for securing social justice. Mr. Fox, rich and handsome, courts a young woman named Lady Mary, who decides to visit the castle where her suitor lives. With its high walls and deep moat, Mr. Fox's castle seems impenetrable, but Lady Mary, "a brave one," enters it and explores its rooms. Over one door is written: "Be bold, be bold, but not too bold / Lest that your heart's blood should run cold." Lady Mary is too bold for sure, and her heart's blood runs cold when she discovers a Bloody Chamber in the castle. "What do you think she saw? Why, bodies and skeletons of

IT IS NOT SO
NOR IT WAS NOT SO
& GOD FORBID IT SHOULD BE SO

BUT IT IS SO
& IT WAS SO
HERE'S HAND& RING I HAVE TO SHOW

John Batten, illustration for "Mr. Fox," 1890

beautiful young ladies all stained with blood." When Mr. Fox appears, dragging a young woman behind him, Lady Mary hides behind a wine cask and witnesses the chopping off of a hand with a ring on it. The hand lands in Lady Mary's lap and provides her with the evidence she needs to indict her betrothed, a man who has turned in an instant from partner into adversary.[10]

Here is how one version of the tale concludes:

Now it happened that the very next day the marriage contract of Lady Mary and Mr. Fox was to be signed, and there was a splendid breakfast before that. And when Mr. Fox was seated at table opposite Lady Mary, he looked at her. "How pale you are this morning, my dear." "Yes," said she, "I had a bad night's rest last night. I had horrible dreams." "Dreams go by contraries," said Mr. Fox; "but tell us your dream, and your sweet voice will make the time pass till the happy hour comes."

"I dreamed," said Lady Mary, "that I went yestermorn to your castle, and I found it in the woods, with high walls, and a deep moat, and over the gateway was written":

*Be bold, be bold.*

"But it is not so, nor it was not so," said Mr. Fox.

"And when I came to the doorway, over it was written":

*Be bold, be bold, but not too bold.*

"It is not so, nor it was not so," said Mr. Fox.

"And then I went upstairs, and came to a gallery, at the end of which was a door, on which was written":

*Be bold, be bold, but not too bold,*
*Lest that your heart's blood should run cold.*

"It is not so, nor it was not so," said Mr. Fox.

"And then—and then I opened the door, and the room was filled with bodies and skeletons of poor dead women, all stained with their blood."

"It is not so, nor it was not so. And God forbid it should be so," said Mr. Fox.

"I then dreamed that I rushed down the gallery, and just as I was going down the stairs I saw you, Mr. Fox, coming up to the hall door, dragging after you a poor young lady, rich and beautiful."

"It is not so, nor it was not so. And God forbid it should be so," said Mr. Fox.

"I rushed downstairs, just in time to hide myself behind a cask, when you, Mr. Fox, came in dragging the young lady by the arm. And, as you passed me, Mr. Fox, I thought I saw you try and get off her diamond ring, and when you could not, Mr. Fox, it seemed to me in my dream, that you out with your sword and hacked off the poor lady's hand to get the ring."

"It is not so, nor it was not so. And God forbid it should be so," said Mr. Fox and was going to say something else as he rose from his seat, when Lady Mary cried out:

"But it is so, and it was so. Here's hand and ring I have to show," and pulled out the lady's hand from her dress, and pointed it straight at Mr. Fox.

At once her brothers and her friends drew their swords and cut Mr. Fox into a thousand pieces.

By producing evidence, Lady Mary has what she needs to recruit her kinfolk and their friends to slay Mr. Fox. The safe space of a dream narrative, told on a festive occasion, enables her to speak, and, surrounded by sympathetic listeners, she can be assured of rescue and relief. By filtering the truth through the medium of the dream, which is ordinarily counterfactual, Lady Mary works up the courage to reveal the facts as she recounts the horrors housed in Mr. Fox's castle, then produces physical evidence, a gruesome little trophy proving that the dream is not mere fantasy but corresponds to a grim reality. This story reads almost like a playbook from times past for victims of sexual assault and marriages arranged to the wrong kind of groom. An exercise in social justice, it is also a reminder that you may need physical evidence to back up your claims.

Campbell's heroes, drawn from myth and religion, embark on adventures and return with healing elixirs. The heroines of fairy tales are more modest in their ambitions. They pursue justice without weapons in hand, telling stories to broadcast misdeeds and to bring outlaws to justice. After a closer look at Campbell's mythical heroes, I will turn to one of the foundational texts of the Western world, Homer's *Odyssey*. In it, Odysseus, the wily wanderer, and Penelope, the stay-at-home mother, reveal a good deal about the gender distortions in our understanding of heroism. The hero on a journey and the heroine on a mission. Drawing this sharp distinction, crude as it may be, is a first step in understanding the driving force behind the protagonists of tales that we have enshrined as "classic." Classic texts are the stories that have found a place in the classroom, in nationwide curricula that are foundational, designed to build cultural values.

Not many teachers have done what Philip Pullman, author of the young adult series His Dark Materials, did while employed as a teacher at Bishop Kirk Middle School in Oxford. Three times a week, the prizewinning author improvised, telling his versions of *The Iliad* and *The Odyssey*, not repeating but retelling. Most other teachers have relied on the letter rather than the spirit of the poem, taking the words on the page and using Homer's portraits of Odysseus and Penelope to educate their students and animate discussions in their classrooms. For that reason alone, how we approach Homer's epic matters, and already a chorus of voices has been raised about the unsettling sexual politics and gender dynamics in myths, epics, and stories from times past. I count my voice in that chorus, and I hope here to identify how those who were silenced, suppressed, and sidelined in those narratives still managed to find strategies for heroic actions, large and small. Writers today, as will become evident later in this chapter, have resurrected marginalized women from times past and given them voices, affirming their resourcefulness and thereby endowing them with agency. Margaret Atwood's *Penelopiad*, Natalie Haynes's *A Thousand Ships*, and Pat Barker's *Silence of the Girls* are among the volumes that give us new perspectives on *The Iliad* and *The Odyssey*, reminding us that there is always another side to a story and also revealing that silencing does not foreclose possibilities for heroic action.[11]

Toni Morrison was quick to understand that she and other writers were not just reanimating figures from the past but making something new. She insisted that she was not repeating but re-signifying, fashioning her own version of archetypes in works like *Beloved* and *Tar Baby*. Madeline Miller reimagines Circe in the 2018 novel of that title, undoing her vilification in *The Odyssey* and enabling us to understand the defensive nature of her magic. The heroine of Fran Ross's *Oreo* (1974) is the mixed-race daughter of a Black mother and a Jewish father, and she borrows tropes from the culture in which she lives to cross racial boundaries while on a quest that closely resembles Theseus's journey into the Labyrinth. These authors enable us to see that the possibilities for heroic words and deeds are limitless, and heroines, like heroes, have features that are infinitely supple and endlessly malleable. But let us first look at heroes to understand just how Joseph Campbell identified the enduring features in their thousand faces.

## The Hero with a Thousand Faces

Occupying a liminal space between men and gods, the heroes of ancient times were often associated with military valor or Herculean feats of strength. When Joseph Campbell set out to develop an understanding of the hero archetype, he discovered a drama that unfolded in a series of combative encounters, with conflicts and ordeals that required stunning high-wire acts ending in a triumphant victory and return home. The consuming idea of Campbell's analysis turns on men of action and the redemptive journeys they take to secure some form of salvation for us all.

Born in 1904 in New York City, Joseph Campbell studied at Dartmouth College and Columbia University, earning a degree in English literature in 1925. After postgraduate work in Romance languages and in Sanskrit studies at universities in Paris and Munich, Campbell withdrew from the PhD program at Columbia and spent five years living in what he described as a low-rent shack in upstate New York, reading nine hours a day and contemplating his future. In 1934 he accepted a position at Sarah Lawrence College, at that time a college for women, and taught well-attended courses on literature and myth there for thirty-eight years.

Campbell sat out the war years at Sarah Lawrence. Turned a cynic by England's history of colonial conquest and the United States' deplorable treatment of Native Americans, even Hitler and his invading armies could not, at first, move Campbell from a position of pacifism. He considered registering as a conscientious objector, but, after reading in the Bhagavad Gita about Arjuna's duty to fight, Campbell decided that, if drafted, he would fight as Arjuna had fought. When the Selective Service announced that it would be drafting only men under the age of thirty-eight, Campbell breathed a huge sigh of relief, for he had no interest in joining the ranks of what he called "shouting warriors," the men who had attached themselves to "the Anglo-Saxon empire of machines and opportunistic lies."

It is hard to imagine that Campbell's 1949 study of the hero was not informed, at least in some subliminal way, by the bravery of American GIs, many of whom returned home triumphant from the ordeals of military combat and were celebrated as war heroes. To be sure, the war years also witnessed Campbell's rising interest in South Asian religions and East Asian myths, with their exercises in self-abnegation. And Campbell had declared himself to be not in the camp of warriors and merchants but in a "third camp," the one inhabited by people writing books, painting pictures, and playing musical instruments. It was their duty, and his of course too, to "discover and represent without compromise the ideals of Truth, Goodness, and Beauty."[12] Still, GI Joe was surely a consideration, if not a vaunted heroic ideal, as Campbell wrestled with a project that chronicled colossal ordeals, bloody conflicts, hard-won conquest, and triumphant returns home.

Campbell's book captured the imagination of twentieth-century writers, artists, and filmmakers not long after its publication. Its popular appeal was amplified through Bill Moyers's conversations with the mythographer and storyteller in *The Power of Myth*, a series of interviews filmed at George Lucas's Skywalker Ranch in 1988. Described as "one of the most popular series in the history of public television," it continues to draw audiences today.[13] Like many other filmmakers, the creator of the *Star Wars* film franchise had found in Campbell's work a blueprint for mythmaking. In radically inventive ways, Lucas drew on the classical motifs of the mythic journey but made them new to create the narrative wizardry of the original *Star Wars* trilogy. "If it hadn't been for [Campbell]," he once said, "it's possible I would still be trying to write 'Star Wars' today."[14]

In some intuitive fashion, Campbell understood that all the heroic figures—Jesus, Buddha, Moses, Krishna, Jason, David, Perseus, King Arthur—who populate his many volumes on the power of myth are not at all so different from the less commanding characters who roam the fairy-tale universe, always also in search of Elsewhere, the Promised Land, a Better Place, Cockaigne, the land of milk and honey, or some other Utopian Ideal (succinctly summed up in fairy tales with the phrase "Happily Ever After"). What he wrote in *The Hero with a Thousand Faces* held true for all stories: "The magic is effective in the tiniest, nursery fairy-tale, as the flavor of the ocean is contained in a single droplet."[15]

Campbell begins his study of the hero with a thousand faces by laying out the concept of what he calls the "monomyth" (a term he borrows from James Joyce, the writer who was the subject of his doctoral dissertation and, tellingly, the author of *Ulysses*). For him, stories about heroes tap into a deep well of human creativity driven by the need to face down our fears about mortality. Every culture "spontaneously" fashions its own myths, but with a tight discipline that orders and controls the flow of the locally inflected story. "Why is mythology everywhere the same, beneath its varieties of costumes?" Campbell asked. The Lakota may call their trickster god Iktomi, but that deity does not operate all that differently from the West African Anansi, the Greek Hermes, or the Mesoamerican Quetzalcoatl. And whether we are listening to the chants of witch doctors in Congo, reading the sonnets of Lao-tzu, or catching the words of an Eskimo fairy tale, he added, the story never changes. Campbell enumerates with stunning confidence the twelve building blocks used to create an interlocking edifice of story, an architecture that structures story with impressive uniformity even in the most remote corners of the world.

1. Ordinary World
2. Call to Adventure
3. Refusal of the Call

4. Meeting with the Mentor
5. Crossing the Threshold
6. Test, Allies, and Enemies
7. The Approach
8. The Ordeal
9. Reward/Rebirth
10. Road Back
11. Resurrection
12. Return with the Elixir

Campbell's one "marvelously constant story" follows the trajectory of the hero from the proverbial womb to the (symbolic) tomb, followed by resurrection in one form or another. Departure, Initiation, and Return: that was the basic formula, as the professor summed it up for his audiences. Initiation is, as it turns out, something of an Ordeal, but since it is little more than a stepping stone to rewards, resurrection, and a return home, Campbell describes it with an abstract term, one that is drained of pain and suffering.

Quest narratives give us something primal: heroic figures banished from home, uprooted from a familiar world that has turned toxic, and in search of a new place to settle down. Long before Campbell's monomyth, there was what scholars called the Rank-Raglan "mythotype." The German psychoanalyst Otto Rank, Freud's trusted colleague and collaborator for nearly two decades, had identified twelve transcultural features of hero myths in his 1909 volume *The Myth of the Birth of the Hero*. We can think here of Moses, King Arthur, or countless other figures who transcend their humble origins and perform deeds that enable them to attain nobility and heroic stature. As Rank put it, "nearly all prominent civilized nations" (and by that he specified Babylonians, Egyptians, Hebrews, Indians, Persians, Greeks and Romans, and Germanic peoples) left a literature full of poetic stories that glorified national figures: "mythical princes and kings, and founders of religions, dynasties, empires, and cities."[16] The origin stories of these supermen, as Rank called them, has a "baffling similarity," and he itemized the features of myths about them as follows:

1. Child of distinguished parents
2. Father is a king
3. Difficulty in conception
4. Prophecy warning against birth
5. Hero surrendered to the water in a box
6. Saved by animals or lowly people
7. Suckled by female animal or humble woman
8. Hero grows up
9. Hero finds distinguished parents
10. Hero takes revenge on the father
11. Acknowledged by people
12. Achieves rank and honors

Lord Raglan's 1936 *The Hero: A Study in Tradition, Myth and Drama* doubled down on Rank's model, emphasizing once again less heroic struggles than family conflict (we are back in the domain of *ordeals* rather than adventures), always based on a troubled and troubling male developmental model, one that can quickly become emblematic of what today, in a stroke of deep irony, we no longer lionize but call toxic masculinity. Myths have been said to enact repressed wishes and have a profoundly antisocial dimension; hence the deep paradox of enshrining as cultural heroes men who are living embodiments of social pathologies.[17]

Campbell's superhuman figures may know tragedy and die as martyrs, but they also acquire transcendent glory and a level of renown approaching immortality. How do they die? Better to ask, How do they live on? "He has been reborn," Campbell tells us of the hero, and "his second solemn task and deed therefore . . . is to return to us, transfigured, and teach the lesson he has learned of life renewed."[18] The superhero, cleansed of sins and purified of offenses, becomes both redeemer and teacher, though it is not entirely clear that he has any real lessons to convey, beyond the singularity of his own life trajectory.

Not to be overly reductive, but all the hero narratives analyzed by these experts in psychology, anthropology, and religion seem deeply motivated by a desire to ward off the chill of death and to bring a reassuring message about redemption and renewal. The features about family life seem to signal more than anything else that the hero begins life as a defenseless victim, one who will rise above the adversities of social circumstances and the hardships of domestic distress to bring wisdom and solace to his culture. Autonomous and unbridled, he makes a name for himself by becoming the storied ancestor of a new tribal formation, kinship unit, or religious order.

Our collective infatuation with Campbell's mythic journey, even many decades after its publication, is evident in the flood of how-to manuals readily available, each designed to help writers realize the dream of producing a Hollywood script for a blockbuster film. Christopher Vogler, in his self-help guide for writers, drew on Campbell's work to identify "a set of principles that govern the conduct of life and the world of storytelling the way physics and chemistry govern the physical world."[19] Syd Field uses Campbell's "template of the classical 'hero' throughout myth and literature" to explain the cinematic triumph of films like *Casablanca*, which feature present-day heroes who "die" and are reborn, sacrificing their lives "for the higher good."[20] Blake Snyder, in his bestselling manual of screenwriting, *Save the Cat!*, tells us that his craft is as much science as art: "It's quantifiable." There are "Immutable Laws of Screenplay Physics" and those rules are "constants, and in some cases eternal (see Joseph Campbell)."[21]

Some writers have resisted playing by the rules, or, at the least, they are not interested in templates, blueprints, or master narratives of any kind. In an interview, Neil Gaiman, a writer who is completely at home in the world of mythology and roams around freely in it, was once asked if Joseph Campbell had influenced his way of telling a story. "I think I got about halfway through *The Hero with a Thousand Faces*," he replied, "and found myself thinking if this is true—I don't want to know. I really would rather not know this stuff. I'd rather do it because it's true and because I accidentally wind up creating something that falls into this pattern than be told what the pattern is."[22] For Gaiman and for other imaginative writers, eccentricity and lack of predictability is paramount, and they have no interest in lifting their foot off the gas pedal to consider whether they are following the rules of the road. Instead they aim to shock and startle readers at every bend in the narrative lane, cutting us to the quick by creating something unprecedented.

Fanatical devotion to the hero's journey or monomyth is evident not just in the world of screenwriting but also in therapeutic contexts, with spiritual and psychological growth as the end goal of treatment. Is it any surprise that the so-called mythopoetic men's movement of the 1990s, formed in reaction to what was seen as the excesses of second-wave feminism, tapped into the popularity of *The Hero with a Thousand Faces* to distill a universal story-language for use in its workshops? Sometimes referred to as the New Age men's movement, it was less interested in social advocacy than in organizing retreats that included drumming, chanting, and gathering in sweat lodges. Like Campbell, the leaders drew on the writings of the Swiss psychologist Carl Jung and his theory of archetypes to navigate their way through what they saw as a crisis of male subjectivity and to find their way back to a deeply spiritual masculine identity.

Sessions led by the charismatic Robert Bly, author of *Iron John: A Book about Men* (1990) and coeditor of *The Rag and Bone Shop of the Heart: Poems for Men* (1992), were designed to enable participants to enact various phases of the hero's journey and to heal themselves by unleashing their "animal-males." In initiation rituals under the banner of the "Great Mother" and the "New Father" (nine-day conferences are held annually in Maine), participants sequester themselves in discussion groups and return with a renewed affirmative consciousness of their masculine identity. They are encouraged to discover kindred archetypes (King, Warrior, Magician, Lover, and Wild Man) that can be recruited as models for daily life. In *Iron John*, Bly drew on a fairy tale with that title, collected by the Brothers Grimm, to make a strong case for embracing the wild man within, a heroic archetype, to guide men to wisdom and self-actualization.

## The Cultural Surround of the Hero's Journey

Reading Campbell's concise summary of the Hero's Journey jolts us into quick recognition of the gender distortions in the monomyth: "A hero

ventures forth from the world of common day into a region of supernatural wonder: fabulous forces are there encountered and a decisive victory is won: the hero comes back from this mysterious adventure with
the power to bestow boons on his fellow man."[23] Driven by conflict and
conquest, this narrative arc utterly fails as a model of women's experience.[24] As Campbell explained to Maureen Murdock, author of *The Heroine's Journey* (1990), "Women don't need to make the journey. In the
whole mythological tradition the woman is *there*. All she has to do is
to realize that she's the place that people are trying to get to."[25] "When
a woman realizes what her wonderful character is," he added in a way
that can only produce exasperation today, "she's not going to get messed
up with the notion of being pseudo-male." Campbell's signature insouci-
ant style—often winningly kindhearted—when talking about matters of
far-reaching consequence can also mask an unconscious form of condescending misogyny. Women can never aspire to undertake the journey:
reservations are restricted to men alone. Besides, who in the world wants
to be a pseudo-male, whatever that may be?

For Campbell, the boon and elixir are the actual goals of the quest-
ing hero, but women also happen to be back home, waiting patiently for
the hero's return. Like Vladimir Propp before him, the Russian folklorist writing in the 1920s about how all fairy tales are alike in regard
to their structure, Campbell gives us a "once upon a time" that begins
with the hero's departure from home and ends when "the hero is married and ascends the throne," united with the princess or "sought-for
person." Along the way there may be Circe-like temptresses (yes, nearly
always female) who seek to derail him on the way to a new home, but
they can be cast aside, sacrificed and abandoned for the sake of a "mys-
tical marriage," a union representing the hero's "total mastery of life."
And in a final flourish, we discover that "the woman is life, the hero its
master and knower."[26] Lurking beneath this plot lies not just a need to
"master" life (and women), but also a profound desire to cheat death and
gain immortality.

These statements ring so quaint and old-fashioned that it is difficult to work up any real contempt for the rhetoric of narcissistic mas-

tery and self-contained masculinity built into them. Still, in many ways it is a wonder that there was no storm of protest when Campbell's book was published. *The Hero with a Thousand Faces* appeared in 1949, a time when postwar prosperity was just getting underway, with boat-sized cars sporting flashy hood ornaments and black-and-white television sets encased in clunky wooden consoles rapidly growing in number. Rodgers and Hammerstein's *South Pacific*, with its chorus of frustrated sailors singing about how there is nothing like a dame, its naïvely sentimental efforts to explore racial prejudice, and its hero finding true love on "Some Enchanted Evening," was attracting crowds on Broadway. And George Orwell's *Nineteen Eighty-Four*, a chilling dystopia in which Big Brother is always listening in, was just about to become obligatory high school reading. Fears about the rise of Communism and the threat of nuclear annihilation were running high and preoccupying minds. But as important, the United States was just beginning to feel the tremors of what would become a seismic shift in women's participation in the labor force. World War II had dramatically, if temporarily, increased women's employment outside the home. The number of women in the workforce rose from eighteen million in 1950 to sixty-six million in 2000, at an annual growth rate of 2.6 percent. In 1950, women were 30 percent of the labor force; by the year 2000, that figure had grown to 47 percent.

Nineteen forty-nine was also the year that marked, on the other side of the Atlantic in France, the publication of Simone de Beauvoir's *The Second Sex*. Translated into English in 1953, it became one of the foundational texts of second-wave feminism in the United States, the phase in which legal equality and reproductive rights became paramount. What the French philosopher did was to reveal how women, "free and autonomous" on the one hand, paradoxically live in a world that compels them to assume "the status of Other." How, de Beauvoir asked, had the cultural difference between men and women been historically defined? In a word, men were conquerors, with women as their enslaved captives. Men invent, create, explore, and exploit, while women stay at home and procreate.

Simone de Beauvoir took seriously the fairy tales and myths that had been part of her childhood and her education in France. She saw them as revelatory. The storytelling repertoire of long ago unapologetically mirrored the rough truths of the gendered divisions in the social worlds. "Woman is Sleeping Beauty, Donkey Skin, Cinderella, Snow White, the one who receives and endures. In songs and tales, the young man sets off to seek the woman; he fights against dragons, he combats giants; she is locked up in a tower, a palace, a garden, a cave, chained to a rock, captive, put to sleep: she is waiting."[27] Women, in other words, are not cut out for action or accomplishment, let alone conquest or victory. Recall the women of Greek myth, with figures such as Danaë, Europa, and Leda, all visited and impregnated by Zeus, when he disguises himself in the form of a golden shower, a white bull, and a swan. After what can only have been wretched sexual encounters (thankfully, we never get the details), they give birth to powerful, adventurous sons. Then there is Andromeda, punished because her mother boasted of her beauty, after which she is forced to languish chained to a rock until the heroic Perseus finds and releases her. Or Arachne, the target of a goddess's wrath for boasting that her tapestries were more beautiful than Athena's. These long-suffering women far outnumber full-scale goddesses like the wise Athena, the fierce Artemis, and the beautiful Aphrodite, all deities embodying abstract concepts, beyond reproach and—fortunately for them—usually, though not always, beyond approach.

There are two powerful gendered plots in our culture. F. Scott Fitzgerald captured them in his pronouncement that "the two basic stories of all times are Cinderella and Jack the Giant Killer—the charm of women and the courage of men."[28] "Charm" is, of course, a loaded term, implying all kinds of possibilities, ranging from agreeable grace to powerful magic, but the author of *The Great Gatsby* was not invested in nuances when he drew a sharp distinction between innocent persecuted heroines and giant slayers. Instead he solidified a contrast that has haunted the Western imagination and has become its default narrative option. On the one hand, there is the autonomous male hero seeking self-actualization through adventure and conquest (Jay Gatsby comes to mind). Then there is the patient, long-suffering, self-effacing heroine—what one critic calls the "afflicted woman trope."[29]

The hero's journey, as Jia Tolentino points out in a study of "pure heroines" and their self-destructive behavior, provided the story grammar for literary works reaching back to Charles Dickens's nineteenth-century *A Tale of Two Cities* and taking us up to Karl Ove Knausgaard's twenty-first-century *My Struggle*.[30] When we rattle off the titles of a host of nineteenth-century novels that foreground women—all firmly installed in the twentieth-century college curriculum—we come up with titles ranging from Tolstoy's *Anna Karenina* and Hawthorne's *Scarlet Letter* to Flaubert's *Madame Bovary* and Wharton's *House of Mirth*, all works that breathlessly evoke suffering heroines, intolerable domestic arrangements, and ominous vulnerability.

Are there exceptions to the rule that women exclusively are the long-suffering victims in our mythical and literary plots? There is, of course, the spectacular example of the biblical Job, who loses his children, his wealth, and his health, and whose faith is tested by what appear to be undeserved trials. At the same time, there are also female exceptions (mainly historical or legendary) that, more than anything else, prove the rule that combat is the domain of men. France's Joan of Arc blocks the English Siege of Orléans; the woman warrior Scáthach trains the Irish hero Cú Chulainn in the art of combat; the beautiful widow Judith of biblical tradition beheads the military invader Holofernes. And then there are the Amazons. But these chaste women (often gender fluid as well as virginal) remind us of how heroic behavior is predominantly in the DNA of men. There is something *unnatural* about them, for these legendary women, unlike their male counterparts, have a touch of the otherworldly or the grotesque. In some ways, they represent a perversion of the feminine by usurping the power of the heroic.[31] Military valor has, above all, served as a hallmark of the discursive field that defines the hero, and for many, the mental image of a hero remains a helmeted *male* warrior. Virgil begins his epic poem *The Aeneid* by declaring that he will sing of "arms and the man." As noted, the genre of epic or national myth, which bestowed on us the concept of the hero in its most conventional sense, turns on conflict and warfare: ancient Greece's *The Iliad*, France's *The Song of Roland*, England's *Beowulf*, Spain's *El Cid*, and the *Mahabharata* of India.

Even today we refer to the cult of the hero and to hero worship when we wish to designate our admiration for those who lead by example, usually in martial terms though sometimes in spiritual ones as well. Hero cults emerged in ancient Greece to commemorate those who had died in battle and to recruit their protective power over the living. More than ancestor worship at the local level, rituals honoring heroes offered a reassuring form of simple and direct piety uncomplicated by the full details of historical lives. Though devoted chiefly to warriors, hero cults occasionally found expression in votaries that included clusters of family members.[32]

Shining Achilles, clever Odysseus—let us remember that these heroes, almost always described with ennobling epithets, emerged from story and song at a time when the spoken word was the only means of transmission. Heroes had to be larger than life, with stereotypical traits that made it easier to learn their stories by heart. Superhuman beings solved a problem in a sense, for they were not just larger than life, but also *all action*, in ways that allowed their stories to circulate with ease, to replicate, and to endure in oral-aural cultures. With the introduction of writing and printing, characters began to lead more complex, subtle, and nuanced lives in psychological terms, and interiority became the hallmark of great fiction.[33] Narrative turned inward and suddenly we catch more than a quick glimpse of what is going on in the minds of those in the narrative arena. Flat figures, as E. M. Forster told us, become rounded, fully realized characters. We can see inside the minds of Dickens's David Copperfield and Jane Austen's Elizabeth Bennet and understand their thinking. Achilles and Cassandra, on the other hand, rarely invite us in, though we can often infer their emotions and motivations from their actions and reactions.

## Odysseus on a Journey and Penelope at Home

Few will doubt that the hero with a thousand faces has dominated the Western imagination, preventing us from seeing how women have figured in fictions that we have turned into timeless and universal cultural expressions. Women may appear in those fictions, but all too often they lack voices and agency, let alone a presence in public life. We see Odysseus in action, held in thrall by his artful ruses and bold deeds. We feel his pain when he parts from Calypso, tremble with him in the cave of Polyphemus, and rejoice when he finds his way back home to Penelope and Telemachus. As a hero of classical antiquity, he performs the "wondrous deeds" that are the hallmark of men seeking glory in those times.[34] Penelope, by contrast, like her many cousins in epic and myth, is confined to the domestic arena, with little to say for herself. In national epics ranging from the Finnish *Kalevala* to the French *Song of Roland* and in works ranging from Goethe's drama *Faust* to Richard Wagner's opera *The Flying Dutchman*, women quietly spin and weave, cook and clean, embroider, bear children, heal, and make things whole, clearing the way for the hero's salvation, or, at the least, not getting in the way of it.

Consider Homer's *Odyssey*. To assess its cultural impact, imagine how many young test takers and essay writers in the United States have been asked to describe the character traits of its protagonist. We can take the measure of that question about Odysseus by surveying sample responses available in a Google search of "Odysseus" and "hero." Their number, as it turns out, is legion. Here is the first entry in a search conducted in January 2020: "Odysseus is brave, loyal, smart, arrogant at times, wise, strong, shrewd, cunning, majestic." Here is SparkNotes: "Odysseus has the defining character traits of a Homeric leader: strength, courage, nobility, a thirst for glory, and confidence in his authority. His most distinguishing feature, however, is a sharp intellect." And CliffsNotes tells us that Odysseus "lives by his wiles as well as his courage" and adds that he is "an intellectual."

What about the other heroes of *The Odyssey*? Achilles, too, gains "a kind of immortality" through "valor and intense, honest devotion to a cause." He is *the* hero of the Trojan War and the "greatest" of all the Greek warriors. Possessing "superhuman strength," he also has "some character flaws" (his protracted sulking, along with his threat to hack the body of Hector to pieces and eat his flesh raw, may count among them). These shortcomings, alas, keep him from acting with "nobility and integrity," but they still enable him to fulfill the mission of winning immortality, and he does it through the poem known as *The Iliad*.

As for Penelope, in the first Google entry for her traits, we find that she is defined not in her own right but by her domestic role as "Odysseus's wife" and "Telemachus's mother." "Penelope's most prominent qualities are passivity, loyalty, and patience (along with beauty and dexterity at the loom)—the age-old feminine virtues," we learn. Then comes the coup de grâce: "She does very little but lie in bed and weep." The commentator for LitCharts concedes that she has some "hidden qualities," among them "cunning and cleverness." eNotes also sees her as "pragmatic" and "shrewd," but underscores the fact that "fidelity" remains one of her "most significant characteristics," while her husband's lack of fidelity fails to get a mention. In a website entitled The Psychology of Penelope, we learn that Penelope is "renowned" because she blends "the faithfulness that every man expects of his wife, but also exudes the sexual desire he wants from a lover." Admittedly, some of these declarations can be dismissed as internet nonsense, but that they have been optimized by search engines suggests that they have played a not negligible role in shaping student thinking and essay writing about *The Odyssey*. And they reflect the standard curricular wisdom of a time well before the internet became a research tool. The young are taught early on and quickly about gender differences—what it takes to be a hero and what it takes to keep your man.

*The Odyssey* gives us female characters who do more than verge on the stereotypical: they are the foundational stereotypes. On the one hand there is the bewitching Helen, the seductive femme fatale who figures as a threat to human civilization because she is irresistible to men, conquering their hearts (note the irony of blaming her for male vulnerability to beauty). Then there is Penelope, the virtuous wife, chaste and faithful, staying at home while her husband exposes himself to the alluring attractions of sorceresses and sirens. Helen is positioned as responsible for death and destruction, her beauty turning heads and launching a thousand (war)ships, while Penelope weaves a shroud even as she carries out household duties while cleverly fending off her sycophantic suitors. And then, rounding out the trio, there is the murderous Clytemnestra, who plots with her lover to kill her husband Agamemnon (a man willing to sacrifice his daughter for fair winds to take him to Troy) by throwing a robe over him and stabbing him to death. She is a reminder that not all women are as chaste, faithful, and dazzlingly beautiful as the two other prominent female figures in the epic. Students have been taught to accept these stories as canonical, authoritative, and normative, and were rarely, if ever, encouraged to question silencing or to challenge gender stereotyping. Until now.

*The Odyssey* emerged from a Greek oral storytelling culture and was composed in the form we know it today in the eighth century BCE. Once written down, orally transmitted epics lost the improvisational energy that drove their tellings and retellings. Turned into sacred texts, immutable and unassailable, they became part of a literary-historical record, stories that no longer challenged listeners to weigh in, respond to, and reshape their terms and values as had been the case with oral performances. Traditional tales, as defined by folklorists, change with each new telling, incorporating the creative contributions of listeners, even as they capture and conserve what has been relayed by earlier narrators, bards, and rhapsodes. But once written down, even when reinterpreted for Anglo-American audiences by new translations, their historically contingent values and beliefs harden into timeless and universal truths. As we shall see, however, the telling of stories and myths from times past can be, and has been, contested, complicated, and reimagined.

## Mythical Heroines Get Make-Overs

Mnemosyne: that is the name of the mother of the muses. She is the goddess of memory, and, without her progeny, song, music, dance, and story would not exist. It is Mnemosyne to whom women writers have appealed in the past decades. It is time, they seem to be telling us, to remember not just the heroes from the ancient world but also the heroines. Through belated acts of mythopoesis, writers today are doing what mythmakers have always done supremely well. From competing and conflicting histories, legends, and stories, they create new accounts. And, like magic, they re-member women from ancient times and bring them back to life.

How about an experiment? the German writer Christa Wolf once asked. "What would happen if the great male heroes of world literature were replaced by women? Achilles, Hercules, Odysseus, Oedipus, Agamemnon, Jesus, King Lear, Faust, Julien Sorel, Wilhelm Meister." Today that experiment is being carried out by women

Dante Gabriel Rossetti,
*Mnemosyne*, 1881

writers in many different cultures, and they are focused less on Faust or Julien Sorel than on Achilles and Odysseus. They recognize the challenges of taking on the ancients (and that is where the action has been), rewriting Homer rather than Shakespeare, though the Bard has received his share of challengers. How have writers like Margaret Atwood, Christa Wolf, and Pat Barker approached the sacred texts of times past? Most are not out to change the story but rather to show us the perspective of the women on the home front, the vulnerable observers on the sidelines who have been, until now, silent—or silenced—onlookers deprived of any real agency.

Homer and other bards made sense of the phantasmagoria of war by focusing on a few idealized figures and compressing the action of their narratives into scenes of vivid and intense drama. Women writers have used a range of strategies to "reenvision" (that is the term they invoke again and again) the past. How do they let us see things with fresh eyes? The dominant tactic has been to take us inside the minds of women so that we can experience their side of the story. The Trojan War, Napoleon's invasion of Russia, the Bourbon Restoration all look different when seen from a new angle and described by a "chatty" narrator, eager to provide all the details and to let us know *what it felt like* to be on the sidelines of bloody conflicts and contests fought by heroes.

Margaret Atwood's *Penelopiad* is told by Penelope and by the twelve "maids" (in reality, enslaved women) who fought off the suitors, successfully or not. Christa Wolf's *Cassandra* is a first-person account from the title figure on the day of her death. And Pat Barker's *The Silence of the Girls* lets us hear the voice of Briseis, a captive woman given as a war prize to Achilles. These "correctives" to *The Odyssey* and *The Iliad* are all first-person accounts, at times rambling, prolix, and wordy to a fault. But they are also personal, confessional reports from those who were victimized, enslaved, and violently subjugated by those in power. They move in a number of modes, ranging from complaint and indictment to self-justification and also self-incrimination. They turn the tables in radical ways, and suddenly the heroes are given new attributes and epithets. "The brute Achilles"—that's how Wolf's Cassandra describes the Greek warrior again and again until the reputation of Homer's shining hero is finally shattered.

The writers who took up the cause of women from the ancient world could be described as Social Justice Storytellers, were it not that the term "Social Justice Warrior" has been appropriated by right-wing political alliances and turned into an insult. The latter term was added to the *Oxford English Dictionary* in 2015, and it was defined as a derogatory noun to describe "a person who expresses or promotes socially progressive views." It was applied to activists with an agenda driven by political correctness and identity politics and with the aim of correcting social injustices. Before 2008, the term was used to describe champions of those left behind economically and socially, the underprivileged and overworked. But soon, in the wake of the Gamergate controversy of 2014 (a right-wing backlash that pitted those who accused the gaming industry of oppressing and harassing women against those who took up arms in the defense of gaming culture), "Social Justice Warrior" became an insult hurled at those who came to the defense of victims of harassment, many of whom in turn became the targets of vicious troll activity and received countless death threats.

Social Justice Storytellers: that descriptor, for all its concerning overtones, still defines what women writers in the last century and in our own century have been after. On a mission to make visible the faces of those who have been marginalized and to let us hear their voices, they tell stories that compel us to reassess how women lived in times past and to discover what strategies they used to survive. These authors document heroic acts of compassion as well as the artful tactics used in times past for airing grievances and bringing about change.

## Margaret Atwood's Penelopiad and #MeToo: The Victims Speak Up

It is the year 2005 and Margaret Atwood is having breakfast with Jamie Byng, a rising small publisher who pitches the idea of rewriting a myth from classical antiquity. Breakfast, the author of *The Handmaid's Tale* later confesses, is her "weakest time of day," and, in a burst of goodwill, she signs a contract—and then hits a wall, with a powerful case of writer's block. Just as she is about to scrap the project and return the advance to the publisher, the Muse taps her on the shoulder, and Atwood begins writing *The Penelopiad*. What irked Atwood in *The Odyssey* and inspired her to engage in rethinking the Greek epic was, surprisingly, not so much Penelope's marginalization as the hanging of the twelve maids, which seemed "unfair at first reading, and seems so still."[35]

*The Odyssey*, as it turns out, became something of a launchpad for rewriting the literary canon, a challenge taken up by several women writers in the late twentieth century and first decades of this century.[36] Rewriting the epic from the perspective of Penelope is not an obvious choice, and it certainly was not that back in 1928, when Dorothy Parker wrote a poem called "Penelope" with the punchline "They will call him brave." Her

Penelope sits at home, brewing tea (a perfect anachronism!) and snipping thread, while Odysseus rides "the silver seas." It did not occur to Parker to go beyond sarcasm, and it took many more decades to see in Penelope a woman who had been restricted to waiting, weaving, and marking time. Atwood's Penelope is forever on the brink of tears. As for Odysseus, "there he was making an inspiring speech, there he was uniting the quarrelling factions, there he was inventing an astonishing falsehood, there he was delivering sage advice, there he was disguising himself as a runaway slave and sneaking into Troy."[37] Penelope, by contrast, is confined to the marriage plot, without access to the world of deeds and action.

John Roddam Spencer Stanhope,
*Penelope*, 1849

There are reasons why Atwood was stumped by the assignment to rewrite a myth. Kathryn Rabuzzi captures precisely the challenge of retelling Homer's epic poem from the perspective of Penelope. "Finding voices authentic to women's experience is appallingly difficult," she writes. "Not only are the languages and concepts we have . . . male oriented, but historically women's experiences have been interpreted for us by men and male norms."[38] The very title of Homer's epic underscores, on its own, the erasure of female experience. The wife of Odysseus is just that, marginalized socially and subordinated domestically. Even her son Telemachus famously tells her to shut up and return to her weaving. What we know of Penelope and other women from classical antiquity has been mediated by male voices, making it something of an impossibility to capture what it was really like for women in that era. The challenge was to find words, not just for Penelope but also for the twelve maids, deputized as spies by Penelope and, under her watch, subjected by the suitors to sexual assault.

In 2006, a year after the publication of *The Penelopiad*, social activist Tarana Burke used the phrase "Me Too" on Myspace (a now-defunct social media platform) as a rallying cry for victims of sexual harassment and assault. Over a decade later, on October 15, 2017, the American actress Alyssa Milano received a screenshot of the phrase from a friend and tweeted it out, adding, "If all the women who have been sexually harassed or assaulted wrote 'Me too' as a status, we might give people a sense of the magnitude of the problem."[39] The next morning she woke up to find more than thirty thousand people had signed on to #MeToo. Suddenly women were empowered to use words and stories to transform secrets tainted with shame into a form of solidarity that banished vulnerability and guilt.

Even before real-life women began telling their stories on social media platforms, as well as to journalists and legal teams, women writers (Atwood was among the first) had already heard a distant drumbeat and were exploring tales from times past, hoping to get another side to stories and a different perspective on epics and myths we have elevated to classical status. Suddenly Penelope was able to come back from the dead and speak to the living. Homer may not have allowed her to say much, but

Margaret Atwood could give her a voice. And Penelope's experience was ripe for revision. It was time to reenvision her life. And if she seems less of a victim than survivors of sexual harassment and assault today, it is worth recalling that Penelope's life began with an act of unspeakable cruelty, when her father Icarius, who had hoped for a son, threw the newborn girl into the sea. Penelope was saved by some ducks, and Icarius then had a change of heart and named her after the Greek word for duck. We do not learn about the circumstances of Penelope's birth in *The Odyssey*, but Atwood's figure starts her narrative by reporting that event and then moving on to her arranged marriage at age fifteen to a man who wins (by cheating) a competition staged by her father. "I was handed over to Odysseus, like a package of meat," she tells us. And let us not forget that in *The Penelopiad*, we also finally hear the voices of the victims of multiple sexual assaults, the murdered maids.

"You think you'd like to read people's minds? Think again," Penelope warns us on the first pages of *The Penelopiad*. We have access not only to her thoughts, but also to the voices of the twelve maids. *"Now that I'm dead I know everything,"* Atwood's Penelope declares in a solo performance meant to assert her omniscient narrative authority. Then we hear the maids, who intone: "We are the maids / the ones you killed / the ones you failed." The twelve have their day in court at last, near the end of *The Penelopiad*, with a judge who consults Homer's *Odyssey* and confirms that "the suitors raped them" and "nobody stopped them from doing so." Penelope's monologue becomes an exercise in self-incrimination, by disclosing that both she and Odysseus used their positions to take advantage of the enslaved women and failed to protect them. But it is only in Penelope's account that we find that eye-opening revelation. It was not a concern for Homer.

How does Atwood create room for heroism? Her Odysseus is cut down to human size, and Penelope does not fare much better. Is it possible to find heroism in the patience and fidelity of a woman on the home front?[40] To drive home the difference between Telemachus and Odysseus on the one hand, and Penelope on the other, Joseph Campbell noted that *The Odyssey* tracked three journeys: "One is that of Telemachus, the son going in quest of his father. The second is that of the father, Odysseus, becoming reconciled and related to the female principle. . . . And the third is Penelope herself, whose journey is . . . endurance. . . . Two journeys through space and one through time."[41]

Penelope's inventiveness in the face of adversity and her ingenuity in warding off aggression remind us that she too is an active agent in her destiny. More than patient, submissive, and doggedly faithful, she is as wily and cunning as the "man of twists and turns." The foregrounding of her weaving on both a literal and metaphorical level—her expert handiwork as well as her skill at plotting and deceiving—reminds us that her so-called journey through time has its own value as story. Penelope's account turns out to be equally compelling and seductive when voiced by a modern bard willing to explore—with ironic distance as well as sympathetic engagement—the hearts and minds of characters from long ago and far away.

Bored, lonely, and weepy, Penelope sits at home, surrounded by suitors, weaving a shroud for Laertes, and refusing to wed until that covering is completed. Each day she works at the loom, weaving "finespun, / the yarns endless" and each night she undoes the labor of the day.[42] In *The Human Condition* (1958), Hannah Arendt described three components of the *vita activa*, or active engagement with and in the world. The first, Labor, is what is required to sustain human life, and it is carried out by *animal laborans*, a creature tied to the biological necessities of life and caught in endless cycles of consumption and reproduction. By contrast, *homo faber* is the exponent of Work, the architect, inventor, or legislator, charged with constructing buildings, institutions, and laws, all of which divide the human world from the natural world. Finally, there is *zoon politikon*, a social and political being who creates and secures spaces of freedom by becoming an actor or agent in the public sphere. Penelope is clearly doomed to dwell in the domain of *animal laborans*, engaging in an activity that leaves no traces whatsoever behind it, while her husband, the man of twists and turns, undertakes a circuitous journey that elevates him to the rank of hero, celebrated in song and story. Driven less by a political mission than by an appetite for literal self-mythologization, Odysseus transcends the limits of the human, becoming an exemplar of the cultural hero: autonomous, adventurous, and ambitious in the pursuit of renown.

But is there more to Penelope's story than what appears to be an utterly pointless activity? Her weaving seems to be even less effectual than the efforts of *animal laborans* in that the labors of the day are undone at night. To be sure, the undoing is strategic, but it secures nothing of real worldly value. Atwood's Penelope rejects all claim to fame, refusing the role of "edifying legend." "What did I amount to?" Penelope asks. "A stick used to beat other women with. Why couldn't they be as considerate, as trustworthy, as all-suffering as I had been? That was the line they took, the singers, the yarn-spinners. *Don't follow my example*, I want to scream in your ears."

Addressing readers as a silent jury, Penelope does what one critic describes as "telling a story in order to name and blame an evildoer."[43] At the same time, the chorus of the maids tells a different story, indicting Penelope for failures that she tries to refute by blaming others or to dismiss because she was "desperate" or "running out of time." Penelope's account reminds us that lurking beneath the abstract principle of justice are social inequalities and asymmetrical power relations, along with personal disputes and vendettas. The maids are Penelope's nemeses, but they are also reminders of how storytellers, no matter how passionate about telling the truth and getting to the bottom of things, can give us only a single perspective that cannot tell the whole story or resolve the question of moral culpability. Or is it possible that the author of *The Penelopiad* escapes that charge and manages to be "the fairest of them all" by giving us multiple perspectives? Is Margaret Atwood, then, our new cultural heroine, who speaks truth to power?

Instead of generic heroes, driven by conflicts and contests and known for their actions (Gilgamesh, Beowulf, Hercules), a new typographic heroine has emerged, known for intellectual powers and literary feats. Thomas Carlyle, back in 1841 in lectures on heroes, hero worship, and the heroic in history, celebrated a new archetype, the "Man of Letters," a singular figure who engages in the "wondrous art of *Writing*, or of Ready-writing which we call *Printing*."[44] Heir to the prophets, poets, and seers of times past, this hero conjures with words. After all, Carlyle adds, "the great deeds of heroes like Achilles, Aeneas, or Regulus would be nothing without the literary labours of Homer, Virgil, or Horace." This form of heroism becomes the trademark of some of our heroines from the past century and in the present one.

## Cassandra and Calliope Speak Their Minds

Today we can speak without hesitation about heroines with a thousand and one faces, and writers may be at the very top of that list. For them, the call to adventure may take the form of an epiphany, a recognition that the old story is no longer true and that a new ideological orientation can transform the story as it was once told. But what specific strategies do authors use to identify the other thousand heroines among their number? Today, many women writers seem to be looking backward, resurrecting figures from times past to reveal that those who are socially marginalized were not as weak and powerless as they may at first blush seem. Finding dignity, value, and significance in the lives of those who were sidelined in one way or another, these writers give us new angles, new perspectives, and new stories.[45] What if we are able to listen to the voices of Europa, Arachne, Hecuba, Psyche, and others? The effect is to defamiliarize the stories that circulate widely in our culture and to interrogate those same old stories, with critical instincts engaged, and to reflect on the old versus the new. But beyond that, these narratives challenge us to make an effort to get our stories right, to recognize that no single protagonist has a hotline to the truth, and to understand how justice is a hard-won social good that requires us to listen to more than one voice and to be open to listening both to individual testimony and to choruses of lamentation and complaint.

The ancient world rarely let women speak their minds, neither in real life nor in myth, story, and history. There are, of course, exceptions, and Euripides lets Hecuba rip into Ulysses, when she learned that she was to be his slave: "My luck is to serve / The foulest man / Alive, back stabber, / Justice hater, / Hell-born snake / Whose slick tongue / Twists everything / To nothing, twists / Love to hate, / And hate to love." But then it is also Euripides who gives us a line blaming the entire Trojan War on "one woman and her evil marriage."[46]

Margaret Atwood discovered that women from the ancient world could be revived and given voices. But even before *The Penelopiad*, Christa Wolf discovered a kindred spirit in a Greek woman whose voice had perpetually gone unheeded and who needed to be heard today. "To speak with my voice, the ultimate," Wolf's Cassandra tells us in the 1983 novel of that title. In Cassandra, Wolf discovers an alter ego, a double who can look into the future because she has "the courage to see things as they really are in the present."

Had Christa Wolf been reading Simone Weil, who wrote an essay about *The Iliad* as a "poem of force"? The true hero of Homer's epic, the French philosopher and political activist had argued, was *force*, a vector that enslaves by turning anyone subjected to it into a thing. In voluminous notes in the form of four documents accompanying the novel and describing its genesis, Wolf explains why she chose to channel Cassandra's voice: the fate of Cassandra prefigures what was to be the destiny of women in general for the next three thousand years—"to be turned into an object."[47]

"To whom can I say that the *Iliad* bores me?" Wolf asks in a moment of uncompromising candor. Stunned by the blunt honesty of that question when I read it, I reflected on how I had long failed to connect fully and passionately with *The Iliad*, with my mind resistant to sorting out all the military details and committing them to memory. Why was I always mixing up Greek warriors with their Trojan counterparts (which side is Ajax on?) and unable to keep their story lines intact? It was not because I could not "identify" with Achilles or Hector or Priam but rather because Homer gave us a story held together by rage, war, violence, homicide, carnage, and "heroic" deeds. Women, Wolf tells us, experience "a different reality," and the world of *The Iliad*, when seen through the consciousness of Cassandra, priestess and seer, can come to life and engage readers in new ways. Suddenly Achilles is given a new epithet: "the brute Achil-

Frederick Sandys, *Helen and Cassandra,*
1866

les" (*das Vieh Achill*, in the original German, which could be translated as "Achilles the animal"). The heroic search for "glory" and immortality suddenly bows down to a different quest: the effort to avoid the ruinous destruction of a city and its people—an *Untergang*, utter annihilation.

The threat of annihilation—in this case nuclear—is the driving force behind *Cassandra*. In 1980 Christa Wolf, living in what was then known as East Germany, traveled to Greece with her husband Gerhard. Two years later she delivered five "Lectures on Poetics," four of them on her Greek travels and the fifth a draft of the novel *Cassandra*. The four introductory lectures were published separately as *Conditions of a Narrative* and take us into the world of tourism and ancient history, poetics and politics.

What motivated Wolf to turn her attention to Cassandra beyond the desire to capture something about a woman who, like the author of the novel, trafficked in words? For Wolf, the stakes were high, and she wanted to offer nothing less than a takedown of the self-destructive logic of the Occidental world, the death drive that had led to the annihilation of a city, the slaughter of men, and the enslavement of women. For her, the threat of nuclear obliteration becomes the occasion for writing about an ancient civilization that followed a path leading to its own destruction. Cassandra, whose words and prophecies have no purchase at all, becomes a proxy for the writer in Wolf's day and age, desperately seeking to warn and dissuade ("He who strikes first will die second") but utterly failing to execute a plan for effective resistance.

In *A Thousand Ships* (2019), Natalie Haynes, a British writer with a University of Cambridge degree in classics, takes up the challenge of orchestrating a polyphonic chorus, enabling us to hear the voices of the many silenced by Homer. Who channels those voices but Calliope, the Muse of Epic Poetry? And what does she sing?

> I have sung of the women, the women in the shadows. I have sung of the forgotten, the ignored, the untold. I have picked up the old stories and I have shaken them until the hidden women appear in plain sight. I have celebrated them in song because they have waited long enough. Just as I promised him: this was never the story of one woman, or two. It was the story of all of them. A war does not ignore half the people whose lives it touches.[48]

Calliope, in her account, pays tribute to Mnemosyne, who helps bring back and memorialize the feats of women from times past. We hear voices from a parade of Trojan women including Hecuba, Polyxena, and others, and also Greek women ranging from Iphigenia to Penelope. Homer, it turns out, told us only half the story, and the silenced half is marked by acts of heroism that exceed what we have in what Haynes calls "one of the great foundational texts on war and warriors, men and masculinity." Who can forget the words of Polyxena as she marches toward her execution: "They would not be able to call her a coward." "Is Oenone less of a hero than Menelaus?" asks Calliope. "He loses his wife so he stirs up an army to bring her back to him, costing countless lives and creating countless widows, orphans and slaves. Oenone loses her husband and she raises her son. Which is the more heroic act?" "No one sings of the courage required by those of us who were left behind," Penelope writes.

Odysseus's wife pens a series of missives to her husband, each steeped in sarcasm. "You are wedded to fame, more than you were ever wedded to me," she writes. "And certainly, your relationship with your own glory has been unceasing," she adds as she ponders all the reasons for Odysseus's delay in returning home to his wife and son. In other words, true heroism is situated not in those striving for glory and immortality but in the fearless women who sought to preserve life—sometimes just to survive—rather than engage in senseless acts of annihilation.

At one point, Calliope whispers into Homer's ear: "She [Creusa] isn't a footnote, she's a person. And she—all the Trojan women—should be memorialized as much as any other person. Their Greek counterparts too." Haynes has become the new bard, inspired by a muse who was fed up with Homer and decided to anoint a new poet to tell the story of the Trojan War. Like Homer, through the agency of the Muse, Natalie Haynes undertakes the task of memorializing, this time remembering and conferring immortality on those once left for dead, buried, and forgotten. Greek and Trojan women alike come alive, speaking to us, haunting us with a new understanding of the courage and care it took to survive and to become our new heroines.

## Lifting the Silence

As we have seen, the men of myth have fared far better than the women, for we often hear about the passions that inflame them—rage, revenge, or romance—and much else. Ursula K. Le Guin's *Lavinia* (2008) begins with a complaint. "The life he [Virgil] gave me in his poem is so dull, except for the one moment when my hair catches fire—so colorless, except when my maiden cheeks blush like ivory stained with crimson dye—so conventional, I can't bear it any longer." Lavinia wants to be heard: "I must break out and speak. He didn't let me say a word. I have to take the word from him. He gave me a long life but a small one. I need room. I need air."[49]

Ursula Le Guin, who called herself a genre buster, once wrote that her "games" were "transformation and invention." Speculative fiction—myth, fantasy, science fiction—enabled her to use imagination not just to subvert and challenge the status quo but also to explore alterity and gender. "All I changed was the point of view," she said in an interview, and, with that change in perspective, we see an entire world "from the point of view of the powerless." Writing fiction enabled Le Guin to get into other minds and to explore the consciousness of other beings. In *Lavinia*, we discover a voice that Virgil never let us hear. Le Guin, who spent years "struggling to learn how to write as a woman," decided at one point not to "compete" with the literary establishment, "with all these guys and their empires and territories."[50]

In a commencement speech delivered at Bryn Mawr College in 1986, Le Guin spoke to the graduates about different language registers, a Father Tongue that is the voice of power and reason and a Mother Tongue, the language of stories, conversation, and relationships. In this ideological dichotomy, the Mother Tongue is devalued as "inaccurate, unclear, coarse, limited, trivial, banal." "It's repetitive," she added, "the same over and over, like the work called women's work." She urged graduates, much like Campbell when he spoke about the power of artists, to raise their voices in a third language, the voice of song, poetry, and literature. "I am sick of the silence of women. I want to hear you speaking. . . . There's a lot of things I want to hear you talk about."[51]

In 2018 the British novelist Pat Barker responded to Le Guin by writing *The Silence of the Girls*, which begins by defamiliarizing heroic behavior in *The Iliad*: "Great Achilles, Brilliant Achilles, godlike Achilles . . . How the epithets pile up. We never called him any of those things; we call him 'the butcher.'"[52] *The Silence of the Girls* gives voice not just to Briseis, queen of one of the kingdoms neighboring Troy and captive slave of Achilles, but to all those who suffered during the siege of Troy. What has been handed down to us? "His story, *His*, not mine"—we have the words and deeds of Achilles but not those of Briseis. "What will they make of us, the people of those unimaginably distant times?" she asks. "One thing I do know: they won't want the brutal reality of conquest and slavery. They won't want to be told about the massacres of men and boys, the enslavement of women and girls. They won't want to know we were living in a rape camp. No, they'll go for something altogether softer." It is almost as if Pat Barker has recruited Briseis for the #MeToo movement to write herself into history, finding her voice and recovering her humanity through the act of writing. "Now my own story can begin," is how her account ends.

Achilles's surrender of Briseis to Agamemnon,
first-century CE fresco from Pompeii

In a sense, once Briseis is given a story and a history, she becomes as heroic as Achilles—if not more so than the Greek "hero" who enslaved her and ensured that we would be kept in the dark about her. Song and story begin to trump deeds as we learn about what matters when it comes to a literary afterlife that bestows "immortality" on a figure. At first Achilles is the one who turns to his lyre to chant songs "about deathless glory, heroes dying on the battlefield or (rather less often) returning home in triumph." But as Briseis unfolds her story, it dawns on her that the simple lullabies sung by Trojan women to their Greek babies (in the Mother Tongue) are making sure that they too will live on: *We are going to survive—our songs, our stories. They'll never be able to forget us. . . . Their sons will remember the songs their Trojan mothers sang to them.*"

In many ways, Barker's novel invokes the trope of the Talking Book, an oxymoronic phrase coined by Henry Louis Gates Jr. in his 1988 book of literary criticism, *The Signifying Monkey*. Gates uses the term to illustrate how the tension between the oral and the written has been represented in the Black literary tradition, which privileges the voice and the vernacular over the written word, and favors autobiography over third-person narrative. Here it is important to remember that Briseis, like African Americans in the antebellum South, is not granted the status of a person. A slave, she is a thing, "an 'it,' a possession to be valued, bartered, coveted, tossed aside. . . . Her identity and humanity have been erased."[53]

At one point, Briseis overhears a squabble between Achilles and Nestor. But she stops listening to the "big words being bandied about"—honor, courage, and loyalty. Why does she tune out? Because it dawns on her that, when the two are talking about her, they refer to her not as "Briseis" but as "it." "For me there was only one word, one very small word: *it. It* doesn't belong to him, he hasn't earned *it*." Reduced to the status of a thing that circulates in transactions and exchanges, she is also denied the power of the spoken word, the right to interrupt and to assert her humanity.

Like Penelope in Atwood's new epic, Briseis comes back from the dead to speak to us, though Briseis, by contrast with Penelope, speaks as a living, sentient being, not as a woman broadcasting from the Underworld. Briseis uses the vernacular in an autobiographical account to reveal the flaws and fault lines in Homer's account and to write herself into history. "Will they tell your story?"—this line from the Broadway musical *Hamilton* is a reminder of how constantly and willfully the distaff side has been neglected, even when lives are filled with words and deeds that measure up to and, in many cases, exceed those of a culture's "heroes." "They" are unlikely to tell your story, and that is why *you* have to tell it, is the implication. Like Eliza in *Hamilton*, though more fully so and not just in a cameo, Briseis puts herself "back in the narrative" and earns, through her voice, the kind of literary immortality bestowed on men like Achilles.

Myths and fairy tales invite us to hit the refresh button, oxygenate the characters, fill in the gaps of the plot, and make new versions. Let us not forget that they were improvised in social spaces as an early form of collective bargaining, with call and response, give and take, and a chatty back-and-forth that often took the form of "That's not how I heard it." The female figures in male-dominated myths are now ready for action, and women writers today have revealed that the minds of those figures can be as deep, rich, and complex as those of the characters in the novels we read today. Centered and rounded, they have become fully realized characters, vocal and outspoken, ready to change the stories that others have told about them or to insert themselves more actively into the story. And change the narrative they do, as you can discover from looking at the titles of twenty-first-century novels inspired by mythical narratives. Just a quick effort to identify re-visions of the story of Hades and Persephone is revealing, with over two hundred retellings in print today, ranging from Emily Whitman's *Radiant Darkness* and Brodi Ashton's *Everneath* to Sasha Summers's *For the Love of Hades* and Tellulah Darling's *My Ex from Hell*.

In *Circe*, Madeline Miller transforms the daughter of Helios from an infamous witch who makes swine of men into a woman with powerful maternal instincts, magical healing powers, and a drive to undo the cruelty she has inherited from the gods and replace it with compassion. Circe has a history, and we learn about her unrequited love for a mortal (a fisherman named Glaucos), how she cleansed Jason and Medea of their crimes, and the role she played in the story of the Minotaur. By the time Odysseus arrives on the island of Aiaia, we know that there is a reason why she casts spells on sailors—she is also the survivor of multiple sexual assaults, defending herself from predators. Unlike the gods, with their limited emotional palette, Circe begins to evolve, moving from the unchanging righteousness and chilly insouciance of the gods to a form of compassionate care that humanizes her. When she proposes to Telemachus that he might have become known as "the Just," he responds by saying, "That's what they call you if you're so boring that they can't think of something better."

In many ways, Miller, like Margaret Atwood before her, becomes the true sorceress, conjuring Circe and bringing her to life with a breathtaking command of the ancient world, both its gods and its mortals. When Circe contemplates her newfound vulnerability and lies in bed worrying about the mortality of her children and husband, she rises and goes to her herbs. "I create something. I transform something," she tells us. Sensing that her witchcraft is "as strong as ever, stronger," she is grateful for the "power and leisure and defense" that she possesses. A crafty double of her character, Miller creates a self-referential narrative, a text about the magic of words as much as of potions. She casts a spell on us as we enter the world of the ancients, discovering the rich inner lives of figures who were once inscrutable but now have a history that resonates with accounts we have read in works by male authors.[54]

Barker saves Briseis and Miller does the same for Circe, memorializing their lives and rescuing them from oblivion. Recall how Hannah Arendt told us about the importance of telling stories. Homer was known as the "educator of Hellas" because he made warriors immortal by memorializing their deeds. Now the time has come for new voices to assume the role of educating the young, keeping the classics alive with counter-narratives and lives reimagined. Storytellers can now channel the histories of heroes and heroines, creating communities of memory that keep alive the words and deeds of those who came before us and earned not just glory but also dignity and humanity.

## Spiders, Storytellers, Webs

For many years, when I taught E. B. White's *Charlotte's Web* in a course at Harvard University called Fairy Tales, Myth, and Fantasy Literature, I always drew a blank when the occasional student asked why there is a character in it named Homer. It seemed like a stretch to connect Homer Zuckerman, Fern's unremarkable uncle, the farmer who displays the pig Wilbur at the fair, with the Greek rhapsode. But over time, I began to wonder if White had cleverly placed what cinephiles call an Easter egg into his narrative about a spider named Charlotte. After all, Charlotte is no ordinary spider: she is an arachnid who knows how to do things with words. And she is also an expert in the art of memorialization.

White famously began *Charlotte's Web* with the question, "Where's Papa going with that ax?"—not exactly what you would expect in a book for young readers.[55] The novel takes us from Wilbur's rescue from death by a girl named Fern to a second liberation from the threat of slaughter, when Charlotte works magic in her web, describing Wilbur as, among other things, "Terrific," "Radiant," and "Humble." In a chapter called "The Miracle," we see (and E. B. White works hard to instruct us on how to visualize) a web that is anything but a death trap: "On foggy mornings, Charlotte's web was truly a thing of beauty. This morning each thin strand was decorated with dozens of tiny beads of water. The web glistened in the light and made a pattern of loveliness and mystery, like a delicate veil." And in the web are written the words, "Some Pig."

What better way to describe the writer at work than this: "Far into the night, while the other creatures slept, Charlotte worked on her web." E. B. White's spider is not just a humble descendant of Arachne, the proud weaver of beautiful tapestries, but also a creature who knows how to work magic with words. She revitalizes language (some of her words are retrieved from the town dump) and wields her authority in ways that transform Wilbur and ennoble him. Beyond that, she teaches Wilbur how to use words so that, after her death, he pays tribute to her memory while her daughters are wafted away by warm spring breezes. "I was devoted to your mother. I owe my very life to her. She was bril-

liant, beautiful, and loyal to the end. I shall always treasure her memory."
*Charlotte's Web* sounds full chords, and we will discover, in a later chapter,
how women's work—spinning, weaving, and fabricating—is connected
with storytelling, as a form of resistance and revelation, an effort to lift
the silence. But first, a look at the work of silencing.

CHAPTER 2

# SILENCE AND SPEECH

## From Myth to #MeToo

*There is the tale of Jupiter, contriving to lie with Danae
by becoming a shower of gold; a story, which, as we
understand it, signifies the corruption of a woman's
chastity by gold. Whoever devised such stories . . .
presumed that there is in the hearts of men a degree
of evil which it is impossible to describe, for they
believed that men could endure such lies with patience.
And men have, indeed, embraced them with joy.*

—SAINT AUGUSTINE, *The City of God*

*As a reader, I claim the right to believe in the meaning
of a story beyond the particulars of a narrative, without
swearing to the existence of a fairy godmother or a wicked
wolf. Cinderella and Little Red Riding Hood don't need
to have been real people for me to believe in their truths.*

—ALBERTO MANGUEL, *Curiosity*

## *Persephone, Europa, and Danaë: Seduced and Silent*

Many of our most familiar Greek myths—stories about Leda, Danaë,
or Europa—swirl with so much violent energy that they seem resistant
to social messaging of any kind at all. Some educators have argued for
banning them in classrooms for the young or, at the least, adding trigger

warnings to them. These are not tragedies of heroic defiance or of human failings, but tales of assault and abduction, injury and trauma. For many decades they produced virtually no moral panic at all on the part of those repurposing the myths for the young, in large part because we live in an era that reveres ancient culture for its timeless beauty, wisdom, and truth. We have generally recoiled from judging the gods, especially when they are Greek or Roman.

Where does the story of Persephone and her abduction by Hades land in Edith Hamilton's table of contents for her bestselling *Mythology* (for decades a standard fixture in the U.S. high school curriculum) but in a section entitled "Flower-Myths: Narcissus, Hyacinth, Adonis"? And what kind of story is it? There is no talk of randy gods with a sense of entitlement. Instead one brother named Zeus is described as generously "helping out" another named Hades. Zeus thoughtfully fashions the delicate beauty of the narcissus as a strategy for luring Persephone away from her friends, thereby enabling Hades to "carry away the maiden he had fallen in love with."[1] Not a word is said about the compulsive philandering of both Titans, nor is there any sympathy for the plight of the girl who is the target of an "abduction" or "rape." Hades needs a queen, and who on earth, aside from Persephone's mother, would object to the abduction?

Persephone is, to say the least, a reluctant bride. She cries out for her father and, once in the lower world, she longs to see her mother again. Only in deference to Zeus's command does Hades allow Persephone to return home. And even then, it is only for a limited period, the spring and summer months of every year, for Hades has tricked his abducted bride into eating a pomegranate seed (a diabolically clever version of a date rape drug) that will force her to return to the gloom of the lower world. "He secretly put the seed in my mouth, a sweet morsel, and forced me to eat it against my will," Persephone tells her mother.[2] Superior physical strength and sorcery collude to keep Persephone captive, away from light and far from the delights of life on earth.

Edith Hamilton, a model of mythological erudition in her time, had no trouble at all including a full-page illustration entitled "The Rape of Europa" in her *Mythology*. It shows the moment of Europa's capture as one of rapture, a frolic on the high seas, complete with dolphins, mermaids, and the figure of Poseidon all cheerfully participating in aquatic pageantry. Europa, we read, was "exceedingly fortunate": "Except for a few moments of terror when she found herself crossing the deep sea on the back of a bull she did not suffer at all." And as for the bull, he is "so gentle, as well as so lovely, that the girls

Frederic Leighton, *The Return of Persephone*, 1891

were not frightened at his coming, but gathered around to caress him and to breathe the heavenly fragrance that came from him."[3]

Note that Edith Hamilton's *Mythology* promises *timeless* tales of *gods* and *heroes* in its subtitle. The heroines in many of these tales are eminently forgettable, effaced and erased in their status as victims. They may be able to procreate, but they are barred from the more creative antics carried out by the pantheon of Greek heroes, shining examples of those who test the limits of human intelligence, cunning, determination, and criminal behavior. Daedalus designs the Labyrinth. Prometheus steals divine fire. Jason recovers the Golden Fleece. Perseus slays Medusa.

Many years after Ovid described Europa mounted on a bull, looking back in panic at the shoreline, and the second-century Greek poet Moschus gave an account of Europa's kidnapping, European artists weirdly reveled in the opportunity to show a bull running off with a girl on his back. Zeus and Europa are found on paintings, prints, Italian wedding chests known as *cassoni*, enamel snuff boxes, and much else. "The Abduction of Europa" or "The Rape of Europa," as it was sometimes

called, became the subject of paintings by countless artists over the centuries. There is Rembrandt, who in 1632 gave us a Europa turning her gaze
backward (terrified, astonished, or just bewildered?) to the fading shore,
where her friends helplessly gape while a ferocious-looking white bull
with serpentine tail upright flees with his victim. One art historian insists
that there is "never any question of violence or rape," but the expression
on Europa's face in many works of art clearly refutes that assertion.[4]

The reaction of critics to this assault? Here is one representative voice:
"A master of visual effects, Rembrandt took pleasure in describing the
varied textures of sumptuous costumes and glittering gold highlights on
the carriage and dresses."[5] An unshakable commitment to aesthetics and
faith in the power of art to transcend its subject matter, no matter how
sordid, has somehow blinded critics to the violence of the event depicted.
To be sure, twentieth-century art historians were famously more invested

Rembrandt, *The Abduction of Europa*, 1632
*Digital image courtesy of the Getty's Open Content Program*

in questions about form and style than in content, but it seems odd that there was, up until the twenty-first century, virtually no discussion of the distraught woman in the scenes depicted, particularly given the outrageousness of the subject matter.[6]

Titian's priceless "The Rape of Europa," painted in the 1560s, is on display at Boston's Isabella Stewart Gardner Museum, where the god who spirits the girl away is described as "mischievous." The commentary further alerts us to Gardner's enraptured pleasure in the purchase: "I am back here tonight . . . after a two days' orgy. The orgy was drinking myself drunk with Europa and then sitting for hours in my Italian Garden at Brookline, thinking and dreaming about her."[7] Spiritual elation is here equated unguardedly with bodily ecstasy. Gardner's breezy

Titian, *The Rape of Europa*, 1562

observation reminds us that "rape" and "rapture" are not only etymo-
logically related but also that rapture, in a now obsolete inflection, could
mean "the act of carrying off a woman by force," according to the *Oxford
English Dictionary*. Inscribed in those paintings and their titles about the
rape of Europa is the notion that the abduction of the girl is less sexual
assault than a euphoric elevation of her spirit and, perversely, also that of
the beholder.

Here is the art-historical commentary on a 1716 *The Abduction of
Europa*: "This delightful painting by Jean-François de Troy ... portrays
the climactic moment from Ovid's story in *Metamorphoses*.... Jupiter
has transformed himself into a handsome bull to lure the lovely princess
Europa onto his back and carry her away to Crete, where she would bear
him three sons."[8] A *handsome* bull? What traits turn a ferocious beast
into a handsome creature? Never mind that the abductor is a bull. And is
that all it takes to entice a lovely princess to ride off into the waters? And
how is it that a scene of forcible capture, known in modern parlance as
rape, comes to be described as "delightful"?

The titles of the parade of European paintings featuring Zeus and
Europa routinely refer to the scene euphemistically as an abduction rather
than a "kidnapping" or "rape." After all, these are gods accustomed to
having their way with mortals, and the protective cloak of abduction
helps to conceal what was most likely the reality of sexual assault. There
are many who even resist the idea that capture implies violence. As one
scholar in the field of classics insisted some years ago, "We should talk
about abduction or seduction rather than rape, because the gods see to it
that the experience, however transient, is pleasant for the mortals. More-
over, the consequences of the unions usually bring glory to the families
of the mortals involved, despite and even because of the suffering that
individual members of the family may undergo."[9] Even this critic, who
refers to a "union" rather than a rape and insists on exonerating the gods
by asserting that they were allowed to engage in behaviors that were "rep-
rehensible" when committed by mortals, registers some misgivings by
recognizing the "suffering" that may be present in the "pleasant" experience. Europa rarely speaks in accounts that have been handed down

to us, but she does say "a few words" in Aeschylus's *Kares*. Her report is terse, and she alludes only fleetingly to Zeus's "trick" of using a "flourishing meadow" to attract her, focusing instead on her procreative powers: fertility, the "travails" of labor, and her distinguished offspring.

When John Keats, a frequent visitor to the British Museum, looked at Grecian urns or studied sketches of the ones showing bulls pursuing young women, he was unsettled enough to write in his famous ode: "What men or gods are these? What maidens loth? / What mad pursuit? What struggle to escape?"[10] Unlike many contemporary critics and commentators on the abductions hanging in art galleries today, the early nineteenth-century British poet understood that the maidens portrayed were not necessarily eager to consent to the desires of bulls and other beasts. Still, he also wrote about "wild ecstasy" even as he revered the "still unravish'd bride of quietness" that is the urn on which the abductions are portrayed. An object that is the "foster-child of silence," the urn is mute yet also a "sylvan historian" that tells tales. Keats's poem takes up and boldly but also cryptically reinterprets the tropes of silenced victims and speaking images that haunt the cultural history of the classical age.

There is another consideration here, one that links the rape of Europa to geopolitical concerns at the most fundamental level, even if it is not entirely clear that there is a direct connection between Europe and Europa. Consider that Europe as continent and the European Union as a larger entity have both claimed Europa, the victim of an abduction, as a namesake. There is some unsettling irony in the title of a recent book by Lynn H. Nicholas about the Nazi looting of art: *The Rape of Europa: The Fate of Europe's Treasures in the Third Reich and the Second World War* (1994). Benita Ferrero-Waldner, Austria's European commissioner, understood the strange oddity of the European continent priding itself on its connection with a myth about abduction, and she actually made it worse by suggesting that Europe's namesake had been a *promiscuous* young woman. "You could of course be forgiven for the myth analogy," she said. "Our very name is rooted in mythology—Europe being a beautiful maiden carried off by the God Zeus in the guise of a bull. But today's Europe, beautiful though she may be, is no longer that kind of girl."[11] It is hardly surprising that most European policymakers and politicians rarely draw a connection between the continent on which they live and the woman abducted by Zeus, yet the building that houses the Council of the European Union in Brussels has on display a statue featuring Europa riding a bull bareback as it triumphantly leaps forward.

Mary Beard reminds us that the first documented instance of a man silencing a woman—telling her that it is unseemly for women to speak in public—appears in Homer's *Odyssey*. Here is what was written down in a scene that begins with Penelope leaving her chambers and entering the palace's great hall, where a bard is singing about the challenges facing Greek heroes on their journeys back home. Penelope asks for an encouraging account and is met with a powerful rebuke. Her son Telemachus

Léon de Pas, *Europa Riding the Bull*, 1997, at the entrance of the Justus Lipsius headquarters of the EU Council of Ministers in Brussels

orders her to return to her quarters and to "take up your own work, the loom and the distaff. . . . Speech will be the business of men, all men, and of me most of all."[12] This humiliating admonition, delivered from son to mother, may not necessarily reflect Homer's worldview, but it tells us much about how women in Greek and Roman antiquity may have had voices yet were not allowed to use them in anything that resembled the public sphere, even when that space was at home. And what was their business? Spinning, weaving, and other forms of handiwork.

As late as the eighteenth century the sage Samuel Johnson was telling his biographer Boswell, "Sir, a woman's preaching is like a dog's walking on his hind legs. It is not done well; but you are surprised to find it done at all."[13] Women may not have been officially banned from speaking in public, but when they did the result was perceived to be comical, for it is evidently not in their genetic makeup to do what comes so naturally to men.

All these abducted mythical women, deprived of access to language and protest, are also presented not just as voiceless but also as mindless, for the tellers of tales avoid letting us see how victims of assault process what happens to them. Take the story of how Zeus begot Perseus by impregnating the beautiful Danaë, an account written down in the first or second century CE in a mythographical work known as the *Bibliotheca*, or *Library*. Acrisius, the father of Danaë, learns from the oracle that his daughter is destined to give birth to a son who will kill him: "For fear of this, Acrisius built a bronze chamber beneath the ground and kept Danaë guarded within it. She was seduced none the less, some say by Proitos [her uncle] while according to others, Zeus had intercourse with her by transforming himself into a shower of gold and pouring through the roof into Danaë's lap."[14] As Edith Hamilton reminds us, we are never told how it was revealed to Danaë that it was Zeus who visited her nor do we learn anything at all about her experience of that visitation.[15] Imprisoned through no fault of her own, impregnated without her consent, and set afloat with her son in the open seas, Danaë is the repeated victim of patriarchal authority in the form of her own biological father and also the father of the gods. And yet, we learn nothing about her inner life. In a recently published, authoritative encyclopedic work called *The Classical Tradition*, her identity is captured with the phrase: the "lover of Zeus."[16]

In the post-classical West, Danaë's story enjoyed a rich and provocative afterlife. On the one hand, Danaë was seen as a symbol of modesty, and the sunken chamber (often changed to a tower) that "protected" her became an allegorical representation of Chastity. But in 1388 things began to take a different turn, when a Dominican cleric named Franciscus de Retza wrote, "If Danaë conceived from Jupiter through a golden shower, why should the Virgin not give birth when impregnated by the Holy Spirit?"[17] In other words, Danaë is, as the renowned art historian Irwin Panofsky argued, a pagan prefiguration of the Virgin Mary, another way of suggesting a strange cultural-repetition compulsion. By emphasizing conception, even if immaculate in at least one case, the monk opened the door to curiosity about the unusual form of sexual congress in the biblical story.

Artemisia Gentileschi, *Danaë*, 1612

In *The Genealogy of the Gods*, written in the late fourteenth century, Boccaccio added momentum to a medieval swerve from chastity to licentiousness in the story of Danaë by repeating scholastic rumors that the Greek maiden had been corrupted by gold or that, pragmatically minded, she had bribed Zeus to help her break out of her prison. She made a bargain with Zeus, "at the price of intercourse with him."[18] With one stroke, it is easier to understand what was behind a portrait painted in 1799 by the French artist Anne-Louis Girodet. To get even with a famed actress for refusing to pay for an earlier portrait, Girodet retaliated by painting her this time as Danaë, catching gold coins (presumably from her lovers) in her lap. What we have in the reception of the Danaë story is an almost literal enactment of the Madonna/whore dichotomy, with the Greek woman deprived of any voice at all in the story and in how it was read through the centuries.

## Philomela Weaves a Story

Let us return to Ovid, for an even more shocking incident of silencing, by looking at his story about Tereus, Procne, and Philomela, once referred to as the "ur-text for women without tongues."[19] On the way from Athens to visit her sister Procne, Philomela is violated by her brother-in-law, Tereus. He drags her into an isolated hut deep in the woods and rapes her. She threatens her brother-in-law with payback in the form of a public denunciation. "Somehow or other I will punish you," she announces. Though imprisoned, her voice "will fill the trees / and wring great sobs of grief from senseless rocks."[20] Note here Philomela's determination to cast aside decorum and to *speak out*. She will use her voice in ways that will not only move others but also evoke grief from inanimate objects, even from the stones that we shall later see as "patient" listeners in folkloric inventions.

How does Tereus respond? With savage violence in the style of a scene from a horror film, he uses pincers to grab Philomela's tongue and cuts it out, even as she is still struggling to speak. Spared no details, we read on as Ovid tells us: "Its stump throbs in her mouth, while the tongue itself / falls to the black earth trembling and murmuring, / and twitching as it flings itself about." Even after his appalling act, Tereus continues ("they

say") to violate Philomela's mutilated body. In this moment of utter deso-
lation, "they say" becomes a beacon of hope, signaling that some are now
finally telling Philomela's story and filling the woods with denunciations.

"What can Philomela do?" Ovid asks. "Great trouble" inspires resourcefulness, and the Princess of Athens, deprived of a voice, reveals Tereus's crime
by weaving its enactment into a cloth delivered to her sister. "Outwardly
silent / yet inwardly ablaze," Procne, outraged by the revelation of Philomela's
rape in the tapestry, invites Tereus to a feast. There, he "stuffs his gut," feed-
ing on the flesh and blood of his own child, the boy Itys, whom Procne has

slain. "You would have thought
/ that the Athenians were
poised on wings: and so they
were!" That sentence intro-
duces a series of Ovidian metamorphoses that put an end to
the horrors. Procne is turned
into a nightingale, doomed, as
the female of the species, never
to sing, while Philomela is
turned into a swallow. Tereus,
a towering figure of sin and
depravity, becomes a bird as
well, the colorful hoopoe. This
is a change that changes nothing, for the conflict ends by
returning the protagonists to
nature, with no hope of finding
justice in the real world. And
now the story showcases an
instance of such monumental
horror that we are led to consider Procne to be as criminally
guilty as Tereus.[21]

The afterlife of Philome-

Edward Coley Burne-Jones,
*Philomela*, 1864

la's story can be found in a number of works, most notably Shakespeare's *Titus Andronicus* (c. 1588–93), a play (fictional rather than historical) in which Lavinia, daughter of the eponymous hero, is raped by men who sever her tongue and cut off her hands to prevent her from speaking, writing, or weaving. Lavinia later places a stick in her mouth to write the names of her attackers down in the dirt, reminding us that new technologies of denunciation emerge over time.

Many features stand out in Ovid's account, but Philomela's rape and the severing of her tongue, along with Procne's murder of her son Itys and preparation of a ghoulish banquet, arouse dread in powerful ways. The cutting out of tongues has a long and tortured history, as does the mutilation of women's bodies. The severing of the tongue was a torture favored by those who engaged in religious persecution (in particular, as a form of punishment for blasphemy), and men and women suffered equally the pains of mutilation. In 484 CE, Hunneric, a Vandal conqueror, cut off the tongues and right hands of sixty Mauritanian Christians. Then there is Saint Christina, daughter of a Roman patrician living in the third century CE, who was locked in a tower, beaten, set on fire, and tortured on the wheel. After that, her tongue was cut out, but she continued to speak and was subjected to new forms of torture.

In the folkloric pantheon there are many examples of women subjected to bodily mutilation, among them the "Girl without Hands," a figure who must forage for food in the woods. Examples abound in literary works as well. In Hans Christian Andersen's "The Red Shoes," a girl's dancing feet are amputated as punishment for her love of beauty by a man dressed in red. The mutilation of the organ of speech lives on as a form of silencing in its most devastating form in Andersen's "The Little Mermaid." The title figure's tongue is severed when she trades her voice for a pair of legs that enable her to advance in her mission of attaining not just a prince but also a human soul. In a different literary climate, there is the strange case of Ellen James in John Irving's 1978 novel *The World According to Garp*. Her tongue is cut out by rapists, and she becomes the inspiration for the Ellen Jamesians, a misguided cult whose members cut out their tongues as a form of solidarity with the eleven-year-old victim.

Amputating a tongue ensures, of course, that victims will be unable to declare bodily violations through speech. They are limited to bodily displays, with gestures grotesque in their desperation. In places where illiteracy is the rule, they also cannot identify perpetrators, thus placing them in a special category of the injured. As one cultural historian puts it, the single physical act of cutting out a tongue comes also to stand in for collective violation and voicelessness—a symbolic representation of how women have, through the ages, been silenced. The trope of a mutilated tongue becomes powerful in terms symbolic and real.[22]

Silenced women are not without tools, and Philomela reminds us that so-called women's work—weaving, sewing, and working with coverings—provides an opportunity not just to create but also to communicate. Tapestries, textiles, and embroidery: all can tell stories. Here is how Edith Hamilton describes Philomela's plight and her resourceful solution: "She was shut up; she could not speak; in those days there was no writing. However, although people then could not write, they could tell a story without speaking because they were marvelous craftsmen. . . . Philomela accordingly turned to her loom. She had a greater motive to make clear the story she wove than any artist ever had."[23] That the language of textile production is closely correlated with the generation of stories and their revelatory power tells us much about women's silent craft in preliterate cultures.[24]

How strange and yet also how logical it is that so many of our metaphors for storytelling are drawn from the discursive field of textile production. We weave plots, spin stories, fabricate tales, or tell yarns—a reminder of how the work of our hands produced social spaces that promoted the exchange of stories, first perhaps in the form of chitchat, gossip, and news, then in the shape of narratives and other dense golden nuggets of entertaining wisdom passed down from one generation to the next. Interestingly, fabrication also implies misrepresentation. Stories may be invented but they may also be true in the form of higher-order wisdom. We have seen how misrepresentations and lies work by indirection in folklore to reveal the horrifying details of violent crimes. Fairy tales like the British "Mr. Fox" stage the possibility of creating fictions about unspeakable harms and injuries, using the supposedly counterfactual to get the facts out.

## *Athena Silences Arachne with a Shuttle*

The Greeks gave us many master weavers, most notably Penelope, who, as we saw, set up a great loom in her palace to weave a shroud for Laertes, and on a nightly basis undid her work. There are also the Moirai, or Fates: Clotho, who spins a thread from her spindle; Lachesis, who measures the thread; and Atropos, who cuts it. Hovering over humans, they seem to control their destinies. And then there is Arachne, the inventor of linen cloth whose son Closter introduced the spindle for the manufacture of wool. She challenges Athena (I will use the Greek names even though our authoritative source on the story is Ovid) to a weaving contest—both use skeins of beautiful threads colored like the rainbow and filaments of gold and silver—and the goddess, worshiped as the protector of olive trees, ships, and weaving, does not turn her down. What does Athena depict? Her tapestry shows the gods, seated on high in all their glory, attending a contest in which the goddess herself defeats Poseidon. As a subtle hint to the audacious maiden with whom she is competing, she places in the corners of the tapestry four scenes of mortals punished for daring to challenge the gods.[25]

By contrast, Arachne uses the contest as an opportunity to showcase the failings of the gods, weaving scenes of violent sexual assault into her "beautiful" tapestry. There is Zeus, "tricking" Europa by turning himself into a bull and abducting her. Next, we see Asterie, mother of Hecate, pursued by the same god, who has now disguised himself as an eagle. Leda cowers under the wing of a swan. Once again it is Zeus, masquerading as an avian creature. Then we see the god again, impersonating Amphitryon in order to dupe Alcmena, who believes he is her husband. And presto, he moves from that cruel deception to take the form of a golden shower, a flame, a shepherd, a multicolored serpent for successive conquests. Poseidon makes it into this gallery of rogues as well, first as a bull trying to seduce Canace, then as a ram to deceive Theophane, and finally, in additional scenes, as a horse, a bird, a dolphin. It does not stop there. We also see Apollo, going about the work of "seduction" as a shepherd, then outfitted in feathers, and later donning a lion skin. The depiction of these orgies of "celestial misconduct" (that is one translator's term)

enrages Athena, who is also incensed by the skill of the weaver. The goddess tears the woven work apart and hits Arachne over the head with a
spindle. A mortified Arachne hangs herself to escape additional beatings
and, after her death, is fittingly turned into a spider, forever spinning
webs that soon become new metaphors for storytelling.

Lest we forget, Athena is the goddess who sprang, full-grown and
motherless, clothed in armor, from Zeus's head. As a favorite of Zeus
and a goddess-warrior, she resents Arachne's challenges to authority, her
refusal to embrace humility and obedience. Ripping apart a tapestry that
gives voice to violations, turning the shuttle into an instrument of silencing rather than revelation, and driving a woman back to nature: these
are all tactics that speak volumes and would seem to win support for
Arachne's cause. Yet translators and educators have, for decades, sided
with Athena. Here is Arachne's story, a representative retelling, as found
in Josephine Preston Peabody's *Old Greek Folk Stories*. In it, as in many

René-Antoine Houasse, *Minerva and Arachne*, 1706

modern versions of the story, Arachne's vanity and foolishness lead to her downfall. I cite it here in full to capture the horror of Arachne's punishment and how every retelling of a story is also an interpretation of it.

There was a certain maiden of Lydia, Arachne by name, renowned throughout the country for her skill as a weaver. She was as nimble with her fingers as Calypso, that nymph who kept Odysseus for seven years in her enchanted island. She was as untiring as Penelope, the hero's wife, who wove day after day while she watched for his return. Day in and day out, Arachne wove too. The very nymphs would gather about her loom, naiads from the water and dryads from the trees.

"Maiden," they would say, shaking the leaves or the foam from their hair, in wonder, "Pallas Athena must have taught you!"

But this did not please Arachne. She would not acknowledge herself a debtor, even to that goddess who protected all household arts, and by whose grace alone one had any skill in them.

"I learned not of Athena," she said. "If she can weave better, let her come and try."

The nymphs shivered at this, and an aged woman, who was looking on, turned to Arachne.

"Be more heedful of your words, my daughter," she said. "The Goddess may pardon you if you ask for forgiveness, but do not strive for honors with the immortals."

Arachne broke her thread, and the shuttle stopped humming.

"Keep your counsel," she said. "I fear not Athena; no, nor anyone else."

As she frowned at the old woman, she was amazed to see her change suddenly into one tall, majestic, beautiful,—a maiden of gray eyes and golden hair, crowned with a golden helmet. It was Athena herself.

The bystanders shrank in fear and reverence; only Arachne was unawed and held to her foolish boast.

In silence the two began to weave, and the nymphs stole nearer, coaxed by the sound of the shuttles that seemed to be humming with delight over the two webs—back and forth like bees.

They gazed upon the loom where the goddess stood plying her task, and they saw shapes and images come to bloom out of the wondrous colors, as sunset clouds grow to be living creatures when we watch them. And they saw that the goddess, still merciful, was spinning, as a warning for Arachne, the pictures of her own triumph over reckless gods and mortals.

In one corner of the web she made a story of her conquest over the sea-god Poseidon. For the first king of Athens had promised to dedicate the city to that god who should bestow upon it the most useful gift. Poseidon gave the horse. But Athena gave the olive—means of livelihood—symbol of peace and prosperity, and the city was called after her name. Again she pictured a vain woman of Troy, who had been turned into a crane for disputing the palm of beauty with a goddess. Other corners of the web held similar images, and the whole shone like a rainbow.

Meanwhile, Arachne, whose head was quite turned with vanity, embroidered her web with stories against the gods, making light of Zeus himself and of Apollo, and portraying them as birds and beasts. But she wove with marvelous skill; the creatures seemed to breathe and speak, yet it was all as fine as the gossamer that you find on the grass before rain.

Athena herself was amazed. Not even her wrath at the girl's insolence could wholly overcome her wonder. For an instant she stood entranced; then she tore the web across, and three times she touched Arachne's forehead with her spindle.

"Live on, Arachne," she said. "And since it is your glory to weave, you and yours must weave forever." So saying, she sprinkled upon the maiden a certain magical potion.

Away went Arachne's beauty; then her very human form shrank to that of a spider, and so remained. As a spider she spent all her days weaving and weaving; and you may see something like her handiwork any day among the rafters.

Arachne weaves a web with creatures that come alive, seeming to "breathe and speak." This creative gift is so powerful that it rivals that of the gods, and the contest between goddess and mortal found in Greek mythology can be found repeated and reconfigured in stories from around the world. The Lenape, or Delaware Indians (an Indigenous tribe originally living in the Northeast regions of the United States and Canada), have a story about "How the Spider Came to Be." It is said to derive from the tale of Arachne, but more than likely it arose independently as a fable about the rivalry between a "Creator" and a "skilled weaver." In it, the woman, who turns out to be the *"second* finest weaver in all of Creation," is punished for the "pride" she takes in her weaving. The Creator turns her into a spider.[26] Women may procreate and create but it is an act of hubris to compete with the powers of divine beings. What we see in the tale of Arachne and in the Lenape fable about the origins of spiders is clear insight into an anxious need to set limits to women's creativity, for their power to procreate and produce more than the mere semblance of life already places them in competition with supreme (male) deities. As tale-tellers and purveyors of rough truths, female weavers represent powerful threats to the status quo, and shrinking them down to the size of spiders, obliged to weave their webs in dark corners or high up in the rafters, means that their work can be ignored or will go unnoticed.

There is more to be said about spiderlore, and, given the connections among webs, weaving, spinning, and storytelling, a figure like Anansi of African lore comes to mind. The patron god of language and storytelling, Anansi came to be known in the Caribbean and in the U.S. South as Aunt Nancy or Nancy or Miss Nancy. These spider storytellers can be both sinister and benevolent. Female cousins of Anansi constantly challenge the rules of the social order, and they also reveal the scandals that are part of the status quo. Before considering how women developed new strategies—verbal rather than visual—for exposing misconduct and indicting those who engaged in wrongdoing, let us look at the afterlife of Philomela's story to see how it still resonates with us today.

## Writing Letters and Sewing Pants:
## Alice Walker's The Color Purple

Alice Walker had women's handiwork on her mind when she reflected on how she wanted "to do something like a crazy quilt" and write a story that can "jump back and forth in time, work on many different levels, and one that can include myth."[27] Walker never explicitly mentions Ovid's *Metamorphoses* in connection with her story about how a young Black woman named Celie reclaims agency and constructs her identity by writing letters and sewing garments. But if we recall that Philomela "had a loom to work with, and with purple / On a white background, wove her story in," it is almost impossible to imagine that Walker was not up to something, connecting a tale set in 1930s rural Georgia to a story from ancient Greece.

*The Color Purple* begins with a letter addressed to God. Celie has been silenced, unable to communicate with anyone but a higher being after she is raped by a man she believes to be her father. He has decreed, *"You better never tell nobody but God. It'd kill your mammy."*[28] God the Father remains her interlocutor until she discovers letters from her sister Nettie. That correspondence was hidden from Celie by her husband, Albert, a man with his own ways of silencing women, through brute physical force and stealth. "I don't write to God no more. I write to you," Celie declares once she discovers Nettie's letters.[29]

How does Walker make the story of Philomela and Procne new, pointing the way to something beyond a cycle that begins with violence and is followed by revenge that repeats and perpetuates the ferocity of the initial act? Celie emerges from the silence imposed on her by double rapes. She struggles to find her voice, tell her story, and create an identity. Her sister Nettie, who narrowly escaped violation at the hands of "Pa" and Celie's husband, Albert, becomes (like Procne for Philomela) her audience as she moves from an inability to say "I am" to taking ownership of what else but a company for selling things sewn from fabric: "Folkspants. Unlimited."

Telling her story in letters is just one strategy used by Celie to reconstitute her identity. Moving from the annihilation of her identity ("You black, you pore, you ugly, you a woman. Goddam . . . you nothing at all," Albert tells her) to something constructive, Celie turns to sewing pants, an activity that blends the feminine with the masculine by using the handicraft of sewing to create garments traditionally worn by men. An odd choice at first blush, but sewing becomes the activity that reconciles Celie with Albert, enabling her to talk with him in ways that had never seemed imaginable: "Us sew, I say. Make idle conversation." Celie finds an alternative to the destructive cycle of violence initiated by the rape that silenced her: "Everyday we going to read Nettie's letters and sew. A needle and not a razor in my hand, I think."[30]

The mythical imagination prides itself on exaggeration and amplification. It gives us the raw rather than the cooked, putting us in touch with the dark side of human nature, with vices so terrible that even philosophers recoil from talking about them, because they are beyond rational thought. Stories in their primal form connect us with the irrational as nothing else does and remind us of our animal nature.[31] The tale of Philomela and Tereus is the stuff of myth precisely because it takes us into the proverbial heart of darkness, enacting the unimaginable and challenging us to think and talk about dark emotions that take us out of our comfort zones. When Alice Walker gives us the story of Celie, she is creating a narrative that *resonates with* rather than reinvents Ovid's account of Philomela. Celie and Philomela become figures in a crowded literary field rather than fictional reinventions parading in linear fashion through the ages, down from Ovid to us.

One critic points out that Celie's pen and needle revisit, revise, and rewrite the story of Philomela's rape as well as the master narrative of women's subordination in patriarchal cultures.[32] But perhaps it makes sense to challenge the notion of Greek influence on modern fiction, as Toni Morrison did in 1989: "Finding or imposing Western influences in/ on Afro-American literature has value, but when its sole purpose is to *place* value only where that influence is located it is pernicious."[33] The Greeks did not invent filicide, but "Medea" has become our shorthand for a mother who murders a child. The ancient world of the Greeks is credited (like it or not) with having produced the foundational text about that subject, with the result that Toni Morrison's *Beloved* becomes an adaptation of Euripides's *Medea* rather than what it is: one link in a golden, global network connecting all stories.

What Alice Walker fashions is a counter-discourse to narratives about muting and silencing women. Her work is something of a liminal text, drawing on the legacy of the mythical past with its silenced women engaging in handicrafts, yet also looking forward to a time when speech, storytelling, writing, and revelation become powerful instruments for women. Scheherazade, a woman whose name has become synonymous with storytelling, will serve, once again, as our guide, this time as we enter the universe of women using words to pass on stories, with tales about telling tales and about the power of finding and using your voice.

## Scheherazade: Storytelling, Survival, and Social Change

Scheherazade has always been a mystery, and we do not know exactly how she became a collecting point for a vast ensemble of texts from the Middle East to the Far East. She first materializes in the frame tale for *The Thousand and One Nights*, which made its way from Persian to Arabic manuscripts in the second half of the eighth century CE, and then she migrated into cultures all over the world.[34] Like Europa, Persephone, Danaë, and Arachne, she is the product of a collective imagination shaped in large part by *men* of letters. But unlike the figures of Greek mythology, she has a voice, a powerful instrument that secures her survival and changes her culture. In what follows I will move from the mute and muted women of Greek mythology, whose efforts to broadcast misdeeds are severely limited, to folkloric inventions that equip women with voices. Scheherazade, alone of all her kind, stands at the head of a procession of women who begin to deploy narrative in strategic ways—using it to protect themselves from peril, to speak truth to power, and to transform their social worlds.

If you read *The Thousand and One Nights* as a child, you probably did not have access to an unexpurgated version. I can still see, in my mind's eye, the magnificent gold-embossed spines of a multivolume *Arabian Nights* in the foyer of a childhood friend's home. Those volumes were among the few books verboten for their racy content (Balzac's *Droll Stories* were on that same shelf), off-limits to the teenagers in the house. Of course, the teens in the family all tried, with varying degrees of success, to see what was inside them. What is tastier than forbidden fruit? Editions of *The Thousand and One Nights* designed for children not only omit some tales and bowdlerize others but also eliminate the shocking details of the frame narrative, with its account of lascivious women, sexual intrigue, and courtyard orgies.[35]

Scheherazade may be celebrated as a cultural heroine, but in her stories womenfolk in general are revealed as dissipated and deceitful. The collection's frame narrative is anything but child friendly and stands as a stark reminder that what we think of as fairy tales for the young were in fact what John Updike correctly called "the television and pornography of an earlier age."[36] *The Thousand and One Nights* starts with accounts of Shah Zaman and Shahriyar and their spectacularly failed marriages. Women's promiscuity, we learn, knows no bounds. In a culture that placed strict restrictions on women's mobility and constrained their social conduct in severe ways, we encounter wives who are boldly lascivious and who routinely engage in sexual mischief.

Shah Zaman of Samarkand declares his plan to visit his brother Shahriyar, but turns back home mid-journey to retrieve a gift, only to find his wife in flagrante. There she is, "lying on a couch in the arms of a black slave" (the tales have been charged with both racism and misogyny) and, in a rage, he kills the "foul" woman and her lover. When Shah Zaman arrives at his brother's palace, he does not immediately share the story of his wife's "treachery," and his wretched mood keeps him from going out to hunt with his brother. Brooding in the palace, he witnesses an even more flagrant example of dissolute behavior in his brother's garden: "As Shah Zaman was looking, a door opened and out came twenty slave girls and twenty slaves, in the middle of whom was Shahriyar's very beautiful wife. They came to a fountain where they took off their clothes and the women sat with the men. 'Mas'ud,' the queen called, at which a black slave came up to her and, after they had embraced each other, he lay with her, while the other slaves lay with the slave girls and they spent their time kissing, embracing, fornicating and drinking wine until the end of the day."[37]

Misery loves company, and Shah Zaman finally tells all, whereupon the two betrayed brothers leave the kingdom in search of other victims of women's treachery. Their first stop is with a jinni who keeps "a slender girl, radiant as the sun" imprisoned in a trunk. While the jinni is sleeping, the girl beckons to the brothers and tells them they must "satisfy her" or she will betray them to the jinni: "Take me as hard as you can or else I'll wake him up." Reluctantly, the brothers agree, "taking turns with her." As a final sign of her depravity, she demands to add rings from Shah Zaman and Shahriyar to her collection, which numbers anywhere from 98 to the 570 listed in Edward Lane's translation, as well as in the later translation by Richard Burton.[38] In a coda to the episode, wisdom is extracted from the tale with the following verse:

> Do not put your trust in women
> Or believe their covenants. . . .
> They make a false display of love,
> But their clothes are stuffed with treachery.
> Take a lesson from the tale of Joseph,
> And you will find some of their tricks.
> Do you not see that your father, Adam,
> Was driven from Eden thanks to them?

Women are not only untrustworthy, false, treacherous, and deceitful but also responsible for the Fall. Never mind the duplicity of the jinni, who abducted the young woman when she was betrothed to another, and now keeps her under lock and key, save for a few moments of liberty when he is sleeping.[39] Eve, too, gave in to temptation. (No mention is made of how Eve does nothing more than commit the "sin" of eating fruit from the Tree of Knowledge and offering some of it to Adam.)

There is more, and in an unnerving addendum, we learn that a poet has written:

> *I am a lover, but what I have done*
> *Is only what men did before me in old days.*
> *A true cause for wonder would be a man*
> *Never before trapped by the allure of women.*[40]

In other words, men have engaged in the very behavior women display, and they also perpetually succumb to temptation. Yet it is never really their fault, for they are constantly "trapped" by seductive women. In some ways the captive girl's behavior does nothing more than remind the two brothers as well as the audience listening to their story about a brazen double standard that sees depravity in behaviors that are not sanctioned or censured when men engage in them.

What about Scheherazade? She enters the picture three years after Shah Zaman and Shahriyar have returned home, once the two have found a man who has suffered a fate worse than their own. Shahriyar's first act on arrival in his palace is to behead the queen who betrayed him before his adventures with Shah Zaman commenced. He then slays all the slaves who cavorted with her. Finally, as noted earlier, he crafts a plan with razor-sharp consequences. Each evening he will take a new bride, and, after a night of pleasure, an execution will follow. The practice commences that night, and for three years it continues, until soon, "no nubile girls" are left in the city. It is then that Scheherazade volunteers.

Who is Scheherazade? First, she is the daughter of the man in charge of procuring brides for Shahriyar and also tasked with dispatching them. Scheherazade's father would have been all too familiar with the daily ritual established by the king; indeed he is a part of its most horrifying aspects. Oddly, Scheherazade, for all her wisdom, seems unaware of her father's daily mission and his connection to the disappearing virgins in her city. Unshaken by Shahriyar's vengeful fury, she insists on marrying him: "Either I shall live or else I shall be a ransom for the children of the

Muslims and save them from him."⁴¹ Both strategic thinker and compassionate idealist, she is a woman ready for action or self-sacrifice.

How did Scheherazade become a master storyteller? The answer may have less to do with immersion in an oral storytelling culture than in a passion for reading. Scheherazade is, in fact, a voracious reader: "She had read books and histories, accounts of past kings and stories of earlier peoples, having collected, it was said, a thousand volumes of these, covering peoples, kings and poets." As one critic points out, she was revered as a reader and a scholar, a "bookish" heroine, whose natural habitat is the library, not the king's bed. Then she combines the two "by turning the king's bed into a place of storytelling."⁴² And what kinds of stories does she tell? There are tales of demons and monsters, thieves and harlots, morality and depravity, pirates and beasts, adventures and puzzles, all manner of tales, as might be expected in a volume of its size. Through storytelling, Scheherazade not only saves her own life but also transforms Shahriyar from a tyrannical despot into an enlightened and compassionate ruler. The cliff-hangers she crafts "educate" the king by exposing him to the entire spectrum of human behavior, arousing his desire to know not just "What's next?" but also "Why?" She tells stories, but she also creates a partnership in which there is much to talk about, so much so that the king presumably comes to a better understanding of how to rule.

Scheherazade is not just a mystery but also a paradox. Her aim is to cure the king of his misogyny. But she tells him stories that seem designed to strengthen his conviction that women are licentious, wily, and crafty. Take the story "The Porter and the Three Ladies," in which three wealthy sisters invite a porter they have hired to join them in the city of Baghdad for a day of carousing. After they have wined and dined the porter, each of the sisters disrobes, sits on the porter's lap, and, pointing to her private parts, asks, "What is this?" The porter plays the same naughty game, asking the sisters to name his anatomical counterpart. Or consider the "Tale of the Husband and the Parrot," with a parrot murdered for speaking the truth about "a woman of perfect beauty and grace" who engages in double deceptions. Then there is "The Semi-

Petrified Prince," in which an enchantress married to a prince engages in hanky-panky with one of the slaves in the household. When her husband discovers the adultery, she casts a spell on him, turning the lower half of his body into marble, and transforming his kingdom into a lake and its former inhabitants into fish.

When the Turkish novelist Orhan Pamuk reflected on his reading of *The Thousand and One Nights*, he recalled how impressed he was, as a child, with its "lies, tricks and deceptions, the lovers and betrayers, the disguises, twists and surprises."[43] But reading it in his twenties, he was "troubled" by much in the stories. "Men and women were perpetually at war," he observed. "I was unnerved by their never-ending round of games, tricks, deceptions and provocations." And most important, the volume sent the message that "no woman can ever be trusted—you can't believe a thing they say—they do nothing but trick men with their little games and ruses." *The Thousand and One Nights*, he concluded, was the product of a culture in which men feared women and the power of their "sexual charms."[44] Only later in life did he find the volume to be a "treasure chest," a book that shows us "what life is made of." His recollections are revealing, for they remind us that Scheherazade's wisdom may turn less on converting Shahriyar to a new value system than on recruiting him as a conversation partner in the interstices of the stories, gaps to which we are not privy, but that we fill in as we read. Stories like the ones in *The Thousand and One Nights* fire us up and demand processing through conversations about the messages they send.

Like Philomela in Ovid's *Metamorphoses*, Scheherazade has a dual mission. She is no mere "clever survivor," but also a "transforming agent."[45] Philomela weaves the story of her rape into a tapestry not only to exact revenge but also to model ways of airing what has been silenced by a culture. Both Philomela and Scheherazade begin as victims, but the arc of their stories takes them to a position enabling them to speak for themselves and to a culture in ways that let them live on in story and song.

The Danish artist Kay Nielsen's illustration for the frame tale to *The Thousand and One Nights* reminds us that Scheherazade, for all her heroic vitality, remains small and weak. Seated before the king, she is naked, exposed literally and figuratively, the target not only of his gaze but also of his regal power. Made to appear superhuman through his oversized turban and flowing royal robes in Nielsen's image, Shahriyar may fall under the spell of Scheherazade's stories, but he remains in charge nonetheless. And Scheherazade looks more like Hestia, goddess of the hearth, than Aphrodite or Athena. Who will not conclude, while contemplating Nielsen's rendering of the relationship between the two, that Scheherazade becomes a figure affiliated with submission and domesticity?[46] Her voice and her body are placed in the service of the king.

Scheherazade may lack the mobility and appetites of male cultural heroes, but she transcends the narrow domestic space of the bedroom through her expansive narrative reach and embraces bold defiance as she sets about remaking the values of the culture she inhabits, using words alone. She not only arouses curiosity but also turns herself into a storytelling transvaluation machine, for she understands at the deepest level that words can change you. Behind her transformative art lurks the ruse of the disempowered, and Scheherazade, despite the physical constraints placed on her, uses language in ways that reveal what the philosopher J. L. Austin referred to as its "perlocutionary" power, its ability to persuade, teach, or inspire. Scheherazade operates at a level that is culturally productive and also biologically reproductive. Creative and procreative, she produces children with Shahriyar and also sets the stage in powerful ways for the literary progeny that spring from her story—the many female storytellers whom we will encounter in the chapters that follow.

Scheherazade will always remain a mystery, a paradox productive in its power to generate an infinite regress of conversational sites. Each time we read *The Thousand and One Nights*, we discover new facets to her identity, features that challenge us to rethink how we once viewed her. Just as Orhan Pamuk revised his understanding of the *Nights* with successive readings, so we modify, adjust, and fine-tune our appreciation for a master storyteller who continues to keep us waiting, breathlessly, for the next installment of her enchantments.

## The Compulsion to Confess: Victims and Stones of Patience

In one version of the story about Philomela, Procne, and Tereus, Philomela does not lose the power of speech. Instead, she uses her voice to tell her story, but in the form of a lament rather than a communication. When an eavesdropper hears her, the story of her rape gets out. Before investigating women's speech—along with rumor, gossip, and storytelling—in the next chapter, I want to explore a story that reveals just how it is that murder (or other shocking forms of criminal behavior) will out. The compulsion to confess and tell all affects not just wrongdoer but also victim, as folktales from around the world tell us.

For centuries, women in fairy tales have made use of veiled speech and clever ruses as they prowled around the margins of storytelling worlds. They have engaged in a practice one expert calls "idionarration," talking to themselves as much as to others, using words to get their story "out there," even when, or perhaps especially when, no one seems to be paying attention.[47] Like children in fairy tales, they are often silenced, by fathers, brothers, and other male relatives, and in some cases even by creatures exceptionally low in the food chain, but also by those high in divine hierarchies.

I will look first at some stories in a collection published by the Brothers Grimm, two German scholars and statesmen determined to use folklore as a way to consolidate cultural identity at a time when their country had been occupied by French forces. What began as a project with nationalistic aspirations turned into the creation of a storytelling repertoire that went global to create a shared body of folklore with a recognition factor far beyond the Grimms' wildest dreams of success. The tales were translated into English soon after the publication of the two volumes in 1812 and 1815 and quickly traveled to England and to the United States, where they became bestsellers and began to rival domestic lore. Then along came Walt Disney, who drew on the Grimms' fairy tales to make the first feature-length animated film, *Snow White and the Seven Dwarfs*. When the film was released in 1937 (and subsequently shown in forty-six countries), the *New York Times* anointed it a "folk-film," a movie that marked the beginning of a new transnational canon of folklore: "As folk-tales were once passed from tribe to tribe and nation to nation, so that few societies have lacked something resembling the Cinderella story, or the Aladdin story, so we may have folk-films." Without any misgivings about the sinister side to this corporate takeover of a heterogeneous folk-loric heritage, the reporter cheered on the process of standardization and commercialization.

Still, the stories appropriated by the Walt Disney Company have hardly suffered setbacks, and a look at some of the tales in the Grimms' collection reveals that what is preserved there resonates with narratives from all over the world, reminding us that the stories will never stop replicating themselves in what Darwin called "endless forms most beau-tiful and wonderful." Nowhere is this more true than in tales about women silenced and women endowed with the power to speak and tell their stories.

Examples of girls silenced abound in the Grimms' *Children's Stories and Household Tales*. In "The Frog King," the famed first story in the collection (recall that Campbell used it as the curtain raiser for *The Hero with a Thousand Faces*), the title figure, with an instinct for authority, tells a princess in tears over a lost golden ball: "Be quiet and just stop bawling." "Don't cry, Gretel" and "Be quiet"—that's also what Hansel tells his sis-ter when they are lost in the woods, unable to find their way back home. And the girl in the Grimms' story "Our Lady's Child" loses the power of speech when she refuses to admit that she opened a door forbidden to her. Constantly deprived of speech, these fairy-tale figures are rendered defenseless and vulnerable. Complaint remains taboo for them.

"The Goose Girl," a story included in the Grimms' collection of 1812, reveals the complex ways in which silence and speech operate in tandem to produce self-reflexive narratives that allude to the power of stories to make things right—in other words, to find justice. In this case, however, a female rival, rather than a predatory male, inflicts suffering on the her-oine, reminding us that villainy can come from any quarter. The rescuer comes in the form of a patient listener, who doubles as suitor and savior.

A princess traveling to foreign lands for her wedding is betrayed by an ambitious chambermaid who usurps her position. Forced to tend geese in the kingdom she was to rule, she cannot reveal her true identity, on pain of death. All the while she retains magical powers, summoning the winds to divert the attentions of unwelcome suitors or communicating with the head of her beloved horse, a creature decapitated by the chambermaid. If speech in its most urgent form is denied her, still she finds, as is the case with Cinderella, Snow White, Thousandfurs, and a host of other fairy-tale heroines in the Grimms' collection, some consolation in her power to commune with and be at home in the natural world.

It is the father of the prince who, after getting wind of intrigue and betrayal from the horse's head endowed with speech, proposes that the goose girl tell her troubles to an old iron stove. Once he walks away, the princess crawls into the iron stove and starts "weeping and wailing." "She poured her feelings out and said: 'Here I sit, abandoned by the whole world, even though I'm the daughter of a king. A false maid forced me to remove my royal clothing and now she has taken my place with my bridegroom. And here I am, forced to do menial work as a goose girl. If my mother knew about this, her heart would break in two.'"[48] The sly king had not moved far from where the princess was and inched his way over to the stovepipe, catching every word of the goose girl's complaint. The truth becomes public thanks to the royal eavesdropper, a sympathetic listener who is also a male intermediary with the authority to validate and air the facts, even when, or perhaps especially when, they are hotly denied. Telling your story, finding the power of speech—even if it seems to take the form of mere breath in the wind—liberates and rights wrongs.

Giambattista Basile's seventeenth-century collection of Italian stories known as *The Pentamerone* contains a tale that resembles the Grimms' version of "Snow White." But there is a crucial difference: in it an aunt plays the role of cruel persecutor. The ill-treated girl one day asks her uncle to bring back for her from his travels a doll, a knife, and a pumice stone. What does Lisa, as the girl is called, do when the doll arrives? She puts it in front of her and begins weeping, recounting "all the story of her troubles to that bundle of cloth, just as if it had been a real person." And what is the point of the knife and pumice stone? When the doll does not respond, Lisa threatens to sharpen the knife on the stone and stab her with it. "All right," the doll quickly declares, "I have understood you. I'm not deaf!"[49]

The doll may be animated, but it is no substitute for a real-life interlocutor, and, one day, Lisa's father eavesdrops at the door. He hears the weeping girl speaking with dark intensity:

> [The Baron] saw Lisa telling the doll all about her mother's jump over the rose-leaf, how she swallowed it, her own birth, the spell, the curse of the last fairy, the comb left in her hair, her death, how she was shut up in seven caskets and placed in that room, her mother's death, the key entrusted to the brother, his departure for the hunt, the jealousy of his wife, how she opened the room against her husband's commands, how she cut off her hair and treated her like a slave, and the many, many torments she had inflicted on her. And all the while she wept and said, "Answer me, dolly, or I will kill myself with this knife." And sharpening it on the pumice stone, she would have plunged it into herself had not the Baron kicked down the door and snatched the knife out of her hand.

Something of a second self, the doll becomes a conversation partner, not human to be sure, but also "not deaf." It is willing to listen to the tale of Lisa's woes without triggering fear of retaliation for "telling" on the aunt. The Baron asks his niece for a full account and then stages a banquet at which he urges her to "tell the story of the hardships she had undergone and of the cruelty of his wife." This is a tale that makes "all the guests weep." Reciting woes to an inanimate object, in this case a kind of personal talismanic figure, creates the opportunity for a sympathetic listener to eavesdrop, which in turn prepares the way for a public performance, a scene of storytelling that elicits sympathy for the victim and leads to a punishment for the persecutor: "Then he drove his wife away, sending her back to her parents." Justice is served, perhaps not entirely cold, at the Baron's banquet.

There are many fairy tales that take as their subject self-imposed muteness or enforced silence followed by disclosures of abuse. The Portuguese story "The Maiden with the Rose on Her Forehead" gives us a heroine who asks her uncle for a talisman. What does she do but take the artifact made of stone to her room and place it on her bed:

> As the prince was curious to know what she would do with it, he hid himself under the bed. The girl began to tell her history to the stone, saying, "Oh! talisman, I am the daughter of a princess, sister to the prince my uncle, who lives in this palace and is married. But he does not know that I am his niece, for I was kept spell-bound in an iron chest; and his wife and her mother burnt my skin all over with a hot iron."[50]

In this case, kinship has been suppressed and is revealed at last through the girl's testimony, overheard by the prince, to an inanimate object. He restores the girl to her royal rank and does away with his wife and mother-in-law by scorching their skin and immuring them behind a wall.

Occasionally, stories about betrayal and abuse feature men as victims, as in "The Lord of Lorn and the False Steward," a ballad recorded in nineteenth-century Britain by Francis James Child.[51] The steward in that story, much like the heroine of the Grimms' "Goose Girl," is forced to trade places with a servant. His true identity is revealed when he tells his story, not to the lady of the house directly, but to a horse that kicked him. As in "The Golden Bracelet," recorded in Kentucky and appearing in a collection called *Tales from the Cloud Walking Country* (1958), an animal rather than an inanimate object becomes the audience for a tale of woe, told this time by a "true bride."[52] "[She] had let her little dog follow her to Spain," we read in that Southern tale, "and it was a heap of comfort to her to talk to it every night and tell how she lost the golden bracelet that was her protection from harm. She held to her promise not to tell it to no human person. But the old king's serving woman heard, and she told the old king." Although there are occasional wronged young men in these stories, women still far outnumber them, and they can be said to suffer as much at the hands of mothers, sisters, aunts, and servants as at the hands of fathers, husbands, brothers, and uncles.

In the early 1940s, Susie Hoogasian Villa decided to collect folktales from informants living in an Armenian community located in Delray, a part of southwest Detroit. Using Gregg shorthand, she wrote down several hundred tales, among them "Nourie Hadig," a story told to her by Mrs. Akabi Mooradian. In an appendix to *100 Armenian Tales*, the highlights from her extensive archive, she added notes about a dozen similar tales told in regions neighboring Armenia, pointing to the widespread dissemination of the story.

"Nourie Hadig," like the Grimms' goose girl and Basile's Lisa, is the victim of a rival who does everything in her power to trade places. In this case, Nourie Hadig has been tending a slumbering prince, and, when he finally awakens after seven years, he believes that a duplicitous female servant has been in charge of his recovery. "Neither girl told the prince the truth about the arrangement"—Nourie Hadig's pride and the servant girl's infatuation get in the way of disabusing the prince of his error. Before the wedding, the prince plans a shopping trip, and he asks Nourie Hadig what she would like. "A Stone of Patience" is the reply. Off the prince goes to a stonecutter, who gives him the required object, along with a speech about its powers:

> If one has great troubles and tells them to the Stone of Patience, certain changes will occur. If one's troubles are great, so great that the Stone of Patience cannot bear the sorrow, it will swell and burst. If, on the other hand, one makes much of only slight grievances, the Stone of Patience will not swell, but the speaker will. And if there is no one there to save this person, he will burst. So listen outside your servant's door. Not everyone knows of the Stone of Patience, and your servant, who is a very unusual person, must have a valuable story to tell.[53]

What is less alive and sentient than a stone? The notion of a stone of patience, a stone that can listen to human sorrows so intense that it feels empathy, swells, and can burst is a stroke of genius. As expected, Nourie Hadig recounts her sufferings to the stone, and we find in the folk narrative a miniaturized version of the events already told, now from the point of view of the heroine:

"Stone of Patience," she said, "I was the only child of a well-to-do family. My mother was very beautiful, but it was my misfortune to be even more beautiful than she. At every new moon my mother asked who was the most beautiful in the world. And the new moon always answered that my mother was the most beautiful. One day my mother asked again, and the moon told her that Nourie Hadig was the most beautiful one in the whole world. My mother became very jealous and told my father to take me somewhere, to kill me and bring her my bloody shirt. My father could not do this, so he permitted me to go free," Nourie Hadig said. "Tell me, Stone of Patience, am I more patient, or are you?"

The Stone of Patience began to swell.

The girl continued, "When my father left me, I walked until I saw this house in the distance. I walked toward it, and when I touched the door, it opened magically by itself. Once I was inside, the door closed behind me and never opened again until seven years later. Inside I found a handsome youth. A voice told me to prepare his food and take care of him. I did this for four years, day after day, night after night, living alone in a strange place, with no one to hear my voice. Stone of Patience tell me, am I more patient, or are you?"

The Stone of Patience swelled a little more.

"One day a group of gypsies camped right beneath my window. As I had been lonely all these years, I bought a gypsy girl and pulled her up on a rope to the place where I was confined. Now, she and I took turns in serving the young boy who was under a magic spell. One day she cooked for him and the next day I cooked for him. One day, three years later, while the gypsy was fanning him, the youth awoke and saw her. He thought that she had served him through all

those years and took her as his betrothed. And the gypsy, whom I
had bought and considered my friend, did not say one word to him
about me. Stone of Patience, tell me, am I more patient, or are you?"

The story within the story mirrors the larger narrative, but also offers
a new perspective and a new audience, with the Stone of Patience mod-
eling empathetic behavior, reminding listeners that stories can be rousingly tender and emotionally charged. More than intellectual exercises in
mapping "What if?" scenarios, the story also contains a dose of magic,
with its stone that swells with pity. By telling a tale, you can communicate pain, suffering, and injustice. And the prince, who eavesdrops on
the scene of storytelling, willingly concedes the hazards of partial knowledge: "I didn't know the whole story." And with that, the gypsy is sent
back into servitude (creating the opportunity for a new tale of injustice),
and Nourie Hadig marries the prince.

Stones of Patience are a rarity in European and Anglo-American folklore, though a German saying about something being capable of moving
a stone to tears or making a stone empathetic (*etwas könnte einen Stein
erbarmen*) suggests some kind of deep chasm separating the cold, mute
silence of a rock-hard surface and the kind, effusive warmth of human
compassion. Persian folklore has a tale called "Sang-e Sabur," and the
patient stone in the title represents the most empathetic listener imaginable. Collecting all the compassion that has been squandered in the
world, it absorbs suffering as it listens to the tribulations of those who
must bear an intolerable burden of misery. The patient stone sacrifices
itself, willingly bursting into pieces by taking on what would otherwise
crush its human interlocutor.

The Stone of Patience made its way into Armenia, and in mysterious
ways other tropes and motifs of the Persian tale about a long-suffering
young woman also migrated into European lore. In 1966 Hafizullah
Baghban collected a story called "The Seventy-Year-Old Corpse" from a
thirty-year-old housewife named Hayā, living in Herat City in Afghanistan.[54] In the next decade Baghban recorded two additional versions of

the tale, a fact that suggests a widespread dissemination of stories about Stones of Patience. Elements of the tale are kaleidoscopically reconfigured in the European repertoire, repurposed in ways that make better cultural sense for the audience. Occasionally, however, they hold the key to fairy-tale puzzles. Why, for example, does the heroine of "The Goose Girl" tell her woes to an iron stove, of all possible things? The answer becomes evident when we look at its distant analogue, the Afghan story about an aging corpse.

A man sells thorn bushes for a living and has a daughter who spins cotton while he is away. One day, a nightingale perches on a wall and tells the girl that she will marry a seventy-year-old corpse. The next day the man and his daughter set out to visit a relative. On the way they run out of water, and the daughter walks to a fort where she fills her jug but is then unable to find an exit. She begins to weep, and a window opens, giving her access to seven rooms. In the seventh lies the corpse of the title, punctured with needles. The girl purchases the services of a concubine, who is given instructions to remove all the needles sticking in the corpse, save one. Instead, she defiantly removes all the needles. The corpse is resurrected, marries the concubine, and makes the spinner his second wife. Here we find the same role reversal of princess and servant, beautiful girl and gypsy, that appears in European analogues.

As in "Beauty and the Beast" and "Cinderella" stories, the heroine makes a modest request, asking the "corpse" to bring her a patience stone and a black-handled knife when he returns from a shopping expedition for wife number one. After securing the items, the "corpse" learns that he must attend to how they are used: "She'll put herself in an oven and cover the top. Then she'll tell her story from the beginning to the end [to the stone]. At the end she'll kill herself [with the knife]." The seventy-year-old heeds these words and sits near the oven, listening to the story of the old man's daughter. How does he react? Stunned by the revelation of wife number one's treachery, he ties her hair to a horse's tail and has the horse run until the woman is "torn to pieces." Then he covers her skull with silver and turns it into a drinking glass. The young woman who succeeded in revealing the truth has the "good fortune" of marrying the seventy-year-old corpse, and one can only hope that the exercise in revelation has transformed him physically as well as emotionally: "God fulfilled their wish."

What happens when the seventy-year-old corpse *is* the patience stone? This is the premise of a 2008 novel by Atiq Rahimi, a French-Afghan writer and filmmaker. *The Patience Stone* is set "somewhere in Afghanistan or elsewhere."[55] In this setting that is both a very real war-torn village and an imagined anywhere in the world, a woman tends her comatose husband, a jihadist shot in the neck during a dispute with a relative. Gradually the woman begins to confide in her husband, revealing her fears and desires, the agony of her marriage, in short, her most closely guarded secrets.

It is the woman who makes the connection between her mute husband and the patience stone. "Before she has picked up her veil, these words burst from her mouth: '*Sang-e saboor!*' She jumps. 'That's the name of the stone, *sang-e saboor*, the patience stone! The magic stone!' She turns to her comatose husband and whispers, 'Yes, you, you are my *sang-e saboor*! ... I'm going to tell you everything, my *sang-e saboor*. Everything. Until I set myself free from my pain, and my suffering, and until you, you ...'" For the first time in her marriage, she is able to talk back, to break the code of silence that prevailed for a decade, with a husband so preoccupied by armed conflict that he failed to exchange words with his wife. For her, the process of speaking to the immobilized husband is therapeutic, even if and because she knows that the words she utters can be said only when her husband is unable to respond with words or blows. "What pours out of her is not only a brave and shocking confession, but a savage indictment of war, the brutality of men, and the religious, marital, and cultural norms that continually assault Afghan women, leaving them with no recourse but to absorb without complaint, like a patience stone," Khaled Hosseini writes in his introduction to Rahimi's novel.[56]

Women who tell their stories candidly are risk takers. There may be some therapeutic gain in telling all, but the risk may not always

Walter Crane, illustration for the Grimms'
"The Robber Bridegroom," 1886

be worth the reward. What would happen if the Afghan woman's husband were to awaken from his coma and reveal that he had heard the entire story of her suffering, along with her awareness of what is described as his sterility as well as her sexual betrayals in order to become pregnant? That question is answered (spoiler alert!) by the end of the novel, when it becomes clear that the wife's confessions have not softened her husband's heart. The patience stone, in this case, does not burst in empathetic identification but instead is animated by homicidal rage, averted at the last moment by the wife's use of the dagger that had once hung on the wall with her husband's portrait. The Afghan woman in *The Patience Stone* finds her voice. Telling her story endows her with agency, enabling her to defend herself from her husband's murderous assault.

The Brothers Grimm included a tale in their *Children's Stories and Household Tales* that reprises the British "Mr. Fox" and gives us a final tableau in which a scene of storytelling turns into a kangaroo court. Encouraged by her fiancé to tell a story at the wedding feast, the young woman in "The Robber Bridegroom" frames her narrative as a dream:

"Very well," she replied, "I will tell you about a dream I had. I was walking alone through the woods and came across a house. No one was living there, but on the wall, there was a cage, and in it was a bird that sang:

> *'Turn back, turn back, my pretty young bride,*
> *In a house of murderers you've arrived.'*

Then it repeated those words. My dear, I must have been dreaming all this. I walked from one room to the next, and each one was completely empty. Everything was so spooky. Finally I went down to the cellar, and there I saw a woman as old as the hills, her head bobbing up and down. I asked her: 'Does my betrothed live here?' She replied: 'Oh, you poor child, you've stumbled into a den of murderers. Your betrothed lives here, but he is planning to chop you up and kill you, and then he'll cook you and eat you up.' My dear, I must have been dreaming all this. The old woman hid me behind a big barrel, and no sooner was I out of sight when the robbers returned home, dragging a maiden behind them. They gave her three kinds of wine to drink, white, red, and yellow, and her heart burst in two. My dear, I must have been dreaming all this. Then they tore off her fine clothes, chopped her beautiful body into pieces, and sprinkled them with salt. My dear, I must have been dreaming all this. One of the robbers caught sight of a gold ring on her finger and since it was hard to pull off, he took an axe and chopped it off. The finger flew through the air up behind the big barrel and landed in my lap. And here is the finger with the ring still on it."

With these words, she pulled it out and showed it to everyone there.

The robber turned white as a ghost while she was telling the story. He jumped up and tried to escape, but the guests seized him and turned him over to the law. He and his band were executed for their dreadful deeds.

Telling stories to inanimate objects and broadcasting injury to a public audience have a long and venerable folkloric history. This is not Scheherazade engaging in a storytelling practice that entertains and instructs, keeping the king animated in ways that delay her execution, teach her husband the value of empathy, and lead him to an understanding of the entire range of human emotions and behaviors. We are in the here and now, and broadcasting injury and harm—telling all—proves to be more than cathartic. It can also secure social justice and punish treacherous women and barbaric men. But it is also not without risk.

## Technology and Talk: From ELIZA to Twitter

Today we continue to talk to things, perhaps not in the form of stoves and stones, but in the shape of hard, metallic objects that seem to patiently, and sympathetically, listen to our stories. New technologies have made it possible to tell our stories to maximum dramatic effect in interactions with machines. Back in 1971, Joseph Weizenbaum developed a software program called ELIZA. The irony of naming the program after Eliza Doolittle will not be lost on older generations of program users. The 1956 Broadway hit musical *My Fair Lady*, based on George Bernard Shaw's 1913 stage play *Pygmalion*, tells of a language professor named Henry Higgins who is determined to prove that he can elevate a woman to a higher social rank by changing the way she speaks. Controlling women's speech continues to be supremely important, then as now.

To program ELIZA, Weizenbaum used what are called the nondirected aspects of Rogerian therapy, which famously advocated unconditional acceptance of a client/patient's views in order to promote the uninhibited expression of feelings. "How do you feel about that?" was the classic response to any declarations of abuse, mistreatment, and victimization. ELIZA of course has no real understanding of her user's statements, but "she" is able to generate a variety of leading questions that encourage the sharing of intense feelings and create an affective bond with an entity that conveys a (false) sense of responsiveness and empathy.

Tech guru Sherry Turkle has observed that those who use the program "want to tell it their secrets." Once there is even "the smallest gesture suggesting [ELIZA] can empathize, the instinct to talk, reveal, and confess sets in." "I have watched hundreds of people type a first sentence into the primitive ELIZA program," Turkle adds. "Most commonly they begin with 'How are you today?' or 'Hello.' But four or five interchanges later, many are on to 'My girlfriend left me,' 'I am worried that I might fail organic chemistry,' or 'My sister died.' "[57] Once given the opportunity, most users willingly commit to dialogic engagement with an inanimate object, a modern-day patience stone that promises therapeutic emotional release. Of course the promise of complete discretion should be factored in to the confessional impulse Turkle describes.

The value of telling your story, beyond its use as evidence, has become clear in a variety of ways in the criminal justice system. Many states have passed amendments creating the opportunity for victim impact statements. "Not everyone finds relief in a courtroom, but many people who have endured a violent crime or lost someone they loved report feeling tremendous catharsis after having the chance to describe their suffering in court. Those who worry about the practice say that there should at least be better, fairer, and more clearly enforced rules about doing it."[58] Telling your story, in settings private and public, can go beyond therapeutic release to become part of a fact-finding effort to secure justice for all, paving the pathway for the kind of restorative justice that has found many advocates today.

The Greeks have a story still told today about a woman named Maroula, whose children are murdered by a treacherous mother-in-law. The crime is blamed on the children's mother, and the enraged husband orders his wife's hands cut off and sewn into a sack with the bodies of the children. Maroula is banished from the kingdom and wanders from one region to the next with the sack tied around her neck. One day, she meets a monk, to whom she tells her story, and the monk brings the children back to life and joins Maroula's hands to her arms. The truth reaches the husband as well, in the form of a story. Justice runs its course when the tale is told a third time at a banquet, where the assembled guests pronounce judgment on the villainous woman: "They reached a decision to put her in a barrel of tar and set fire to it on the sea."[59]

Women have always spoken up and acted up, but, as we have seen, they were often silenced in ways that forced them to channel their feelings by confiding in artifacts associated with women's work. In acts of desperation, they talked to themselves or to inanimate objects, discovering that justice could come only when a male intermediary listened in and made things right. Today, we have developed new technologies and new courtroom procedures that enable the telling of stories. Social media platforms provide public outlets for airing grievances and exposing injustices. In a short time span, we have established an alternative system that at times rivals our legal institutions in its power to shame, punish, and chasten—to conjure Nemesis. ELIZA may promise confidentiality but Twitter, Facebook, and Instagram ensure maximum exposure. The premium on storytelling, along with all the attendant anxieties about reliability and concerns about hearing one side alone, has never been higher. The challenges that lie ahead remind us of the vexing complexities implicated in the difference between telling a good story and telling one that is true. As always, aesthetics and ethics dance a tango in dramas, real and embellished, that are compelling, unsettling, and sometimes maddeningly enigmatic at their core.

## Strategies for Silencing:
## Tales about Shutting Down Storytelling

Our word for silence comes from the Latin *silentium*, meaning "quiet, still, calm," a condition of being free from noise. But there is a strong bifurcation of meaning embedded in the term. When we use "silence" as a verb, it signals something imposed or inflicted, yet "silence" is also golden (as the Tremeloes sang in their hit song from 1967), a condition of serenity associated with physical and spiritual well-being and with doing no harm. With the writer Rebecca Solnit, we can think of "silence as what is imposed, and quiet as what is sought," thereby reserving "silence" (especially in its verb form) for a coercive form of behavior, one that ranges from the violent cutting out of tongues to the illocutionary force of a command to shut up.[60]

Our own culture has provided us with all too many instances of purchasing the silence of women who have been the victims of sexual assault. In an interview described in *Catch and Kill*, a detailed account of efforts by Harvey Weinstein to pay hush money to the victims of his criminal behavior, film producer Alexandra Canosa told the book's author, Ronan Farrow: "He creates the situation in which your silence will benefit you more than speaking out will." On the nondisclosure agreements Weinstein's team of lawyers prepared, Rosanna Arquette observed, "He's gonna be working very hard to track people down and silence people."[61]

In *Know My Name: A Memoir*, Chanel Miller wrote about her sexual assault on Stanford's campus as well as about her victim impact statement, published online by BuzzFeed. She described in vivid detail the treatment of sexual assault cases in a court system designed to protect perpetrators. "For years, the crime of sexual assault depended on our silence," she wrote. "The fear of knowing what happened if we spoke. Society gave us one thousand reasons; don't speak if you lack evidence, if it happened too long ago, if you were drunk, if the man is powerful."[62] Her story led not only to changes in California laws but also to the recall of the judge hearing the case, revealing the strength of extrajudicial testimony in deciding guilt and innocence and appropriateness of sentencing.

"How to Silence a Victim"—that is a chapter title in *She Said*, Jodi Kantor and Megan Twohey's account of how they broke the sexual harassment story "that helped ignite a movement." It quickly dawned on the two reporters that, in order to move beyond the "he said, she said" problem, they would have to find hard evidence for the veracity of the autobiographical accounts to which they had become privy. And it was finally in nondisclosure agreements that they found that evidence, ironically the very legal documents designed to mute claims of sexual assault and harassment. The settlements and confidentiality agreements had evolved out of a legal apparatus developed by teams of lawyers more invested in earning high payouts than in getting stories out to the public: "Cash for silence; that was the deal." For lawyers working on contingency and taking as much as one-third of the client's award as their fee, the incentive was to settle out of court, avoiding the possibility of losing their case and getting nothing, as well as the risk of having a client withdraw a claim for fear of humiliation in a courtroom setting. The result was a system that "enabled the harassers instead of stopping them."[63]

The next chapter will take up the stakes in women's storytelling and explore the profound commitment of tales told in the Voice of the Mother (to reprise Ursula Le Guin's term) to revelation, resistance, and restoration. But first I want to consider how the folkloric imagination can, paradoxically, be invested in silencing as much as it promotes talk. In three tales—one from Kenya, one from Japan, and one from Russia—a counter-discourse to women's storytelling emerges. The tales are shocking enough to warrant inclusion, for they tell us much about the vulnerability of those who use stories to transmit wisdom, counsel, and values.

"We tell ourselves stories in order to live," Joan Didion states epigrammatically in *The White Album*, and the stories women have told give us a rousing confirmation of that view. The "shifting phantasmagoria" of actual experience, Didion adds, demands a "narrative line," along with a "sermon" and a "social or moral lesson." In other words, we instinctively try to *learn* from the stories we tell, and the past is not worth talking about unless there is some kind of takeaway for those hearing about it.[64] All the more important to ask: Who tells, who listens, and to what end?

With the phrase "in order to live," Didion captures something more than survival. Stories give our lives meaning, nourishing us and nurturing connections. Recall how Philomela's story reveals how women have made their stories heard, often in the form of a simple cry for justice. The possibility of having a voice is inserted into the silent spaces of women's work (spinning, sewing, and weaving) and of Philomela's tapestry. When she turns into a bird, Philomela will sing a song of lament, becoming a proxy for the poet's voice. In some ways, the story of Philomela and Procne reveals a powerful form of storytelling envy, for Ovid is unable to put *lived experience* on display through image and song, as Philomela does. He can only tell the story secondhand. But that is also, of course, his great good fortune and privilege.

And now for the Voice of the Father, a few counter-narratives to the tales of caution and courage told by women among women. Is it any surprise that the first documented folktale tells a story about a false accusation of sexual assault? In the thirteenth century BCE, there was a story called "The Two Brothers," with one brother named Baîti, the other Anupu.[65] It is Anupu's wife who tries to seduce her brother-in-law, and when her advances are rebuffed (Baîti generously promises not to rat her out), the wife reports to her husband that Baîti assaulted her, going so far as to produce bogus injuries. The story ends with Anupu learning the truth, killing his wife, and throwing her corpse to the dogs. This inaugural tale of a fabricated accusation mingles with a range of folktales that offer a counter-tradition to what dominates the folkloric repertoire.

"Tongue Meat" is a story found in African countries on the eastern part of the continent, at the crossroads of Islamic traditions and tribal cultures. The version printed below was collected in the 1960s in Kenya, as part of a project to preserve oral storytelling traditions. It reveals just how vital storytelling is to human well-being. Disguising its narrative energy with an unappetizing title, it materializes the need for story. But, in a stunning move, it also invests men alone with the power to tell stories—to speak, to sing, to nourish, nurture, and heal. In the contrasting fates of the two wives, we have a clear sense that we need stories *in order to live,* but in this case, men alone understand the "secret" power of stories and pass that secret on to each other.

A sultan lived with his wife in a palace, but his wife was unhappy. With each passing day she grew thinner and less animated. In that same town there lived a poor man whose wife was well nourished, healthy, and happy. When the sultan heard about the couple, he summoned the poor man to his court and asked for his secret. The poor man replied, "It's very simple. I feed her meat of the tongue." The sultan summoned a butcher and told him to buy up the tongues of all the animals slaughtered in town and bring them to him, the sultan. Every day he sent all the tongues to the palace and ordered his cook to bake and fry, roast and salt these tongues in every known way and to prepare every tongue recipe ever written down. The queen had to eat those dishes three or four times a day, but it did no good. She grew ever thinner and was faring poorly. The sultan now ordered the poor man to exchange wives, to which the poor man grudgingly agreed. He took the thin queen with him and sent his own wife to the palace. Alas, there she lost more and more weight in spite of the good food the sultan offered. It was clear that she would not thrive at the palace.

The poor man, after returning home at night, would greet his new wife, tell her about the things he had seen, especially the amusing things. He told her stories that made her shriek with laughter. Then he would take his stringed instruments and sing her songs, of which he knew a great many. Until late at night he would play and amuse her. And lo! the queen put on weight in a matter of weeks. She was beautiful to look at, and her skin was shining and taut, like that of a young girl. And she smiled all day long, remembering the amusing things her husband told her. When the sultan summoned her back, she refused to return. So the sultan came to fetch her and found that she had changed and was happy. He asked her what the poor man had done, and she told him. Then he understood the meaning of meat of the tongue.[66]

Long before therapists and how-to manuals courted the attention of troubled couples, folktales offered up wisdom about how to make a marriage work. But they also did more than that. "Tongue Meat" is a story that resonates in powerful ways with other tales about tongues, tales tragic and hopeful, catastrophic and confident. "This is exactly what stories can do," as one critic puts it: "they fold all of their tellers and places together—and therein lies their mystery and their magic."[67] We have a tale in which we hear first about tongues severed from animals—as a reminder of stories in which the same can be done to torture humans, who can be robbed of the power of speech, communication, and healthy partnerships. In "Tongue Meat," the husband controls language, using it as a device to add weight to his wife and to make her more beautiful. And it is he who is able to go out into the world and return with amusing stories, telling "about the things he had seen," in all the places she is unable to be. The Kenyan tale offers wisdom and truth about how stories entertain and invigorate but it is also a reminder of how—like Ovid in ancient times, the Brothers Grimm in Germany, or Andrew Lang in England—those who wield the power to speak and write are able to appropriate and claim ownership of storytelling. It is hard to imagine why Angela Carter, who gathered together stories about "wise" and "clever" women, included this particular tale in her *Book of Fairy Tales*, for the two wives have little agency and are instead freely exchanged between the two men, who transmit a lesson about the power of storytelling to keep a wife "beautiful" and "happy." On the other hand, there is also a cautionary logic to its inclusion.

If we look at the Russian "How a Husband Weaned His Wife from Fairy Tales," a story of exemplary conciseness, it quickly becomes evident that efforts to get in a word edgewise, as it were, to disrupt, interrupt, and improvise—in short, to be part of the conversation and part of the story-making process—are discouraged. In this story, recorded in the mid-nineteenth century by Alexander Afanasev (the Russian answer to the Brothers Grimm), the pleasures of telling and listening to tales are short-circuited, producing a horror story more than anything else, a chilling account of a need to deprive women of the pleasures of narratives that formed an antidote to the repetitive labors of daily life.

There was once an innkeeper whose wife loved fairy tales above all else and accepted as lodgers only those who could tell stories. Of course the husband suffered loss because of this, and he wondered how he could wean his wife away from fairy tales. One night in winter, at a late hour, an old man shivering with cold asked him for shelter. The husband ran out and said, "Can you tell stories? My wife does not allow me to let in anyone who cannot tell stories." The old man saw that he had no choice; he was almost frozen to death. He said, "I can tell stories." "And will you tell them for a long time?" "All night."

So far, so good. They let the old man in. The husband said, "Wife, this peasant has promised to tell stories all night long, but only if you do not argue with him or interrupt him." The old man said: "Yes, there must be no interruptions, or I will not tell any stories." They ate supper and went to bed. Then the old man began: "An owl flew into a garden, sat on a tree trunk, and drank some water. An owl flew into a garden, sat on a tree trunk, and drank some water." He kept on saying again and again: "An owl flew into a garden, sat on a tree trunk, and drank some water." The wife listened and listened and then said: "What kind of story is this? He keeps repeating the same thing over and over!" "Why are you interrupting me? I told you not to argue with me! That was only the beginning; it was going to change later." The husband, upon hearing this—and it was exactly what he wanted to hear—jumped down from his bed and began to berate his wife: "You were not supposed to argue, and now you have not let him finish his story!" And he thrashed her and thrashed her, so that she began to hate stories and from that time on forswore listening to them.

This tight allegory juxtaposes improvisation and renewal with the deadening effects of rote repetition, with a clear victory for the latter. The wife's understanding of how words can create communal contact zones and animate speaker and listeners alike—but only when the teller is creative, inventive, and collaborative—is challenged by the old man's insistence on the same old story and the husband's validation of repeating a story ad infinitum and ad nauseam. The conflict between the living spirit and the dead letter has rarely been captured so vividly and compactly. Here, as in "Tongue Meat," the activity of storytelling is appropriated by men, but it is also controlled and orchestrated by them in ways that end up punishing women's desire not just to tell but also to listen and to be part of storytelling as an embodied presence.

In Japan, the tale of the tongue-cut sparrow is widely disseminated. It tells of a woman who hacks off the tongue of a bird (recall that Procne and Philomela were turned into a swallow and a nightingale) and is then punished for shutting down song and its beauty. Here is "The Tongue-Cut Sparrow" in a version recorded in the early twentieth century:

In a village in Japan an old man lived with his wife in a cottage.

One morning the old woman saw on her doorstep a poor little sparrow. She picked him up and fed him. Then she held him in the bright morning sunshine until the cold dew on his wings dried off. She let him go so that he could fly back home to his nest, but he stayed awhile and thanked her with his songs.

Each morning, the sparrow perched on the roof of the house and sang out his joy. The old man and woman thanked the sparrow, for they liked to be up early and at work. But near them there lived a cross old woman who did not like to be awakened so early. Finally she became so angry that she caught the sparrow and cut his tongue. Then the poor little sparrow flew away to his home, but he could never sing again.

When the kind woman found out what had happened, she was very sad. She said to her husband, "Let us go and find our poor little sparrow." So they started together, and asked each bird, "Do you know where the tongue-cut sparrow lives?"

At last they saw a bat hanging head downward, taking his daytime nap. "Oh, friend bat, do you know where the tongue-cut sparrow went?" they asked.

"Yes. Over the bridge and up the mountain," said the bat.

At last the man and woman reached the home of their little friend. When the sparrow saw them coming, he was very happy indeed. He and his wife and children all came and bowed their heads down to the ground to show their respect. Then the sparrow rose and led the old man and the old woman into his house, while his wife and children hastened to bring them boiled rice, fish, cress, and saké.

When the sun began to sink, the old man and woman started for home. The sparrow brought out two baskets. "I would like to give you one of these," he said. "Which will you take?" One basket was large and looked very full, while the other one seemed very small and light.

The old people decided not to take the large basket, for that might have all the sparrow's treasure in it, so they said, "The way is long and we are very old, so please let us take the smaller one."

They took it and walked home over the mountain and across the bridge, happy and contented. When they reached home they decided to open the basket and see what the sparrow had given them. They found many rolls of silk and piles of gold, enough to make them rich.

The cross old woman who had cut the sparrow's tongue was peering in through the screen when they opened their basket. She saw the rolls of silk and the piles of gold and planned how she might get some for herself.

The next morning she went to the kind woman and said, "I am so sorry that I cut the tongue of your sparrow. Please tell me the way to his home so that I may tell him I am sorry."

The kind woman told her the way and she set out. She went across the bridge, over the mountain, and through the woods. At last she came to the home of the little sparrow. He was not so glad to see this old woman, yet he was very kind and made her feel welcome. When she started home, the sparrow brought out two baskets as before. Of course the woman chose the large basket. It was very heavy, and caught on the trees as she was going through the woods.

When at last she reached home she was half dead, but she pulled
the screens shut so that no one could look in. Then she opened her
treasure.

Treasure indeed! A whole swarm of horrible creatures burst from
the basket the moment she opened it. They stung her and bit her,
they pushed her and pulled her, they scratched her and laughed at her
screams. At last she crawled to the edge of the room and slid aside the
screen to get away from the pests. The moment the door was opened
they swooped down upon her, picked her up, and flew away with her.
Since then nothing has ever been heard of the old woman.[68]

"Nothing has ever been heard of the old woman." The sparrow is silenced
when the old woman cuts its tongue, and the woman too is silenced when
"horrible creatures" assault her and carry her off. The last sentence in the
story silences the woman as powerfully as the cutting of the sparrow's
tongue, and it seems almost perverse that it is an old woman, living on
her own, who is demonized as the enemy of song and beauty.

Is this some kind of phantasmagoric reshuffling of the tropes that
appear in Ovid's story of Procne and Philomela, reconfigured in ways
that mark women as agents of violence? Or is it some kind of strange
denial of how women are silenced, a reproach to all old wives, accusing
them of severing tongues and shutting down song? The fate of the sparrow, as we see from our three suggestively characteristic folktales about
songs, stories, and silencing, is emblematic of how words, while circulat-
ing freely in social circles where women's work was carried out, were
also stifled and checked in multiple ways. In this allegory of silencing,
a woman becomes the agent rather than the victim of speech cut off.
Recall that language, speech, and plots were among the few instruments
of challenge and change available to women in times past. Recognition
of their authority and discovery of their audacity could come not just
in fables of empowerment but also in the form of stories—often written down by male collectors—that discouraged idle chatter, improvisa-

tion, and argument while at the same time projecting onto women cruel actions designed to silence the beauty of song and story.

The #MeToo movement revealed our culture's deep investment in silencing women, preventing them from talking to each other and speaking out in public spaces. Confidentiality agreements, nondisclosure agreements, and so on—these were part of a larger legal strategy used to make sure victims of sexual harassment, trapped by shame and guilt, kept quiet. The chapters that follow document the history of women's speech, and it is one marked by efforts to devalue, discredit, and dismiss. When Julia Louis-Dreyfus spoke at the Democratic Convention of 2020, she made an important statement about our legal system when she asserted: "I have a gut feeling about fairness and what's right," suggesting that our institutions are not always attuned to women's voices and that now may be the time to correct the flaws in them by paying attention to them. In the past decade, we have discovered a truth universally acknowledged in fairy tales—that there are times when our instinctive sense of what is right or wrong can and should prevail and that the legal system should invest its efforts (challenging as it may be to undertake that project) in investigating how to embed that straightforward premise into its practices in ways that are just and impartial rather than in crafting lucrative agreements that cover up criminal behavior.

# CHAPTER 3

# RESISTANCE AND REVELATION

## Storytelling and the Unsung Heroines of Fairy Tales

*I thought all the stirring tales of courage and adventure*
*were opening a door into my own future, though a*
*few years later—ten, eleven years old, perhaps—the*
*world began to close in around me and I realized*
*the songs belonged to my brothers, not me.*

—PAT BARKER, *The Silence of the Girls*

*The story might sound like common gossip*
*when told by another person, but in the*
*mouth of a storyteller, gossip was art.*

—BARBARA NEELY, *Blanche on the Lam*

## *Speaking Out: Resistance and Revelation*

When Chanel Miller published her victim impact statement in BuzzFeed in 2016, she used the pseudonym Emily Doe. "Here's the Powerful Letter the Stanford Victim Read to Her Attacker" was the headline for the account of her sexual assault. Almost instantly the story went viral, viewed by eleven million people in just a few days. Anonymity, as Miller later wrote, had been her "golden shield," protecting her from humiliation, retaliation, online threats, and other forms of harassment. Silence meant safety, she later wrote in an essay for *Time* magazine. But speaking out and telling her story in public became, as she discovered, an exercise in reconstituting her identity: "No more fragmentation, all my pieces aligning. I had put my voice back inside my body." And before long, she could say, "I felt my own authority."[1]

"Speaking out" may sound like a cliché, or an all-too-easy alternative to political action, particularly in a culture that enables us to express narcissistic injury, personal anguish, and virtue-signaling outrage through social media outlets. But talk has always gotten us somewhere, as we know from the profound silence surrounding matters ranging from child abuse (it took Oprah Winfrey's *talk* show, rather than the courts, to challenge and change that) to sexual assault (there, change came from women talking to each other and not from legal teams). It quickly becomes evident that our understanding of heroism must be shaped by talk, plain and simple, as much as by legal or political action, by words as much as by deeds. "Deeply buried secrets only prolonged my suffering," Gretchen Cherington wrote in *Poetic License* (2020), a memoir about growing up in a household with a father who was a distinguished poet and an abusive parent. "Silence is isolation, as bad as the abuse itself."[2]

The refusal to remain silent becomes the hallmark of today's new heroines, in art as in life. Speech in the form of contradiction becomes their tool, the way to reveal that timeless truths are in fact nothing but socially constructed and historically contingent fictions. Think here of Jane Eyre, heroine of Charlotte Brontë's 1847 novel of that title, a girl who shows us the power of language to speak fresh truths to elder power, to talk back, to undermine authority, and to make a new world by claiming agency through storytelling. Hers is among the first passionate outbursts by a girl in a novel, and it displays the power of words to resist subordination. This is the young Jane speaking—not the "older and wiser," socialized version of Jane who emerges later in her account. It is no coincidence that Jane herself has been seen as a fairy-tale amalgam, a young woman who is part Cinderella, part Donkeyskin, and part Bluebeard's wife. Here is Jane's full-throated outburst when she challenges the authority of her cruel guardian, Mrs. Reed:

"How dare I, Mrs Reed? How dare I? Because it is the truth."

F. H. Townsend, illustration for *Jane Eyre*, 1847

If anyone asks me how I liked you, and how you treated me, I will say the very thought of you makes me sick, and that you treated me with miserable cruelty. . . . I shall remember how you thrust me back—roughly and violently thrust me back—into the red-room, and locked me up there, to my dying day; though I was in agony; though I cried out, while suffocating with distress, "Have mercy! Have mercy, aunt Reed!" And that punishment you made me suffer because your wicked boy struck me—knocked me down for nothing. I will tell anybody who asks me questions, this exact tale. People think you a good woman, but you are bad; hard-hearted. You are deceitful![3]

Accused of "deceit," Jane denies the charge and engages in a reversal of values, repeating to Mrs. Reed, *"You* are the deceitful one." That Jane picks up a book, "some Arabian tales," after this surge of emotion, is no mere coincidence. She and Scheherazade are linked—through tale-telling and the transmission of stories—in closer kinship than seems at first evident. That contemporary reviewers were shocked by Jane's behavior is a reminder of just how daring it was to have a *girl* speak up and talk back. As Elizabeth Rigby wrote in the *Quarterly Review* in 1848, "the tone of mind and thought which has overthrown authority and violated every code human and divine abroad, and fostered Chartism and rebellion at home is the same which has also written *Jane Eyre*."[4] Reading Rigby's reaction today, we can only cheer Jane on.

There are other strategies for claiming agency and authority, and Zora Neale Hurston gives her character, coincidentally named *Janie*, a different path. *Their Eyes Were Watching God* (1937) takes up matters of love, courtship, and marriage, and it also reveals just how the drive to tell a story is entangled with gossip. Janie Crawford is a woman who knows that she has been the object of local gossip: "They got *me* up in they mouth now."[5] On her front porch, the traditional gathering place for storytelling in postbellum Black communities, she sits with her neighbor Pheoby and takes control of the narrative by telling it herself.[6] And that tale becomes the volume in the reader's hands, the proverbial "talking book" of African American writing.[7] Using the vernacular, the speech forms of everyday life, Janie breaks out of her isolation and silence and, in a double irony, takes gossip and transforms it into a form of truth-telling that in turn is a fictional account authored by a woman writer named Zora Neale Hurston.

Janie is a woman accustomed to being silenced. She is twice married, and each of her two husbands worked hard to limit her speech and movement, treating her like property. Her second husband, a store owner who rose to the position of mayor, humiliates her in public when he declares at the store, "Mah wife don't know nothin' 'bout no speech-makin'. Ah never married her for nothin' lak dat. She's uh woman and her place is in de home." It is just there, at home, on the front porch, that threshold space betwixt and between, that Janie begins her story: "If they wants to see and know, why they don't come kiss and be kissed? Ah could then sit down and tell 'em things. Ah been a delegate to de big 'ssociation of life. Yessuh! De Grand Lodge, de big convention of livin' is just where Ah been dis year and a half y'all ain't seen me." And there, huddled together with Pheoby on the porch, Janie does what women have been doing through the ages, telling her version of the story: "They sat there in the fresh young darkness close together. Pheoby eager to feel and do through Janie, but hating to show her zest for fear it might be thought mere curiosity. Janie full of that oldest human longing—self-revelation."[8]

Jane Eyre talks back and stands up to authority; Janie opens up and confides in a friend to tell her story. Both are authorities who become authors of their life stories. Resistance and revelation are paired in these two accounts that reveal how to put muteness, shame, resignation, and submission on the run. Both fictional autobiographies challenge the prevailing social order, using narrative as a confessional, a pulpit, and a lectern.[9]

## Telling Your Story:
## Talking Skulls and a Princess Wearing a Suit of Leather

The folkloric imagination is a storytelling machine gone wild, and it is not surprising to find that it has built-in advertisements for itself, with many stories about the power of stories. Poetry makes things happen, no matter what W. H. Auden may have declared, and symbolic stories have their own high-voltage power.[10] Many tales from oral traditions broadcast the upside to narrative, even as they candidly disclose the downside to confabulation. These made-up stories may not report factual events, but they can capture razor-sharp truths that belong to the wisdom of the ages. Self-referential with a vengeance, they reveal what can happen when you tell a story even as a story is being told. One of these stories is widely disseminated, as folklorists have shown, with analogues in Nigeria, Ghana, and Tanzania, as well as in the United States and the West Indies.[11] A version of it was recorded in 1921 by Leo Frobenius, a German ethnologist who collected stories from the African continent. The teller is clearly exploiting anxieties about skulls, bones, and mortality to produce maximum dramatic effect and to remind listeners that a good story can be a matter of life and death.

> A hunter goes into the bush. He finds an old human skull. The hunter says, "What brought you here?" The skull answers, "Talking brought me here." The hunter runs off and finds the king. He tells the king, "I found a human skull in the bush, and, when I spoke to it, it talked back."
>
> The king said, "Never since my mother bore me have I heard that a skull could speak." The king summoned the Alkali, the Saba, and the Degi and asked them if they had ever heard anything like this. None of the wise men had heard anything like it, and they decided to send a guard out with the hunter to find out if his story was true. The guard accompanied the hunter into the bush with the order to kill him on the spot if he was lying. The guard and the hunter find the skull. The hunter says to the skull, "Skull, speak." The skull remains silent. The hunter asks as before, "What brought you here?" The skull remains silent. All day long the hunter pleads with the skull to speak, but it remains silent. In the evening the guard tells the hunter to make the skull speak, and when it does not, they kill him as the king commanded.
>
> After the guard leaves, the skull opens its jaws, and asks the dead hunter's head, "What brought you here?" The dead hunter replies, "Talking brought me here."[12]

A cautionary tale about reporting what you have seen and heard, "The Talking Skull" also self-reflexively creates a meaningful narrative that undermines its own message. On the one hand we learn about the risks of bringing back news about outlandish things, but on the other hand we have a story that revels in reporting a shocking, startling, scandalous event. The tellers of this tale knew about the compulsion to reveal, confess, air, and just simply *talk*. But they also understood, at a profound level, that the temptation to tell all can take a wrong turn and lead to a sentence of death.

"I'm afraid they'll kill me. They said they'd kill me if I told on them." That's what Recy Taylor told a reporter after she had been abducted and raped by six white men after leaving church on a Sunday evening in Alabama in 1944. That telling tales can have fatal consequences is driven home with a vengeance in this shameful chapter of American history. Taylor received death threats from white vigilantes, who also firebombed her home and set her front porch on fire. If Black victims of sexual assault in the United States rarely found justice in the courtroom, their stories helped mobilize leaders in the civil rights movement to build legal and political coalitions.[13] It was Rosa Parks who helped organize Recy Taylor's defense and who went to Abbeville in 1944 to gather the facts in the case and to make sure her story was told.

Given the enormous stakes in telling your story or speaking truth to the custodians of power, there is always risk. Even when you are reporting the facts, your audience might remain skeptical or hostile, indicting you for false claims, duplicity, or gross exaggeration. The talking skull is, of course, a wonder, an embodied oxymoron that defies belief. The story of its duplicity endlessly replicates itself in a metaphorical hall of mirrors as it is passed down, repeated, and varied, from one generation to the next. There is "The Skull That Talked Back," collected by Zora Neale Hurston in the 1930s in the Deep South, the Ghanaian story "The Hunter and the Tortoise," and the Ozark tale about a talking turtle.[14] In Hurston's story, Old Skull Head tells a man named High Walker: "My mouth brought me here, and if you don't mind, yours will bring you here too."[15] The folktale reminds listeners to keep their mouths shut even as the actual teller of the tale is running off at the mouth, turning a story about storytelling into an allegory of diction as contradiction.

The risk involved in voicing public denunciations becomes evident when we see how girls and women in folkloric inventions resort to subterfuge, wearing costumes and using all manner of stealth measures before telling their tales. In the tales themselves, they are forever engaging in deception, sometimes putting on animal skins (as in "Donkeyskin," "Thousandfurs," or "Catskin"), occasionally hiding in boxes, barrels, and baskets ("Fitcher's Bird"), or covering themselves with cinders, pitch, green moss, or feathers ("Mossycoat"). The heroines profit from mimicry and masquerade, engaging in mysterious parlor games of hide-and-seek, concealing their identity and then revealing it.

In the Egyptian story "The Princess in the Suit of Leather," Juleidah—the girl who wears that odd costume named in the title— flees from home when a "wrinkled matron" advises her widower father to marry his own daughter. She leaps over a palace wall, commissions a suit of leather from a tanner, becomes a servant in a sultan's palace, and wins the heart of the ruler's son, whom she weds. One day, she receives visitors that include her father and the troublemaking matron who had proposed the ill-advised marriage. Putting on the robes and headcloth of her husband, she tells stories to "entertain" her guests. The matron keeps interrupting her accounts, nervously asking, "Can you find no better story than this?" It is then that Juleidah tells the "history of her own adventures," and, when she finishes, she announces: "I am your daughter the princess, upon whom all these troubles fell through the words of this old sinner and daughter of shame." The matron is flung over a cliff; the king gives Juleidah half his kingdom; and all the survivors live in "happiness and contentment."[16]

Many so-called old wives' tales give us, near the end of the story, a compact digest of the narrative, which itself may have been fragmented by interruptions, from stirring the soup to quieting a squalling infant. This dense nugget of elder wisdom was an insurance policy against cultural amnesia and guaranteed that stories mapping escape routes from bad betrothals, abject circumstances, and toxic marriages had a good chance of surviving and enduring. On the one hand, the tales proclaim the importance of disclosing the facts in the here and now ("Speak out! Tell your story"), but they also endorse committing told tales to memory, ensuring their replication and survival, in the form of fiction rather than fact, as a meme that can, in the positive sense of the term, go viral.

"The Princess in the Suit of Leather" was put into print in the twentieth century. But the story circulated in oral traditions long before that in the form of fairy tales, as one of those stories we classify as an "old wives' tale." These confabulations have a long and venerable history as late-night entertainments told by gossips, grannies, nannies, and female domestic servants among themselves and to younger generations. Plato tells of the *mythos graos*, the "old wives' tales" told to amuse or punish children (note the use of the term *mythos*, from which our term "myth" derives).[17] There is also the *anilis fabula* ("old wives' tale"), a term used in the second century CE by Apuleius, who staged a scene of storytelling in *The Golden Ass*, when a "drunken old crone" tries to comfort the victim of an abduction by telling her a tale called "Cupid and Psyche."[18] Even before the rise of print culture and the production of anthologies of fairy tales explicitly for children, traditional tales told by old women were demoted to the status of fare for the younger crowd.

Stories like "The Princess in the Suit of Leather" can give us pause and make us wonder if the women telling these stories were in fact only "old wives"—the elderly women and female domestics to whom they are usually attributed. For centuries the collectors of fairy tales described their sources as aged, invariably misshapen, old crones (that's the term used by the seventeenth-century Neapolitan writer Giambattista Basile), or as servants and nursemaids (Madame de Sévigné labeled them as such in the nineteenth century), or as old women, grandmothers, and nurses (Charles Perrault attributed his seventeenth-century collection of French stories to them). Tadeo, host of the storytelling sessions in *The Pentamerone*, chooses ten women, the ones who are "most expert" and "quick-tongued" in the art of speaking. Here is the parade of crones: "lame Zeza, twisted Cecca, goitered Meneca, big-nosed Tolla, hunch-back Popa, drooling Antonella, snout-faced Ciulla, cross-eyed Paolla, mangy Ciommetella, and shitty Iacova."[19]

Frontispieces to fairy-tale collections picture the tellers as crooked women, bent with age, leaning on canes, often surrounded by grandchildren. By attributing authorship of fairy tales to older generations belonging to the laboring classes, the collectors, educated men from a higher social class, distanced themselves from female voices even as they took command of them. They deprived fairy tales of their authority by disavowing the broad cultural ownership of the tales, which belong to young and old, educated and literate, aristocrats and commoners.

## Discrediting the Wisdom of Old Wives' Tales

Old wives' tales can be encoded with valuable knowledge. The fact that wisdom is preserved through conversation in female domestic circles and in routine tête-à-tête moments between women becomes evident from a tale collected in 1931 by a British colonial administrator in what is today Ghana. It was given the title "Keep Your Secrets." Like the story of the talking skull, this tale too is aggressively didactic, admonishing its listeners to exercise discretion. It warns about the hazards of divulging lifesaving strategies passed on from one generation of women to the next.

In "Keep Your Secrets," a young woman decides to choose her own husband and weds a man who is not a man at all but a hyena. At night, the husband asks his wife what she would do were they to quarrel, and the wife replies that she would turn herself into a tree. "I should catch you all the same," the hyena-husband replies. The wife's mother, eavesdropping on the conversation about her daughter's various tactics for a quick getaway, shouts from her room, "Keep quiet, my daughter, is it thus that a woman tells all her secrets to her man?" The tale concludes by describing the wife's decision to leave her hyena-husband and the tricks she uses to escape. He is on to all her subterfuges, save one, the "thing" she managed to keep to herself.

> Next morning, when the day was breaking, the husband told his wife
> to rise up as he was returning to his home. He bade her make ready to
> accompany him a short way down the road to see him off. She did as

he told her, and as soon as the couple were out of sight of the village the husband turned himself into a hyena and tried to catch the girl, who changed herself into a tree, then into a pool of water, then into a stone but the hyena almost tore the tree down, nearly drank all the water and half swallowed the stone.

Then the girl changed herself into the thing which the night before her mother had managed to stop her from betraying. The hyena looked and looked everywhere and at last, fearing the villagers would come and kill him, made off.

At once the girl changed into her own proper form and ran back to the village.[20]

"Keep Your Secrets" wisely and mischievously avoids disclosing the lifesaving secret, leaving us as readers wondering not just about the wife's strategy but also about what came up in conversations that followed the telling of the story. Was it resourceful speculation about the identity of the "thing" shared between guarded mother and loose-lipped daughter? Or about how to find protection against violent men, even husbands? Could it have been about the beastly nature of husbands? The wonders in this story surely gave rise to wondering why and how, as well as considering the many ways to navigate the risks and perils of domestic arrangements.

That kind of talk among women was dangerous, and there were ways to discredit the stories that gave rise to it. The German writer Christoph Martin Wieland protested what he believed to be a lowering of literary standards when he declared in 1786, just a few years before the Grimms started putting fairy tales between the covers of a book: "It is all right for popular fairy tales, told by the people, to be transmitted orally, but they ought not to be printed."[21] His resentment-inflected caveat is a sharp reminder of a deep need to secure the boundary separating the printed eloquence of educated men from the mere chatter of women. The literary canon as created by an elite had to be cordoned off from the improvisational storytelling of ordinary folk, especially gossipy and silly old women.

*The Dismal Tale*, painted by Thomas Stothard (1755–
1834) and engraved by H. C. Shenton
*Wellcome Collection*

Fairy tales from women's storytelling circles were further segregated
and kept in their place by transplanting them into the culture of childhood. Passed down from one generation to the next, the stories—minus
the ones that took a turn into the edgy and subversive—could be deployed
to offer lessons in values, beliefs, and moral principles. They became part
of a free-floating pedagogical agenda that preceded the rise of literacy
and offered wisdom packaged in wit. The French author Marie-Jeanne
L'Héritier de Villandon defended the resourceful intelligence of nurses
and governesses by pointing to the "moral features" of the stories they

told. At the same time, unlike her male contemporaries, she understood that the tales could still operate effectively in adult salons for a social elite, enabling listeners to indulge in aristocratic romanticism, serving as conversation starters, and constructing platforms for the sociability so highly prized in those settings.[22]

As Marina Warner has insightfully pointed out in a cultural history of fairy tales, arguments like Madame L'Héritier's for coaxing the stories out of the nursery and repurposing them for elite audiences were doomed, for old wives' tales came to be trivialized, dismissed as nonsense and idle chatter. "On a par with trifles, 'mere old wives' tales' carry connotations of error, of false counsel, ignorance, prejudice and fallacious nostrums."[23] And as Angela Carter put it, once the stories were associated with old women, they could readily be dismissed. "Old wives' tales—that is, worthless stories, untruths, trivial gossip, a derisive label that allots the genuine art of storytelling to women at the exact same time as it takes all value from it."[24]

A look at the frontispieces to fairy-tale collections reminds us of why so many were determined to exclude the tales from *literary* culture. In most of those images, an elderly female domestic figure (think again stern grannies, nannies bent over by age, or servants in patched clothing) recites stories to boys and girls. Fairy tales now belong to the very young or the very old, but not to anyone in between. Parents are absent, and how could adults in their right minds possibly number among the enraptured listeners of such trifles? Controlling the traffic between the oral and the literary and holding the line against enabling the oral a right-of-way into print culture reflects the strong determination to keep what had become old wives' tales in the home and far away from the printing press, which created pathways into the public sphere. Otherwise, they might be widely disseminated rather than obstinately existing in pockets of local oral storytelling cultures.

As fairy tales moved from spinning rooms, sewing circles, and the hearth into the nursery, they lost much of their subversive energy. The editors of the famed collections that we continue to publish today (the Brothers Grimm, Charles Perrault, Joseph Jacobs, Alexander Afanasev, and so on) were for the most part men, prominent literary figures and political actors who had no reservations about taking control of and repurposing those vexing voices that had transmitted tales from one generation to the next.

Like the common scold—the designation for a cantankerous woman who became a public nuisance by engaging in forms of negative speech such as complaining, bickering, and quarreling—the tellers of tales talked in ways that could be irritating, provocative, and inflammatory. Giambattista Basile let one of those foul-mouthed women slip into the frame narrative for his *Tale of Tales*. When a court page shatters the jar used by an old woman to collect cooking oil, she lets loose a torrent of curses:

George Cruikshank, frontispiece for *German Popular Stories*, 1823
Richard Vogler Cruikshank Collection, Grunwald Center for the Graphic Arts, UCLA

"Ah you worthless thing, you dope, shithead, bed pisser, leaping goat, diaper ass, hangman's noose, bastard mule! . . . Scoundrel, beggar, son of a whore, rogue!"[25] Is it any wonder that a fifteenth-century British playwright compared women's speech with the waste products of animals: "Go forth, and let the whores cackle! / Where women are, are many words: / Let them go hopping with their hackle! / Where geese sit, are many turds."[26] The words of poets can be revelatory, but scolds generally give more offense than pleasure. What better way to marginalize the tellers of fairy tales than to affiliate them with crones and hags, who, through their close proximity with scolds and witches, hardly seemed trustworthy sources of wisdom and guidance? That the word "scold" is derived from the Old Norse *skald* ("poet") is suggestive, pointing to the possibility that those crabby old women might have been on to something, sharing arsenals of satirical weapons with poets.

Fairy tales go far back in time, and they entered the literary canon as print culture with collections like Giovanni Francesco Straparola's freewheeling *The Pleasant Nights* (1550–53) and Giambattista Basile's

Charles Perrault, frontispiece to
*Contes de ma mère l'Oye,* 1697

burlesque *The Pentamerone* (1634–46), which both feature tales told by women, ladies in the one case, wizened old crones in the other. Both Chaucer and Boccaccio borrowed from oral traditions, with women's voices mixing and mingling with those of men and with themes and motifs that derive from fairy-tale lore.

The anxiety about transporting fairy tales and folktales into the domain of print culture continued well into the twentieth century as well as into our own time. It resurfaces in the pronouncements of someone as reasonable as Karel Čapek, renowned as the Czech author of the play *RUR* (1920). In an essay on fairy tales, he insisted that "a true folk fairy tale does not originate in being taken down by the collector of folklore but in being told by a grandmother to her grandchildren," once again perpetuating the myth that the sources are all superannuated women and that the audience for the tales is limited to the young. "A real fairy tale," he added, is a "tale within a circle of listeners."[27] Fairy tales should be kept in their place and are best confined to the home.

## Gossip and Storytelling

Chatter, chitchat, gossip, idle talk, and conversation have always done deep cultural work for us, and today they continue to serve as sources of knowledge, helping us make sense of the world, providing opportunities for social bonding, and shaping our ways of understanding the values of the world in which we live. For centuries, philosophers condemned "meaningless talk," excluding from their consideration bodies of conversation that take up personal matters and local affairs rather than large-scale public issues. "Pay no attention to gossip," Immanuel Kant warned, for it emerges from "shallow and malicious judgment" and is a "sign of weakness." Yet a recent biography of the German philosopher suggests he routinely indulged in it at dinner parties he regularly hosted.[28] Kierkegaard condemned gossip as trivial and ephemeral, contrasting it with "real talk" that takes up subjects of profound importance with a lasting influence. He worked hard to diminish the power of gossip, even as he understood its muscle and clout, for a local paper, much to his distress, was forever belittling his work and disparaging his physical appearance—he looks like "Either/Or," they wrote.[29] "Idle talk [*Gerede*] is something that anyone can rake up," Heidegger intoned, condemning the egalitarian nature of gossip and its value for the socially marginalized even if conceding its pragmatic value.[30] Being seen and being heard, Hannah Arendt tells us, are both possible only in the public arena, a space of organized remembrance. All else is ephemeral and unworthy of commemoration. High culture's disdain for gossip is strategic, and it is symptomatic of deep anxieties about the subversive power of gabbing, trading stories, and engaging in the seemingly frivolous activity of small talk, malicious or benign.

It is something of a challenge to identify any culture that has not belittled and maligned women's speech and branded it as gossipy. "The chattering, ranting, gossiping female, the tattle, the scold, the toothless crone, her mouth wind-full of speech, is older than fairy-tales," one critic tells

Punishing the common scold in a ducking stool,
from a British chapbook, 1834

us, inadvertently connecting gossip with folklore and cementing the connection between gossip and elderly, deformed women.[31] Juvenal describes
women's loquacity in cacophonous terms: "Her speech pours out in such
a torrent that you would think that pots and bells were being banged
together."[32] The idea of loose talk spills over into the concept of loose
morals, reminding us that the verbal and sexual freedom of women creates high anxiety and incites efforts to contain and police their liberties
and especially any libertine behaviors. Is it necessary to add that those
efforts are redoubled by those who deeply understand the attractions of
the desires that they so vigorously seek to suppress?

The horror of the oral, of stories that lack the luster of the literary,
stems in part from the link between old wives' tales and gossip, or idle
chatter. How could these trifles possibly be dignified with print? But gossip has value precisely because it creates opportunities for talking through
the emotional entanglements of our social lives. Its participants jointly
construct narratives from the stuff of everyday life, spicy plots charged
with speculative glee. Gossip takes up a range of topics, among them
scandal, which invites us to engage in talk about moral dilemmas and
social conflicts.[33] And, more important, it serves as a resource for those
without access to other options for securing knowledge, operating as a
licensed form of release that may not upend the order of things but still
serves as an expressive outlet.

What is gossip's greatest sin? One possibility is that gossip knits
women together to create networks of social interactions beyond patriarchal control and oversight. It can be seen as a counter-discourse that operates against prevailing communal norms, a strategy for collecting talk in
the form of compelling stories that can be parsed and analyzed to turn
into useful sources of wisdom and knowledge. It becomes a storytelling
resource built into a preexisting support system for those limited in their
mobility and confined to the domestic sphere.

That there is something threatening about gossip becomes evident in
the account of F. G. Bailey, a social anthropologist studying a village in the
French Alps. He contrasted two groups, divided by gender. When men
sit around, and the conversation turns gossipy, that is considered socially

acceptable, for the exchanges are viewed as "light-hearted, good-natured, altruistic," a way of gathering information and expressing opinions. When women are seen chatting, then it is an entirely different matter: "Very likely they are indulging in . . . gossip, malice, 'character assassination.' "[34] "Character assassination": those are fighting words. Clearly there is the perception of something dangerous, dodgy, and malevolent in these women gossips and the stories they tell.

Language has, of course, always been the one resource available to those who have been subordinated, disenfranchised, or dispossessed. Unless you are gagged and bound or your tongue is cut out (as we have seen, one of many unimaginably cruel forms of torture and punishment invented by humans), you can still speak. The words may be limited but speech is still possible. The African American writer Audre Lorde once wrote that "the master's tools will never dismantle the master's house," implying that language, shaped by the masters, cannot be deployed to undermine them and can never bring about "genuine victory."[35] All that can be gained through language is partial and provisional, without lasting effect. Still, gossip can create a liberating sense of solidarity for those without a voice. It can become an effective weapon in the hands of the subordinated, as it modulates from idle talk into something more potent, especially if it can leave home in some surreptitious way to enter the public sphere.

The etymological history of "gossip" is complex. The word started out meaning "god-related," then modulated, as a noun, into a term used to designate a godparent. Gradually it was extended to include the social circle of all possible godparents and was applied to kinfolk and friends in general. Only later did the term take a negative turn, used to designate a mode of conversation defined by the *OED* as "idle talk, trifling or groundless rumour; tittle-tattle." The swerve into the trivial and mendacious suggests a steady devaluation of what is talked about, among intimates and friends, in the domestic sphere.

Once degraded, gossip transformed itself from a form of social support and bonding into social sabotage. "Gossip" began to signal not only idle, vindictive talk (is there anything worse than being a gossip columnist?)

but also its source, and "a gossip" is almost exclusively gendered female in most languages. In German-speaking regions, male gossips (*Klatsch-vater* is the term) may exist, but they are outnumbered by their female counterparts (*Klatsche, Klatschweib, Klatschlotte, Klatschtrine, Klatschlise,* and so on). Anthropologists have studied gossip in places ranging from the Antilles island of Saint Vincent to student dorms at an American university. Despite evidence that women gossip only marginally more than men, anecdotes, proverbs, folktales, jokelore, and conventional wisdom all conspire to turn gossip into a female form of communication and bonding, one boiling over with malice more than anything else.[36]

Folklorists and anthropologists tell us that when gossip turns into story—when it becomes a hybrid of truth and fiction, a kind of confabulation—it helps us address collective social anxieties and cultural contradictions. Folktales enable us to process feelings, giving a name to our fears and challenges, turning them into "a representative and recognizable symbolic form."[37] A made-up story might have its origins in the real-life account of, say, a woman's dread of marriage or of another woman's resentment of a stepchild, but it will also disguise those accounts by depersonalizing their content, projecting them into an imaginary world, and exaggerating and enlarging their stakes.

Here is one example of the kind of story that begins as news, turns into a legend, and ends as a fairy tale. It is a Native American tale, told by the Salishan people living in the northwest United States and southwest regions of Canada:

> Once some people were camped on the hills near Lytton, and among them were two girls who were fond of playing far away from the camp. Their father warned them against the giants, who had infested the country.
>
> One day they rambled off, playing as usual, and two giants saw them. They put them under their arms and ran off with them to their house on an island far away. They treated them kindly and gave them plenty of game to eat.
>
> For four days the girls were almost overcome by the smell of the

giants, but gradually they became used to it. For four years they lived with the giants, who would carry them across the river to dig roots and gather berries which did not grow on the island.

One summer the giants took them to a place where huckleberries were plentiful. They knew that the girls liked huckleberries very much. They left them to gather berries, and said they would go hunting and come back in a few days. The elder sister recognized the place as not many days' travel from their people's home, and they ran away.

The giants returned, and, when they found the girls gone, they followed their tracks. The girls saw that they were about to be overtaken, and they climbed to the top of a large spruce-tree, where they could not be seen. They tied themselves with their tumplines. The giants thought they must be in the tree and tried to find them. They walked all around the tree but could not see them. They shook the tree many times and pushed and pulled against it, but the tree did not break, and the girls did not fall down. And so the giants left.

The giants were still looking for the girls, and they soon saw them in the distance. They pursued them, and when the girls saw that they were about to be caught, they crawled into a large hollow log. They covered the openings with branches. The giants pulled at the branches but they did not move. They tried to roll the log downhill, but it was too heavy. After a while, they gave up.

Once they were gone, the girls started running and finally reached a camp of their own people in the mountains. Their moccasins were worn out, and their clothes were torn. They told the people how the giants lived and behaved. They were asked if the giants had any names, and they said they were called Stosomu'lamux and TsekEtinu's.

"This is the essence of play," the celebrated folklorist Roger Abrahams tells us, "objectifying . . . anxiety situations, allowing the free expenditure of energies without fear of social consequences."[38] Suddenly there is no need for seclusion and secrecy, two distinctive features of idle chatter and gossip. The story can now be broadcast, told in public without fear of payback. It is also "under control," in ways that are never the case in real life. Encapsulating a high-stakes conflict, it locates the problem in the long ago and far away of "once upon a time," turning the protagonists into figures with generic names or descriptors and magnifying the monstrousness of the villains, who are now giants, dragons, stepmothers, and ogres. And suddenly the story has become "harmless," mere entertainment, just a fairy tale or a myth. But it continues to haunt us, working its magic by pushing us to talk through all the conflicts it puts on display, magnifying them to create a sensation.

For a vivid sense of how news, rumor, and gossip can modulate into myth, we can turn to anthropological observations from Melville J. Herskovits and Frances S. Herskovits, a couple who studied and documented the storytelling protocols of villagers on the island of Trinidad: "Old and young delight in telling, and hearing told, all the little incidents that go on in the village. To the outside the speed with which news spreads never ceased to be a source of amazement. Equally amazing was the celerity with which the story acquired a texture that made of the commonplace a thing of meaningful or ironic sequences."[39] Texture: that is what is added to the story to turn it from the banal, trivial, and ordinary to something of mythical weight. And that texture comes through conversational exchange, with responses from listeners that put in motion a "weaving backwards and forwards in time of tales of supernatural deeds, and of retribution." In sum, the ancestral wisdom captured in the folklore of the past enriches and narrativizes gossip, producing new stories that will, in turn, be passed on to the next generation. Suddenly we move from the particularities of everyday life to the broad, general strokes and higher truths of mythical thinking.

The Herskovitses witnessed how villagers in Trinidad turned life into art, or what Clifford Geertz called a "cultural form." And cultural forms are not merely "reflections of a pre-existing sensibility" but also "positive agents in the creation and maintenance of such a sensibility." Geertz's famous analysis of the Balinese cockfight reveals how symbolic forms operate: "It is this kind of bringing of assorted experiences of everyday life to focus that the cockfight, set aside from that life as 'only a game' and reconnected to it as 'more than a game,' accomplishes, and so creates what, better than typical or universal, could be called a paradigmatic human event."[40] "Only a game" and "more than a game" captures how story is both low stakes and high stakes, commanding our attention and allowing us to play and be in turn entertained. Operatic and melodramatic, stories told in a communal setting capture lightning in a bottle and put it on display for all to contemplate, wonder at, and begin the hard work of speculation—in short, to philosophize, to engage in an activity that humans do supremely well.

Geertz does not, I think, pay sufficient attention to how interpretive work done in the storytelling arena can disrupt the status quo. Storytelling is a way of creating an alternative discourse, one that may deviate from and contest what is heard in political and public speech. As we have seen, the power of gossip and storytelling to challenge prevailing norms has been vibrantly enacted in the United States by the #MeToo movement. And the real-life stories told by that movement have seeped into our entertainments—Apple's 2020 streaming series *The Morning Show* recycled the scandal that rocked NBC's *Today* show. Entertainments like that one and like others give us much to talk about as we watch how art processes life and enlarges it.

## Unsung Heroines

With the Great Migration of old wives' tales into the nursery, much was lost, with many stories performing a vanishing act. Fairy tales about domestic violence (all those "Bluebeard" tales with their mysterious, charismatic, cruel husbands), accounts of sexual abuse ("Donkeyskin," for example, in which a girl narrowly escapes from a father who demands her hand in marriage), and stories of confinement and mutilation ("The Maiden without Hands") were thinned out, disappearing from the repertoire, for all the obvious reasons. These tales, with their raised scimitars, amputated limbs, and sleepless nights under the covers with hedgehogs or snakes, were hardly suitable reading for the young. They were, of course, never designed for the young, but for women, young and old, as they imagined all the disturbing turns that could occur in courtship and marriage, the path and the goal for most women.

Charles Perrault, the Brothers Grimm, Joseph Jacobs, and the many other philologists, antiquarians, and men of letters (as they were once called) who put together national anthologies of folktales began the slow, steady process of eviscerating the storytelling archive, removing the darker content, expunging scenes alluding to sexual assault, domestic violence, and incest. They did not immediately do away with stories like "Donkeyskin," "Thousandfurs," "Catskin," "The She-Bear," and "The King Who Wishes to Marry His Daughter"—all of which featured incestuous desire—but they worked hard to make tale types like that less prominent in their collections. And some editors of those stories lifted blame from the father by making it clear that the king's councilors, rather than the king himself, were bent on the perverse alliance. Still others attributed the grieving king's pursuit of his daughter to a temporary fit of madness after the loss of his beloved wife.

Later in the nineteenth century, folklorists like Andrew Lang, who put together the popular British Rainbow series of fairy-tale volumes (it was his wife and a team of her friends and collaborators who did the actual collecting legwork), tried to make stories like "Donkeyskin" child friendly.[41] The girl in Lang's rendition of the story is an "adopted" daughter, and we are told repeatedly that the king is not her real father—she just calls him that. Even in its bowdlerized form, stories like that had no appeal for someone like Walt Disney, who favored tales featuring wicked queens (*Snow White and the Seven Dwarfs*), cruel stepmothers (*Cinderella*), and evil sorceresses (*Sleeping Beauty*) over fathers with designs on their daughters. He and others ignored the many stories about fathers who lock their daughters up in towers, chop off their hands, or sell them to the devil.

Tales about abusive fathers and harassing brothers disappeared from the fairy-tale canon. Giambattista Basile's "Penta with the Chopped-Off Hands" shows us a woman talking back to a brother, a man determined to make his sister his wife: "I'm amazed that you let those words come out of your mouth! If they're in jest, they're worthy of an ass, and if they're in earnest they stink like a billy goat. I'm sorry that you have the tongue to say those ugly and shameful things, and that I have the ears to hear them. Me, your wife? Who did this to you? What kind of trap is this? Since when have people made these blends? Since when these stews? These mixtures?" The brother answers by singing the praises of his sister's hands. How does she respond? By chopping them off and sending them to him on a platter, whereupon the brother locks her in a chest that he then tosses into the sea. A sorcerer restores the hands in the end, in a final tableau of reconciliation.[42]

Why have all the heroines who show fierce determination in the face of domestic violence disappeared? The loss of these stories is of real consequence, for Bluebeard's wife, Catskin, the Maiden without Hands, Thousandfurs, and a host of other heroines with names that we would not recognize today model heroic behavior, demonstrating how victims of dreadful family circumstances can find ways not just to survive but to prevail, even after enduring the unimaginable. Endurance: that is the trait that Clarissa Pinkola Estés, author of *Women Who Run with the Wolves*, saw as the guiding lesson of stories like "The Handless Maiden" (as she calls it). The word "endurance," she points out, means not just to continue without cessation but also "to harden, to make sturdy, to make robust, to strengthen." "We don't just go on to go on," she adds. "Endurance means that we are making something."[43]

Along with the oral storytelling cultures that bound together domestic servants, women in sewing circles, wet nurses, and cooks at the hearth, tales about domestic violence have gradually faded and been forgotten, transformed into "innocent" child's play rather than remaining the grown-up business of talk and conversational give-and-take. While it is true that the undisguised and unembellished versions of these tales have gone missing, the tropes of some of these stories have real staying power. There are plenty of forbidden chambers, bloody keys, and husbands with skeletons in their closets in our entertainments today. And, as we shall see, these are precisely the stories that women writers took up in the late twentieth century, resurrecting traditions that would otherwise have been lost.

"A woman without a tongue is as a soldier without his weapon," the British poet George Peele wrote in his 1595 play *The Old Wives' Tale*.[44] Silencing women's voices, keeping their stories out of the official canon, became something of a mission, consciously or not, and the strategy of belittling fairy tales was a powerful way of preventing them from becoming a form of cultural capital available to women belonging to the educated classes, as the stories had once been for the unlettered. It also impeded the wider dissemination of an entire genre of stories that tell of the complications of courtship, love, and marriage, of the underdog who succeeds in turning the tables on the wealthy and powerful, of utopian fantasies that end with a "happily ever after."

Before turning to the afterlife of some of these stories in the works of women writers, let us look at one of the old wives' tales that performed a vanishing act. "Fitcher's Bird," included in the Grimms' *Children's Stories and Household Tales*, gives us a heroine who is not only courageous and clever but also a healer and rescuer. Here is her story, a variant of the tale of "Bluebeard," a fairy tale that conventionally ends with the liberation of the heroine by her brothers:

> Once upon a time there was a wizard who used to disguise himself as a poor man and go begging from door to door in order to capture pretty girls. No one had any idea what he did with them, for they all disappeared without a trace.
>
> One day the wizard appeared at the door of a man with three beautiful daughters. He looked like a poor, weak beggar and had a basket strapped to his back, as if he were collecting alms. When he asked for something to eat, the eldest girl came to the door to give him a crust of bread. All he did was touch her, and she had to jump right into his basket. Then he made long legs and hurried off to bring her back to his house, which was in the middle of a dark forest.
>
> Everything in the house was grand. The wizard gave the girl

whatever she wanted and told her: "Dearest, I'm sure you'll be happy here with me, for you'll have whatever your heart desires." After a few days had gone by, he said: "I have to go on a trip and will leave you by yourself for a while. Here are the keys for the house. You can go anywhere you want and look around at anything you want, but don't go into the room that this little key opens. I forbid it under the punishment of death."

He also gave her an egg and said: "Carry it with you wherever you go, because if it gets lost, something terrible will happen." She took the keys and the egg and promised to do exactly as he had told her. After he left, she went over the house from top to bottom, taking a good look at everything in it. The rooms were glittering with silver and gold, and she thought that she had never seen anything so magnificent. When she finally got to the forbidden door, she was about to walk right past it when curiosity got the better of her. She inspected the key and found that it looked just like the others. Putting it into the lock, she turned it just a bit, and the door sprang open.

Imagine what she saw when she entered! In the middle of the room there was a big basin full of blood, and in it were the hacked off limbs of dead bodies. Next to the basin was a block of wood with a gleaming ax lodged in it. She was so horrified that she dropped the egg she was holding into the basin. Even though she took it right out and wiped off the blood, it didn't help. The stain came right back again. She wiped and scraped, but it just wouldn't come off.

Not much later the man returned from his journey, and the first things he asked for were the key and the egg. She gave them to him, but she was trembling, and when he saw the red stain, he knew that she had set foot in the bloody chamber. "You went into the chamber against my wishes," he said. "Now you will go back in against yours. Your life has reached its end."

The man threw her down, dragged her into the chamber by her hair, chopped her head off on the block, and hacked her into pieces so that her blood ran down all over the floor. Then he tossed her into the basin with the others.

"Now I'll go and get the second one," said the wizard, and he went back to the house dressed as a poor man begging for charity. When the second daughter brought him a crust of bread, he caught her as he had the first just by touching her. He carried her off, and she fared no better than the first sister. Her curiosity got the better of her: she opened the door to the bloody chamber, looked inside, and when the wizard came back she had to pay with her life.

The man went to find the third daughter, but she was clever and sly. After handing the keys and the egg over to her, he went away, and she put the egg in a safe place. She explored the house and entered the forbidden chamber. And what did she see! There in the basin were both her sisters, foully murdered and chopped into pieces. But she set to work gathering all the body parts and put them back where they belonged: heads, torsos, arms, and legs. When everything was in place, the pieces began to move and to knit back together. Both girls opened their eyes and came back to life. Overjoyed, they kissed and hugged each other.

On his return home, the man asked right away about the keys and egg. When he was unable to find a trace of blood on the egg, he declared: "You have passed the test, and you shall be my bride." He no longer had any power over her and had to do her bidding. "Very well," she replied. "But first you must take a basketful of gold to my father and mother, and you must carry it on your back. In the meantime, I'll make plans for the wedding."

She ran to her sisters, whom she had hidden in a little room, and said: "Now I can save you. That brute will be the one who carries you home. But as soon as you get back there, send help for me."

She put both girls into a basket and covered them with gold until they were completely hidden. Then she summoned the wizard and said: "Pick up the basket and start walking, but don't you dare stop to rest along the way. I'll be looking out my little window, keeping an eye on you."

The wizard hoisted the basket up on his shoulders and started off with it. But it was so heavy that sweat began to pour down his forehead. He sat down to rest for a while, but within moments one of the girls cried out from the basket: "I'm looking out my little window, and I see that you're resting. Get a move on." Whenever he stopped, the voice sounded, and he had to keep going until finally, panting for breath and groaning, he managed to get the basket with the gold and with the two girls in it back to the parents' house.

Meanwhile the bride was preparing the wedding celebration, to which she had invited all the wizard's friends. She took a skull with grinning teeth, crowned it with jewels and a garland of flowers, carried it upstairs, and set it down at an attic window, facing to the outside. When everything was ready, she crawled into a barrel of honey, cut open a featherbed and rolled around in the feathers until she looked like a strange bird that no one could possibly recognize. She left the house and, on her way, she met some wedding guests, who asked:

> *"Oh, Fitcher's feathered bird, where have you been?"*
> *"From feathered Fitze Fitcher's house I've come."*
> *"And the young bride there, how does she fare?"*
> *"She's swept the house all the way through,*
> *And from the attic window, she's staring down at you."*

She then met the bridegroom, who was walking back home very slowly. He too asked:

> *"Oh, Fitcher's feathered bird, where have you been?"*
> *"From feathered Fitze Fitcher's house I've come."*
> *"And the young bride there, how does she fare?"*
> *"She's swept the house all the way through,*
> *And from the attic window, she's staring down at you."*

The bridegroom looked up and saw the decorated skull. He thought it was his bride, nodded, and waved to her. But when he reached the house filled with his guests, the brothers and relatives who had been sent to rescue the bride were there ahead of him. They locked the doors to the house so that no one could get out. Then they set fire to it, and the wizard and his crew were burned alive.[45]

The German heroine engineers her own rescue from the wizard Fitcher, an expert in the art of division and a master of dismemberment. He uses his chopping block to separate into pieces what was meant to be whole. The third sister must reverse this process, rejoining the dismembered parts of her sisters, healing them, and restoring them to life.

Arthur Rackham, illustration for the Grimms'
*Little Brother & Little Sister and Other Tales*, 1917

The German word *heilen* (to heal) in this tale, despite its many damaging associations with the political rhetoric of the Third Reich, is in fact the holy grail of many wonder tales, for making whole, restoring equilibrium, and evening out are so often their aim. Fairy tales give us melodramas packed in a tight frame, propulsive yet also spare and contained, with the result that appearances count more than in most narrative forms. Hence the frequency with which healing and wholeness are embodied in beauty, an attribute of the heroine. As Elaine Scarry notes in a philosophical treatise on beauty: beautiful objects make visible "the manifest good of equality and balance."[46] Especially in earlier ages, "when a human community is too young to have yet had time to create justice," she adds, the symmetry of beauty can model justice. It is in the fairy tale that beauty and justice are supremely well suited to mirror and amplify each other, for what is the moral code in that genre but a kind of naïve morality—"our absolute instinctive judgment of what is good and just."[47] The signature attribute of fairy-tale heroines, beauty, comes to function as an index of fairness in both senses of the term. Beauty, magic, healing, and social justice thus operate in tandem in many wonder tales to produce restorative outcomes, final tableaus in which, as the old chestnut declares, virtue is rewarded and vice is punished.

The "cleverest" of the trio of sisters, the third sister also becomes the preserver of life. Not only does she defy the powers of the wizard by making her sisters whole again, she also preserves the egg, protecting it from bloodied defilement by placing it in a bed of goose down. She then transforms herself into a hybrid creature—half human, half animal— dipping her body in honey and rolling in feathers. And to entice her bridegroom to his death, she fashions what is to function as her own double: a skull decorated with flowers and jewels, which Fitcher will believe, at least from a distance, to be his bride. The display created through the adorned skull produces a symbolic nexus linking the bride with beauty and death. The sly sister creates a second self that corresponds precisely to the desires of her groom, while she herself escapes his fatal touch by transforming herself into a thing with feathers, a living creature affiliated with lightness, safety, life, and hope. The heroine claims the powers of the magician, but she uses them to restore life rather than to engineer scenes of slaughter.

## Speaking Up and Writing

We have seen how rumor and gossip turned into old wives' tales, which in turn morphed into fairy tales that landed directly in the culture of childhood with the almost instant loss of stories about women surviving, triumphing, and prevailing, always against the odds. Tales that raised the specter of not-so-happily-ever-after and addressed anxieties about courtship, nuptials, and married life also disappeared from the repertoire as spheres of social activity for women reconfigured themselves. Gone were storytelling sessions that once provided channels for socialization and acculturation as well as for problem-solving and philosophical soundings. At the same time, the myths of antiquity, along with epics such as *The Iliad* and *The Odyssey*, hardened into belief systems that were viewed as the cultural heritage of the West and became a standard fixture in the curriculum of the U.S. education system. Schoolchildren discovered how to be a hero by reading about Achilles, Odysseus, Prometheus, and Hercules.

That women's voices have been silenced, beyond the realm of fairy tale and myth, was acknowledged by the poet Adrienne Rich when she read her acceptance speech for the 1974 National Book Award in poetry, for which she was chosen co-recipient with Allen Ginsberg. Rich and the two other nominated women had formed a pact to share the award with each other should one of the three be named, and this is what Rich read: "We, Audre Lorde, Adrienne Rich, and Alice Walker, together accept this award in the name of all the women whose voices have gone and still go unheard in a patriarchal world, and in the name of those who, like us, have been tolerated as token women in this culture, often at great cost and in great pain." The award was dedicated to "the silent women whose voices have been denied us, the articulate women who have given us strength to do our work."[48] Those voices may not have made it into print, but they were anything but silent, as a look at oral storytelling traditions from earlier times reveals. It is time to bring back some of those ancestral voices, and a number of women writers have done just that in the past decades.

As writers, women have faced daunting challenges, never occupying as prominent a place in the literary canon as their male counterparts. As of 2019, of the 116 Nobel laureates awarded the prize for literature, only 15 have been women. "A woman writing thinks back to her mothers," Virginia Woolf wrote, and those mothers, as we have seen, presided over a social sphere that was domestic, prosaic, and deeply invested in the ordinary and everyday as well as in the sentimental and sensational.[49] It was not just the lack of a room of one's own that prevented women from becoming writers. It was the utter absence of a social environment that supported women at a desk, pondering plots, writing them down, and sending words out into the world.

It has not helped that, for centuries now, women novelists have disparaged their own work in ways that echo the voices of those who wished to discredit old wives' tales. The British novelist Frances Burney felt pressured to give up writing as an "unladylike" practice. For a time she wrote in secret, and she ended up burning her first manuscript, *The History of Caroline Evelyn*. When she published *Evelina* a year later, in 1778, she described it as "the trifling production of a few hours." Mary Wollstonecraft Shelley, whose *A Vindication of the Rights of Woman* was published in 1792, referred to "stupid novelists" and expressed contempt for their works. And George Eliot (who disavowed her female identity by using a male pseudonym) wrote an entire essay called "Silly Novels" in which she denounced the work of lady novelists as "busy idleness." Around the same time, Jo March, the bold, defiant, and spirited second-born of the four March sisters, burned a set of stories that she had decided were "silly" (after a conversation with Professor Bhaer), something her real-life author had also done. As late as 1959, Sylvia Townsend Warner, a British writer who was at the vanguard of female emancipation and empowerment, worried that "a woman writer is always an amateur."[50]

Listening to Rich, Woolf, Burney, and others, it becomes evident that the challenge for women writers is to listen to the voices of their ances-

tors (that's how Toni Morrison put it)—to excavate, unearth, and rediscover stories that were anything but frivolous and trivial. It may be true
that mythological worlds are forever being shattered, as the renowned
anthropologist Franz Boas once wrote, but they are always also in the
process of being rebuilt.[51] Oddly, it is often writers in the avant-garde who
undertake projects of reclamation and inadvertent preservation. We have
seen how Margaret Atwood, Pat Barker, Madeline Miller, and Ursula
Le Guin refashioned myths, giving us a different perspective on heroic
behavior by foregrounding marginalized figures from the mythical past
and discovering how to restore the power of speech to those who had
been silenced by their culture. The writers in the section that follows
used many of the same strategies, going back in time to reimagine stories from times past, giving us tricksters in many cases rather than pure
victims (what folklorists refer to as the archetype of the "innocent, persecuted girl"). By acquiring authority through analytic skill and verbal
wizardry, these women authorized themselves and elevated the genre of
the old wives' tale to what is now dignified by the name of literature. It
was, after all, by listening to the ancestors that the Nobel Prize–winning
Toni Morrison breathed new life into tales about flying Africans, taking
the tropes of those stories, remixing them, mashing them up, and producing what else but *The Song of Solomon*.

Mary Lefkowitz tells us that the Greeks' most important legacy is
not, "as we would like to think, democracy; it is their mythology." That
mythology has been instrumental in perpetuating myths about femininity and naturalizing patriarchal discourses that position women as suffering in silence and lacking any form of real agency unless they weaponize
their looks to bewitch and bewilder. The same holds true for folklore,
with fairy tales doing the same cultural work of perpetuating myths—
which is exactly why some writers decided, in the late twentieth century,
to "demythify" them.[52]

Stories about women dancing to death in red-hot iron shoes, about
girls forced to labor in kitchens as scullery maids, and about the myriad
wicked stepmothers and witches who feast on their children and grandchildren are meant to shock and startle, and no one will dispute that high

coefficients of weirdness and brutality are part and parcel of the genre. The symbolic language of fairy tales sets off alarm bells, but it has also given them a certain staying power and profundity. All the more reason to interrogate the never-ending affiliation of women with cannibalism and curses—all the evil that fuels the plots of fairy tales—and to look under the hood, as Angela Carter put it. She and others made it their mission to revive tales that had vanished and to take the old stories apart, breaking them up into their constituent parts and reassembling them, all the while mending, repairing, and making new.

## Rebels Writing with a Cause: Anne Sexton, Angela Carter, Margaret Atwood, and Toni Morrison

If anyone lived a fairy-tale life in the most harrowing sense of that metaphor, it was the poet Anne Sexton. A likely victim of incest who was guilty of abusing her own children, Sexton's life ended when she committed suicide on a sunny autumn day in New England. After having lunch with the poet Maxine Kumin, she returned home, poured herself a glass of vodka, removed the rings from her fingers, dropped them into her handbag, and put on a fur coat that had belonged to her mother. She then went into the garage, carefully closing the door behind her. Climbing into her 1967 red Mercury Cougar, she turned on the ignition, switched on the radio, and sipped the drink she had made for herself as the exhaust from the engine did its slow work.

In his introduction to *Transformations* (1971), Sexton's collection of seventeen poems that rewrite the Grimms' canon, Kurt Vonnegut Jr. tells us that he once asked a friend to contemplate what it is that poets do. "They extend the language," was the reply. Anne Sexton does us a "deeper favor," he added. "She domesticates my terror."[53] What did Vonnegut mean by that phrase? That Sexton was transplanting horror into the home? That the poet was naturalizing dread? Or that she was taming fear? Perhaps all of the above, for Sexton was determined to show that the terror of fairy tales was not just the product of imaginations gone wild. The stories may feel over the top, extravagant, baroque, and full of excess, but that does not mean that they are not true.

How did Sexton, writing in 1970, hit upon the idea of using the Grimms' fairy tales to domesticate terror? For the origins of *Transformations*, we have to turn to Linda Gray Sexton's memoir: *Searching for Mercy Street: My Journey Back to My Mother*. What did Linda do after school while her mother was busy in her home office? She fixed herself something to eat and propped a book on the table to read while sipping a bowl of soup. One day, "Mother" comes into the kitchen and asks, "What are you reading, honey?" Linda's answer: *Grimms'*. "You never get tired of those stories, do you?" Anne Sexton observed. And the adult Linda muses on how often she "read and reread" those fairy tales.[54] Sexton reappropriated the stories, moving them back from the culture of childhood reading into her own poetry studio, taking the tales her daughter loved best and then repurposing them for grown-ups. The real-life episode enacts a process of reappropriation that began in the 1970s, picked up speed in the next two decades, and has now become an unstoppable cultural force.

At Houghton Mifflin, Sexton's editor, Paul Brooks, worried that the poems in *Transformations* lacked the "terrific force and directness" of her "more serious poetry."[55] The dark humor of the poems must have masked—at least for him—their seriousness, for it is hard to miss the gut punch delivered by *Transformations*. In that slim volume, Anne Sexton embodies fairy-tale villains and victims alike. She is the witch who terrorizes young and old. She is Briar Rose, not slumbering serenely in the castle but lying in bed "still as a bar of iron" with her father "drunkenly bent over [her] bed." And in her version of "Little Red Riding Hood," secrets creep, "like gas," into the house she inhabits. The folkloric becomes personal as she welcomes the horrors of fairy tales, not just embracing them but inviting them in to stay.

The opening poem in *Transformations* is the title of the final story in the Grimms' collection: "The Gold Key." In it, Sexton positions herself as "speaker," not as "writer" or "poet." She is the new bard or inspired rhapsode who has inherited the oral tradition, taking up where the two German brothers left off. The poems may have found their way into a book, but they were reinvigorated by her *voice* ("my mouth open wide"), using the speech register of what her social world calls "a middle-aged witch." She is "ready to tell you a story or two."[56] That she does, and she also transforms the Brothers Grimm in ways that turn the ordinary and quotidian into exactly what Vonnegut found in the collection: domesticated terror. The poems fuse fairy-tale fantasies from "once upon a time" with the "here and now" to take us into the dark world of the nuclear family as the crucible of domestic violence, with all its disturbing conflicts and traumas.

Both a part of the fairy tale and also its teller, Sexton gives us a split consciousness that transforms, as it were, the tale from times past into the living present. Fearlessly acknowledging the dark side to family life and her own sinister role in it, the poet performs her own act of heroism in confessional verse that positions her as victim and villain. It is no accident that she was drawn to fairy tales, for they gave her an opportunity to become a literalist of the imagination (to speak with Yeats)—to turn make-believe into something very real. If Sexton failed to become the heroine of her own life story, she succeeded in transforming herself into a heroine for the literary world by acknowledging the harsh truths in ancestral wisdom.

Just two years after Anne Sexton's suicide, Angela Carter rediscovered fairy tales (she had read them with her grandmother as a child) and was shocked by the toxic mix of death and desire in them. During the summer months of 1976, she was commissioned by the venerable British publishing firm of Victor Gollancz to translate into English the famed French collection of fairy tales published in 1697 by Charles Perrault. "What an unexpected treat," she wrote, "to find that in this great Ur-collection—whence sprang the Sleeping Beauty, Puss in Boots, Little Red Riding Hood, Cinderella, Tom Thumb, all the heroes of pantomime—all these nursery tales are purposely dressed up as fables of the politics of experience." But as she read more deeply in what is known as children's lore, she began to understand the perversity of the fables.

All those "destructive animals" in the fairy tales—what else were they but stand-ins for our own animal nature, "the untamed id . . . in all its dangerous energy."[57]

Not that Angela Carter was against the id. But she planted herself firmly in the camp that worried about how the wolves, beasts, and Bluebeards of fairy tales give us sexual ferocity trained on women as prey. "Old wives' tales, nursery fears!" From childhood onward, women learn about the beasts out there who will "GOBBLE YOU UP." And they collude in their own victimization by giving in to "delighted terror" or trepidation, "cozily titillated with superstitious marvels." "Desirous dread"—that's what the heroine of "The Bloody Chamber" feels for the "mysterious being" who has made it his mission to tame, master, and eventually murder her. The cult of love and death, Eros and Thanatos, requires joint effort. And though it may be co-created by husband *and* wife, it is the wife alone who is imperiled.[58]

Angela Carter was determined to change the narratives from times past, and that meant going beyond the task of translating French fairy tales and putting together collections of fairy tales like her *Wayward Girls and Wicked Women* (1986). At the top of Carter's notes to Perrault's tales are written the words: *"Code Name*: The New Mother Goose."[59] This was the first inkling of *The Bloody Chamber and Other Stories* (1979), a collection of refashioned fairy tales that uncovers not just the "repressed sexuality" of the tales but also reveals our kinship with beasts, a connection that becomes nowhere more clear than in "human" sexuality. By retelling the stories, Carter aimed to point the way to accepting our animal nature even as we discover how to make peace with the animal kingdom and the beastliness in us.

"I was taking . . . the latent content of those traditional stories," she explains, "and using that; and the latent content is violently sexual. And because I am a woman, I read it that way."[60] "The Company of Wolves," her version of "Little Red Riding Hood," does not end with the wolf devouring the girl (as Perrault's French version did) but with reconciliation and reciprocity. When the jaws of the wolf begin to "slaver" and the room is invaded by the forest's seductive blend of love and death (*Liebes-*

*tod*) what does the girl do but burst out laughing and declare that she is "nobody's meat." In a twist that no one had ever thought to give the tale (either the girl outwits the wolf or the wolf gobbles her up), Carter offers a final tableau of the two living happily ever after in a tale where sexual appetite does not imply the annihilation of one of the two partners: "See! sweet and sound she sleeps in granny's bed, between the paws of the tender wolf."

"Beauty and the Beast," another story about the beastliness of male predators, becomes "The Tiger's Bride," a tale in which "nursery fears made flesh and sinew" modulate into another scene of tenderness, with white light from a "snowy moon" shining down on a purring beast: "And each stroke of his tongue ripped off skin after successive skin . . . and left behind a nascent patina of shining hairs. My earrings turned back to water and trickled down my shoulders; I shrugged the drops off my beautiful fur." "The Courtship of Mr. Lyon" takes a less dramatic turn, but here too the heroine takes the initiative, flinging herself on Beast to bring about a "soft transformation" from beast to man. Turning the tales on their heads, setting them in modern times, exploring the consciousness of the characters, and reversing the roles of hero and villain, Carter reimagines the mythical past and makes good on the promise to undo the toxic effects of repressed sexuality.

The cultural perversion of desire becomes evident in the title story of the collection, "The Bloody Chamber." On the face of things, the tale is a literary recycling of "Bluebeard," with a heroine who is both attracted to and repulsed by her lascivious husband: "I longed for him. And he disgusted me."[61] She is tricked into her own betrayal by enacting a "charade of innocence and vice" and playing a "game of love and death," which leads to a sentence of decapitation, whispered "voluptuously" in her ear.[62] The plot takes an unexpected swerve into mythical territory, with a Demeter-like mother swooping down like a *dea ex machina* to rescue her daughter from the blade about to descend on her neck. On horseback and armed with a service revolver, she does what no other fairy-tale mother manages to accomplish, becoming the heroine of her daughter's story.

"I'm in the demythologizing business," Angela Carter once declared.

"I'm interested in myths—though I'm much more interested in folklore—just because they *are* extraordinary lies designed to make people unfree."[63] Like the French literary theorist Roland Barthes, Carter saw myth as an ideologically charged construct, an effort to naturalize man-made concepts and beliefs. We take certain ideas, images, and stories "on trust" without really reflecting on what they communicate, she tells us. Religious parables, nationalist slogans, mythical narratives all come under suspicion. We should uncompromisingly interrogate their terms. Think of Danaë, who is described as "no longer lonesome" and as the "happy bride" of Zeus, after the god visits her in the sealed chamber in which her father Danaüs locked her up.[64] Or how Beauty is required to feel passion for a wild boar, a lion, or a snake in the many versions of her story. Angela Carter was determined to rewrite stories that have been enshrined as sacred and that assert how things "have been and always will be." Disavowing the moral and spiritual authority of tales from times past, she was determined to tinker with them, creating the shock of the new as a reminder that it must not always be as it was "once upon a time."

In a final stroke of genius, Angela Carter sought to conclusively break the magic spell that has taken us all in ever since Charles Perrault and the Brothers Grimm codified the story of Sleeping Beauty and Disney made sure that the story would remain fixed in one single, stable version. "In a faraway land long ago": Disney's *Sleeping Beauty* begins with those words, reminding us of the drive to preserve the mythical power of tales from times past, to perpetuate the cult of what Angela Carter will turn into a beautiful corpse in "The Lady of the House of Love"—the fairy-tale canon in the form told once upon a time.

Carter's "Lady of the House of Love" becomes an allegory of the fairy tale, an enactment of the fate of fairy tales in an age of print culture. Her Sleeping Beauty in that story repeats "ancestral crimes," just as the fairy tale as a genre enables us to lose ourselves in a mindless cycle of repetition compulsion that reproduces and reinforces social norms. The house of fairy tales, like the House of Love, can degenerate into ruins—"cobwebs, worm-eaten beams, crumbling plaster"—when left to its own devices, visited only by sycophantic suitors, driven more by the lure of beauty than the desire to reanimate. Without the right suitor, Carter's somnambulant beauty becomes "a cave full of echoes," "a system of repetitions," "a closed circuit." Leading a "baleful posthumous" existence, she feeds on humans to sustain her dark existence.[65]

What is at stake in Carter's rewritings of fairy tales? Nothing less than a focused protest, an unrepentant rebuke, and a powerful retort to stories that once duped us, taking us in with their cozy bedside manner. Carter's heroines, bent on self-actualization and reconciliation—the word "peace" recurs mantra-like in *The Bloody Chamber and Other Stories*—repudiate the cult of self-effacement and self-immolation in fairy tales that continues to perpetuate itself through films like Disney's *Beauty and the Beast* (1991). That film did not look to Angela Carter for inspiration, but rather followed the advice of Christopher Vogler, author of *The Writer's Journey: Mythic Structure for Storytellers and Screenwriters*. As noted earlier, that was the book that famously used Campbell's Hero's Journey to produce what has been called a CliffsNotes for Hollywood. Belle hears the call to adventure, refuses it at first, crosses a threshold, and so on. It took another ten years for DreamWorks to come up with the kind of surprise twist to "Beauty and the Beast" that would have met with Angela Carter's approval. In DreamWorks' *Shrek*, the male lead discredits fairy-tale romance by flushing its scripts down the toilet, and the film's heroine embraces alterity to live happily ever after as a green monster.

If Angela Carter sends a powerful message about repudiating the emotional terrorism built into old wives' tales when they moved into the culture of childhood and promoted "nursery fears," Margaret Atwood finds much to be admired in the tales once told by our ancestors, seeing in them a form of transformative energy or consciousness-raising, as feminists from the 1960s and 1970s put it. Fairy tales, Atwood recognized early on, are not at all as culturally repressive as some critics have made them out to be. There was much to admire in the Grimms' collection, which was far superior in ideological terms to the French tales that Angela Carter had been translating into English.

The unexpurgated *Grimm's Fairy Tales* contain a number of fairy tales in which women are not only the central characters but win by using their own intelligence. Some people feel fairy tales are bad for women. This is true if the only ones they're referring to are those tarted-up French versions of "Cinderella" and "Bluebeard," in which the female protagonist gets rescued by her brothers. But in many of them, women rather than men have the magic powers.[66]

Margaret Atwood's observation about the need to go from "now" to "once upon a time" remains more relevant than ever. But it is not just writers who are duty bound to undertake the journey to that site. "All must commit acts of larceny, or else of reclamation, depending on how you look at it. The dead may guard the treasure, but it's useless treasure unless it can be brought back into the land of the living and allowed to enter time once more—which means to enter the realm of the audience, the realm of readers, the realm of change."[67] In other words, we have to take those stories from times past and make them our own.

Atwood, who weaves fairy-tale motifs throughout her narratives with almost unprecedented creative energy, translated theory into practice when she wrote a new version of "Bluebeard." "Bluebeard's Egg," in the short-story collection of that title, is told in the third person, but from the point of view of a woman named Sally, an aspiring writer struggling with her social identity and also with her "puzzle" of a husband. Ed is a heart surgeon, a man who avoids intimacy and is notoriously difficult to read.[68] The instructor of Sally's creative writing class assigns the students an exercise in point of view. In class, the creative writing guru, in an effort to replicate how stories were transmitted in times past, dims the lights and tells her students the story "Fitcher's Bird." In this version of the Bluebeard story, as noted earlier, the heroine reassembles the bodies of her dead sisters, engineers their escape, and arranges the incineration of the wizard Fitcher in his own house. In true Bluebeard fashion, Fitcher is a serial murderer who has slain all his "disobedient" wives, one after the other.

The writing assignment coincides with Sally's project of facing up to the hard truths of Ed's likely infidelities. Ed may not sport a beard but he has one quite obviously encrypted in his nickname—Sally's nickname for him is "Edward Bear." Ed's "inner world" becomes a kind of secret chamber, a space that Sally is unable to penetrate, for it is not as transparent as she once had thought. Soon we realize that the story has many hidden chambers—from the broken-down shed at the end of Sally's yard and the "cramped, darkened room" that is Ed's medical examination space to the anatomical cavities of the human heart and Sally's newly purchased keyhole desk —and they all present potential brushes with infidelity. Sally's growing suspicions are corroborated when she sees Ed pressed "too close" against her friend Marylynn and notes that "Marylynn does not move away." It dawns on her that she has made the mistake of using the wrong fairy tales to decode Ed's "inner world." The man she had once thought of as the "third son," "a brainless beast," and a "Sleeping Beauty" is in fact a master of calculation and duplicity who has dictated the terms of their marriage and her subservient role in it.

Atwood unsettles the traditional story of "Bluebeard," showing how the old tale (in its French version) repeats itself down through the ages. But her story of "Bluebeard's Egg" proposes an alternative version, one that is closer to old wives' tales. Sally must produce a story that is "set in the present and cast in the realistic mode." "Explore your inner world," the instructor urges her students. In many ways, Sally will be following a set of instructions that define just how we, as listeners and readers, should process fairy tales. When she bombards herself with questions—"What would she put in the forbidden room?" "How can there be a story from the egg's point of view?" "Why an egg?"—she is enacting exactly what the stories are designed to do: provoke us with their magic, entangle us in their surreal complications, and inspire us to rethink the story and understand its relevance to our own lives.[69]

Sally's struggle with the terms of "Fitcher's Bird" leads to powerful revelations about her own life. Atwood's metafictional exercise (a story about storytelling) suggests that the process of internalizing and retelling can open your eyes to realities that—however disruptive, painful, and disturbing—are not without a liberating potential. Just as the telling of stories in fairy tales leads to discovery and disclosure, so the rewriting of the story can lead to some kind of liberating rebirth. Hence, Atwood's story ends with the image of Sally in bed with her eyes shut, dreaming of an egg "glowing softly, as though there's something red and hot inside it." One day that egg will hatch: "But what will come out of it?" Something pulsing with life, at the least, which is exactly what has been missing from Sally's depleted existence, full of self-consuming acts of sacrifice. As the title of Atwood's story suggests, Bluebeard has been displaced by the Egg, and what hatches from it will become the new leading figure in the story—a heroine in her own right.[70]

"Bluebeard's Egg" gives us a metamyth, a tale that recycles bits and pieces from the Great Cauldron of Story to create a new, personal mythology that is about the power of myth. Fairy tales have much the same cultural force as myths from ancient times, and in many ways they are no different from them. Each is just recruited for different social rituals. It was Italo Calvino who once wrote: "Through the forest of fairy tale, the vibrancy of myth passes like a shudder of wind."[71] Atwood tells us how stories from times past challenge us to reengineer our own lives, not following the old scripts but rather creating new narratives in which women can become heroines rather than resign themselves to playing supporting roles.

Few writers understood the social capital of folklore as well as Toni Morrison, who looked with a benevolent eye on stories that captured ancestral lore. In an interview published as "The Art of Fiction," Ralph Ellison had called attention to how folklore "preserves mainly those situations which have repeated themselves again and again in the history of any given group" and how it "embodies those values by which the group lives and dies."[72] For Morrison, folklore is the living embodiment of the ancestor. And in fiction written by African Americans, Morrison noted that the absence of that ancestral wisdom is experienced as a devastating loss: "It caused huge destruction and disarray in the work itself."[73] Morrison likely had Zora Neale Hurston's *Their Eyes Were Watching God* in mind when she wrote that sentence. In Hurston's novel, Nanny tells her granddaughter Janie, "Us colored folks is branches without roots and that makes things come round in queer ways."[74]

Morrison may have had another work in mind, one in which the sheer excess of "destruction" and "disarray" is unnerving: Ralph Ellison's *Invisible Man*. After a brush with death in a paint factory, the protagonist is hospitalized. How is he treated? He is subjected to shock therapy, and, in the aftermath of those jolts, his doctor displays a series of cards. WHO WAS YOUR MOTHER? one asks, in an effort to determine whether his autobiographical memory is intact. Another card bears the inscription: BOY, WHO WAS BRER RABBIT? In this case, it is Invisible Man's cultural memory that is put to the test, but in a way that demeans the narrator and disparages the folkloric character. Mystified, he asks, "Did they think I was a child?" But ironically it is the crash course in cultural memory that galvanizes Invisible Man into action, making him determined to be, like his folkloric antecedent, "sly" and "alert."[75]

The doctor in *Invisible Man* might just as well have held up a card asking WHO IS TAR BABY? and Toni Morrison more or less gave an answer to that question in her 1981 novel *Tar Baby*. What Morrison does is to breathe new life into the folktale, repurposing the story as one about "how masks come to life, take life over, exercise the tensions between itself and what it covers."[76] More than that, the story of Brer Rabbit and his encounter with a sticky snare becomes an allegory of entrapment, and *Tar Baby* restages the tale in mysteriously complicated new ways. The two protagonists of the novel—one glamorous, privileged, and nomadic and the other strong-willed, penniless, and rooted—enact a conflicted attitude toward African American race consciousness. Jadine, Morrison's heroine, has measured success by the standards of white culture, all the while internalizing its values. An orphan in social terms, she is also unanchored in cultural terms. Son, by contrast, the man who challenges Jadine's success story, orients himself toward the past, reverting to home and to a cultural heritage that refuses to accept conventional markers of success. It is he who must remind Jadine of the Tar Baby story.[77]

Brer Rabbit and the Tar Baby were never really on life support, but Ellison and Morrison resurrect those stories in ways that make them relevant to the lives of African Americans today. Committed to the need for ancestral lore, the two writers—often at political odds with each other—go back and retrieve the wisdom of voices from the past. In *The Grey Album*, the poet and essayist Kevin Young described his ambition to engage in a project of reclamation, of the need to "rescue aspects of black culture abandoned even by black folks, whether it is the blues or home cookin' or broader forms of not just survival but triumph."[78] Reclaiming a heritage means building a foundation that is the ancestor, in its literal and literary meanings—a foundation that provides a cultural legacy on which to construct personal identity.[79]

Anne Sexton, Angela Carter, Margaret Atwood, and Toni Morrison as a literary quartet reclaimed stories that provided a "vital connection" with the resilient imaginations of their ancestors. Anne Sexton implemented a powerful strategy of reappropriation when she took stories from a book for children and renewed the oracular power of the oral for adults, identifying with and embodying the characters in her verse renditions of fairy tales. Angela Carter, who had heard the story of "Little Red Riding Hood" from her grandmother—in an unforgiving French version that ends with the girl in the belly of the wolf—understood the stories as ways of demythifying the timeless truths that have led to the subordination of women. Margaret Atwood challenged us to go back and pick up the pieces, assembling them in new ways that reanimate and remythify as they transform. And Toni Morrison, in daring high-wire acts, revealed the importance of ancestors—of stories and histories that built a foundation on which to create something akin to the novel of manners (as she described it tongue in cheek). They are our guides on how to manage, even if never resolve, cultural conflicts. The title of one of Morrison's essays, "Rootedness: The Ancestor as Foundation," speaks volumes.

Fairy tales belong to the domestic arts, and the recipes for putting them together vary endlessly. "Who first invented meatballs?" Carter asks. "Is there a definitive recipe for potato soup?" All four women writers considered here channel oral traditions, reminding us that modern-day notions of intertextuality (the understanding of all writing as part of a web connected through acts of borrowing, theft, plagiarism, piracy, and appropriation) mirror the techniques our ancestors used to create myths. Claude Lévi-Strauss famously called mythmakers *bricoleurs*—experts in the art of tinkering, mending, and using what is close at hand to make something new. Angela Carter's description of tellers of tales applies also to writers of fiction: "The chances are, the story was put together in the form we have it . . . out of all sorts of bits of other stories long ago and far away, and it has been tinkered with, had bits added to it, lost other bits, got mixed up with other stories." And then, depending on the audience ("children, or drunks at a wedding, or bawdy old ladies, or mourners at a wake"), it is trimmed and tailored until it becomes just the right garment for the occasion.[80]

"I was talking to a friend this weekend & I mentioned your name & she said she didn't go in much for hero worship but you were her heroine." That's what Lennie Goodings, who worked at Virago Press for over forty years, as publicist, publisher, and editor, wrote to Angela Carter shortly before the writer's death from lung cancer. "I guess that's another way of saying what I feel too," she added. "Except that heroes are usually distant & cool, until you get too close to them & then they have lead feet."[81] Carter had anything but feet of lead, or clay. Her brilliant irreverence, spirited talent, and heartfelt generosity turned her into a heroine for her time, a writer who shared the honors with the other courageous women included in these pages, along with the many others who renewed and revitalized old wives' tales from times past.

# CHAPTER 4

# WONDER GIRLS

## Curious Writers and Caring Detectives

*Please do not think I am unduly curious. It's not
idle curiosity that is driving me. I too, am on—not
a pilgrimage—but what I should call a mission.*

—AGATHA CHRISTIE, *Nemesis*

*The only reason people do not know much is because
they do not care to know. They are incurious. Incuriosity
is the oddest and most foolish failing there is.*

—STEPHEN FRY, *The Fry Chronicles*

NOT LONG after the American psychiatrist Fredric Wertham was worrying about the seduction of the innocent (that was the title of his 1954
book) through comics, I was, like many girls in my generation, immersed
in the world of Wonder Woman. Wertham had asserted that juvenile
delinquents, or JDs as they were then known, were more or less the product of the morbid themes and violent images in comic books. After all, 95
percent of the children in what was then called reform school read comics, he argued, with impeccably flawed logic. As for Wonder Woman,
she is, gasp! not a homemaker and she does not raise a family. At the
time, that was a winning combination in my book. What was not to like
about a female superhero who was an omniglot with a golden lasso and
bulletproof bracelets, along with heightened empathy bestowed on her
by Artemis? For girls who read comic books, she was a real heroine,

even if she dressed in a bathing suit that looked as if it had been stitched together from a flag.

Wonder Woman was the first female action figure in the Marvel Universe of comic-book superheroes. Although she was wildly successful in commercial terms, it took Hollywood seventy-five years to bring her to the big screen. Superhero films had been oriented toward audiences of teenage boys, and it was not until Jennifer Lawrence's success as Katniss Everdeen in the *Hunger Games* franchise that DC Films was moved at last to make *Wonder Woman*. The film, released in 2017, depicts the Amazon princess Diana facing the challenge of ending World War I.

"Look at the images of the male. They are always *doing something*, they're always representing something: they are in action," Joseph Campbell remarked when talking about the art of the Paleolithic era. By contrast the female figures of that same era are "simply standing female nudes." "Their power is in their body," he added, and "their being and their presence." He worried about the "very important problems" that emerge when women believe that their value lies in achievement rather than simply "being."[1]

Joseph Campbell would surely have recoiled at the idea of female overachievers like Wonder Woman, who was being developed as a superheroine by a man named William Marston living not far away from him, in Rye, New York. Just when Campbell was busy writing *The Hero with a Thousand Faces*, Marston was dreaming up Wonder Woman. "Not even girls want to be girls," Marston complained, "so long as our feminine archetype lacks force, strength, and power." And for him, the obvious antidote to a culture that devalues girls is the creation of a "feminine character with all the traits of Superman plus all the allure of a good and beautiful woman."[2]

Most of the literary heroines in this chapter live by their wits. Innately curious, they are also seen as curiosities in their fictional worlds. They could all become honorary members of the Justice Society formed by DC Comics, for each is on some kind of mission, with a calling driven by progressive ideas. From Jo March in Louisa May Alcott's *Little Women* to Starr Carter in Angie Thomas's *The Hate U Give*, these girls—and most of the figures I will discuss are just that—set out on journeys that may not require them to leave home but rather confront them with challenges that remove them from the domestic arena. I will have more to say about Wonder Woman in the next chapter. For now, as we look at girl wonders who are writers and detectives, it is important to remember that Wonder Woman remained for many decades firmly anchored in the cultural world of girls. It took her cinematic incarnation to finally give her purchase in the world of entertainment for adults. She may be more action than words (though she is that too), and she also deviates somewhat from many other heroines, who are, for the most part, wedded to the word. But the girls and women in what follows are all united by a trait that has been seen, ever since Eve succumbed to it in the Garden of Eden, as the quintessential failing of women: curiosity.

## Curiosity and Its Discontents

Curiosity is in our DNA, and it turns us into extraordinary learning machines, from the day we are born. In a book entitled *A Curious Mind* (2015), the screenwriter Brian Grazer credits curiosity for his professional success, reminding us that Einstein did not feel that he had special gifts—he was just "passionately curious." "No matter how much battering your curiosity has taken, it's standing by, ready to be awakened," Grazer tells his readers in a book designed for those committed to self-improvement. He guarantees a "bigger life" as a reward for cultivating curiosity.[3]

Today we live in a culture that claims to value curiosity, promotes it, and even professes a rage for it. But that has not always been the case, especially when the trait was associated with grown women, those sexually adventurous ladies who, in the nineteenth century, almost single-handedly created a new genre, the novel of adultery. Tellingly, Benito Pérez Galdós's *Fortunata and Jacinta* (1887) is probably the only canonical nineteenth-century novel of adultery that gives us a male philanderer.[4]

Simone de Beauvoir confirms what was noted in an earlier chapter, that for a woman, securing liberty means engaging in infidelity: "It is only through lies and adultery that she can prove that she is nobody's thing." The French philosopher found that, by 1900, adultery had become "the theme of all literature," with cheaters like Tolstoy's Anna Karenina, Flaubert's Emma Bovary, and Fontane's Effi Briest feeling imprisoned by their marriages and longing for something beyond the confines of house and home.[5] By contrast, the heroes from that time and in that literary genre are often courageous adventurers, swashbuckling, fearless, spirited, and smart. Think here of all the voyagers, explorers, and revolutionaries in works such as Jules Verne's *From the Earth to the Moon* (1865), Alexandre Dumas's *The Count of Monte Cristo* (1844), Charles Dickens's *A Tale of Two Cities* (1859), and Herman Melville's *Moby-Dick* (1851).

The nineteenth century gave us the novel of adultery, but it also witnessed the flourishing of the coming-of-age story, adapted by Louisa May Alcott to show that girls possess as much, and possibly more, imaginative energy, investigative drive, and social concern as their male counterparts. Since it might not be safe to write about bold, ambitious women, why not engage in a stealth maneuver and construct heroic girls and portray all the forms of care and concern that constitute their larger social mission? Who better to lead the charge than Jo March, the girl who writes to make her own way in the world?

Scribbling girls, with their passion for using words to further their causes, are close cousins of girl detectives such as Nancy Drew, also driven by curiosity and positioned as an agent of social justice. Oddly, there is something of a midlife crisis in the universe of woman detectives in the first half of the twentieth century, for it is dominated either by girls investigating or by spinsters sleuthing (among them, Dorothy L. Sayers's Miss Climpson and Agatha Christie's Miss Marple) who take on all the allegorical qualities of Nemesis. Before looking more closely at the writers and detectives at the youthful end of the age spectrum, it is worth contemplating women's relationship to knowledge over the centuries, along with some biblical and mythical women who want to know too much.

The history of the English word "curiosity" is full of surprises, with unexpected shifts in meaning over the centuries. The *Oxford*

*English Dictionary* prefaces its definitions of "curious" by noting that the term has been used over time "with many shades of meaning." Given how curiosity has attached itself to a certain type of female heroine, it makes good sense to explore those meanings, the one, now obsolete, signifying "bestowing care or pains, careful, studious, attentive"; the other, as used today, defined as "desirous of seeing or knowing; eager to learn; inquisitive," and often used with a slightly negative connotation.

Curiosity seems to invite judgment. "I loathe that low vice—curiosity," Lord Byron wrote in Canto 23 of *Don Juan* (1819), surely a tongue-in-cheek aside from a poet renowned for love affairs that led to one paramour calling him "mad, bad and dangerous to know."[6] More than a century later, the French sociologist Michel Foucault found himself dreaming of an "Age of Curiosity" and reminded us that curiosity evokes "concern" and "the care one takes for what exists and could exist."[7] A look at the etymology of the term goes far toward understanding how curiosity came to be seen as a trait both valuable and constructive as well as problematic and sinister, with moral and religious judgments constantly being pronounced, for and against.

We can begin by looking at a fable collected by the Roman author Hyginus (born 64 BCE) that tells of a Roman goddess named Cura ("Care" or "Concern"), who molded the first human from clay or earth (*humus*). A narrative competing with Christian accounts, in which woman is a minor character in a creation story with a male God, the story of Cura was taken up by the philosopher Martin Heidegger. What fascinated Heidegger was the way in which Cura represented care for something in the sense of concern or "absorption in the world" and also "devotion."[8] Cura has slipped into oblivion today, just as "curiosity" in the sense of "care," "worry," or "concern" is now obsolete. But that obsolete meaning captures something paradoxical, reminding us that the affirmative and restorative value of care can quickly shade into domineering fussiness and anxious (and anxiety-producing) attention. Is it any wonder that the allegorical embodiment of "cura" is a woman?

Today we use the term "curiosity" to mean "the desire to know or learn," but that appetite, as the *Oxford English Dictionary* reveals, can be judged in multiple ways—as "blamable," "neutral," or "good," with the "good" instinct defined as "the desire or inclination to know or learn about anything." We have a deeply conflicted attitude toward curiosity, seeing it as both annoying addiction and generous attentiveness. Curiosity is a conduit to knowledge, but like all forms of desire, it can lead to excesses and risks pivoting into a Faustian thirst for knowledge that can never be quenched. In sum, care for others and the desire for knowledge are folded into "curiosity," but both can be carried to excess in the form of cravings that push the boundaries of what is appropriate or permissible. And the negative valence given to "curiosity" in both senses of the term implies that there is an authority making decisions about what is illicit or forbidden and what is a legitimate object of care and inquiry.[9]

Our cultural stories about curiosity and knowledge bifurcate as well, giving us an emphatically gendered account of what it means to have an inquiring mind. When Aristotle declared that "all men by nature desire to know," he was paving the way for the belief that desire can lead to good things, foremost among them scientific knowledge.[10] But there are things off limits to human intelligence, and the twelfth-century French abbot Bernard de Clairvaux was among the first to set limits to curiosity in its social form: "There are people who want to know solely for the sake of knowing, and that is scandalous curiosity"—scandalous in the sense of outrageous but also associated with the creation of scandals, with nosy inquisitiveness and meddlesome prying.[11]

## Pandora Opens a Jar and Eve Eats Fruit from the Tree of Knowledge

Women's problematic and persistent desire for knowledge instantly becomes evident in the stories of Pandora and Eve, two women whose intellectual curiosity leads them to engage in forms of transgressive behavior that introduce evil and misery into the world. In those cautionary tales, curiosity is framed in derogatory terms, signaling a need to rein in curiosity when it manifests itself in women.

Scientists and philosophers living in Early Modern Europe (spanning the three centuries from 1500 to 1800) had sought to demonstrate that curiosity was morally neutral—in large part, in the spirit of Aristotle, to legitimize scientific inquiry. But scientific inquiry remained at that time a distinctly male domain. The more powerfully curiosity was endorsed and rehabilitated in the name of science, the more forcefully a form of "bad curiosity" asserted itself, one that was gendered female and associated with rumormongering, disorder, and transgression. Cesare Ripa's *Iconologia*, a highly influential emblem book published in Italy in 1593, represented curiosity as a wild-haired, winged woman, her features distorted into an enraged expression. "I am no angel," she appears to be saying, despite those wings.

Before turning to Eve, it is worth a look at Pandora, the woman who was fashioned on the orders of Zeus to punish humans for Prometheus's theft of fire. It is she who brought evil into the world by opening, not a box (as the Dutch humanist Erasmus erroneously called it), but a jar filled with "countless plagues." The Greek poet Hesiod, writing around 700 BCE, gave us the two standard accounts of Pandora's origins and her powers. In *Works and Days*, we learn that she is fashioned by Hephaestus, with contributions from other gods and goddesses, including Aphrodite and Athena, who each endow Pandora with gifts, much like the good fairies in our familiar story of Sleeping Beauty. Hermes gives Pandora her name (a richly nuanced term that can mean "all-gifted" or "all-giving"), and he also furnishes her with "a shameful mind and deceitful nature," along with the power of speech, bestowing on her a gift for telling "lies" and using "crooked words and wily ways." Hesiod's *Theogony* describes Pandora as a "beautiful evil," a creature of "sheer guile, not to be withstood by men."

Zeus orders Hermes to take Pandora to Epimetheus, the brother of plucky Prometheus. Naïve Epimetheus fails to heed his brother's warning about gifts from Zeus, and revenge for the theft of fire is exacted: "He took the gift and afterwards, when the evil thing was already his, he understood. Previously men lived on earth free from ills and hard toil and sickness. But the woman took off the great lid of the jar and scattered all these and caused sorrow and mischief to man."[12] Only one item remains in the jar—hope.[13]

Combining the seductive allure of surface beauty with the intellectual traits of deception and treachery, Pandora, the first mortal woman, stands as a perverse model of woman as femme fatale. Her looks and adornment are nothing but a trap. Like Prometheus, she is wily, but her duplicity takes a bad turn with a tragic outcome, becoming a perversion of intelligence and craft. The many otherwise magnificent gifts of the gods are corrupted and distorted, used for evil ends when bestowed on her.

Every age seems to reinvent Pandora, re-creating her in ways that capture cultural anxieties about women and power, evil and seduction. But up through the nineteenth century, her desire for knowledge was generally rebranded as sexual curiosity and she came to be linked with Eve and seduction. In countless paintings, she is depicted without the glittering silver clothing given to her by Athena. Instead she is nude, a jar or box at her side, resembling Venus herself more than anyone else. Occasionally she gets back some of her clothes, though the attire is usually still revealing by the standards of the time.

The nineteenth-century French painter Jules Lefebvre gives us a nude Pandora, perched on a cliff, in side view, to be sure, but with little left to the imagination, since her red hair and gauzy scarf cover virtually nothing. More boldly, John Batten, in his 1913 *Creation of Pandora*, gives us a full frontal view of Pandora on a pedestal, fresh from

John William Waterhouse, *Pandora*, 1896

the forge of Hephaestus. John William Waterhouse's painting *Pandora* (1896) catches the beautiful deceiver in the act of opening the box, her eyes trained on the contents, her shoulders bare in a revealingly diaphanous dress. Dante Gabriel Rossetti's 1879 *Pandora* offers a more chaste representation, exposing only shoulders and arms. The preponderance of European paintings show Pandora either as a seductive, naked figure or as an equally beautiful clothed woman, on the brink of succumbing to temptation. She is positioned as both captivating temptress and guilty troublemaker.

Like many Greek myths, the story of Pandora was uprooted from adult literary culture and transplanted into the playground of stories for children. At first Pandora's evil nature was magnified—but once she shed a few years, she became a "naughty" girl, guilty of being seduced by a combination of beauty and mystery. The box (and, after Erasmus, it is always a box) is generally a glittery, jewel-encrusted, luminous container, and although its size varies, it becomes more like a toy chest than a jewelry box as its proprietor sheds years. *D'Aulaires' Book of Greek Myths* keeps her a woman, but one who is "beautiful and silly," cursed with "insatiable curiosity."[14] Edith Hamilton is much harder on Pandora, calling her a "beautiful disaster." From her, we learn, comes "the race of women, who are an evil to men, with a nature to do evil." Pandora was a "dangerous thing," Hamilton writes, laying it on even more thickly. After all, Pandora, "like all women," has a "lively curiosity." "She *had* to know what was in the box," Hamilton adds in a way that lets us feel her own personal sense of exasperation with the mythical being.[15]

It was Nathaniel Hawthorne who started the trend of turning Pandora into a girl. Just a few miles from where Herman Melville was shaping out "the gigantic conception of his 'White Whale,'" Hawthorne decided, shortly after the birth of a daughter, to rewrite Greek myths. *A Wonder-Book for Girls and Boys*, published in 1851, retells the stories of Perseus and the Medusa, King Midas and his golden touch, Pandora, Hercules and the Golden Apples of the Hesperides, Baucis and Philemon, and the Chimæra. Hoping to purge the tales of their "classic coldness" and "old heathen wickedness," Hawthorne planned to add morals wherever it was "practicable."[16]

Under the title "The Paradise of Children," Hawthorne retold the story of Pandora, turning her and Epimetheus into two orphaned children living in a cottage. Pandora falls under the spell of a beautiful box in the cottage and talks endlessly about it. One day, her curiosity grows so great that she is determined to open the box. "Ah, naughty Pandora!" the narrator scolds. Then, as she is about to open the box, he amplifies his disapproval with "Oh, very naughty and very foolish Pandora!" But Hawthorne does not leave Epimetheus blameless: "We must not forget

Walter Crane, illustration for Nathaniel Hawthorne's
*A Wonder-Book for Girls and Boys,* 1893

to shake our heads at Epimetheus likewise," for he failed to prevent Pandora from lifting the lid of the box and was equally eager to discover the contents of the box.[17]

In 1893 the British illustrator Walter Crane added images to Hawthorne's *Wonder-Book* for the publishing house of Houghton, Mifflin in the United States. His teenage Pandora and Epimetheus are stylized figures, looking more Greek than American or British. For the 1922 edition of Hawthorne's *Wonder-Book*, Arthur Rackham, famous for his illustrations of fairy tales by the Grimms and by Hans Christian Andersen, added images that turned Pandora and Epimetheus into naked, pixielike preadolescents living in a lush natural paradise. The target for a lesson about curiosity has now become the child, both in the story and in the illustrations for it.

The nineteenth century, which witnessed the rise of print culture and higher literacy rates, provided unprecedented access to information and knowledge, not just for men, but for women and children as well. Is it any surprise that curiosity came to be demonized in that century and

Arthur Rackham, illustrations for *A Wonder-Book for Girls and Boys,* 1922

the next, with Pandora as Exhibit A? The incarnation of curiosity in its most damning and damaging form, Pandora provided an alibi not just for reining in women's unruly need to investigate arenas of action traditionally cordoned off from them but also for scolding young boys and girls, but first and foremost girls.[18]

Pandora's desire for knowledge was first rebranded as sexual curiosity. Then her story became a cautionary tale for children, warning them to beware of violating prohibitions. Today the message we take from the story is largely about the survival of hope and our need for resilience in the face of cataclysmic or catastrophic events. Pandora's biblical cousin, Eve of Genesis, has never fully escaped the role of culprit in the Fall of Mankind and expulsion from Paradise. Merging with Pandora in the title of a painting by the French artist Jean Cousin the Elder, she reclines nude in a bower, one arm resting on a skull, the other on some kind of urn. *Eva Prima Pandora*: Are there not striking similarities between the first woman fashioned by Hephaestus and the sinner of Judeo-Christian beliefs? Perhaps it is in fact Pandora on the canvas?

Jean Cousin the Elder, *Eva Prima Pandora*, c. 1550

The temptress Eve became the main biblical source of seduction (with the snake as mere enabler rather than agent) and her desire for knowledge was sexualized, turned into something carnal rather than intellectual.[19] As Stephen Greenblatt tells us in his magisterial *The Rise and Fall of Adam and Eve*, Eve, the mother of all humans, shoulders the blame for our loss of innocence and for the accompanying curse of mortality, bringing death into the world. She is the sinner, embodying the spirit of transgressive desires. Recall, however, that the serpent tempts Eve with nothing but knowledge: "Your eyes will be opened, and you will be like God, knowing good and evil." Eve has done little more than accept the invitation to become a sentient human being endowed with moral awareness and wisdom, and yet she is likened to the serpent, indeed in some cases she *is* the real serpent.[20]

Pandora and Eve both pale in comparison with one biblical creature who reminds us of the powerful anxieties invested in female sexuality. Few can outdo the Whore of Babylon, an allegorical figure who wears on her forehead a banner announcing her wickedness to the world: MYSTERY, BABYLON THE GREAT, THE MOTHER OF HARLOTS AND ABOMINATIONS OF THE EARTH. Representing Extreme Debauchery, she has committed fornication with the "kings of the earth" and sits upon the waters in the wilderness. With seven heads and ten horns, she is "arrayed in purple and scarlet color, and decked with gold and precious stones and pearls, having a golden cup in her hand full of abominations and filthiness of her fornication."[21]

Female carnality was writ large in allegories of excess that became the foundational myths and stories of many cultures. The desire for knowledge becomes dangerous, with what philosophers call epistemophilia (the love of *knowledge*) quickly shading into unrestrained sexual cravings. Philandering men are legion in myth as in fiction, but they are rarely described as figures of ill repute—instead they are legendary libertines, mischievous rogues, conniving cads, insolent scoundrels, and endearing rascals. They are seldom denounced as cravenly seductive and duplicitous—those attributes are reserved for mythical and biblical women like Pandora and Eve.

That curiosity stems from care and concern is a fact rarely acknowledged in the moral calculus of our foundational cultural stories about women. The fairy tale about Bluebeard and his wife is exceptional in its framing of curiosity as a lifesaving strategy. Much as the heroine's drive to explore and investigate may be reviled and attacked, it also saves her neck. "Bluebeard, or the Fatal Effects of Curiosity and Disobedience," the title of an 1808 version of the story, reminds us of how easy it was to misread the tale, turning a story about the value of knowledge into a parable about the perils of an inquisitive mind.

Charles Perrault was the first to write down the story of Bluebeard in his collection *Tales from Times Past, with Morals* (subtitled *Tales of Mother Goose*), published in 1697 under the name of his teenage son, Pierre Darmancourt. Twice removed from authorship, via the attribution of the tales first to old wives and then to a boy who was presumably a listener to the tales, Perrault no doubt feared that these trifles would tarnish his literary reputation. After all, he was a distinguished member of the Académie Française and secretary to Jean-Baptiste Colbert, finance minister to King Louis XIV, the French monarch notorious for the number of his mistresses and illegitimate children. One of those mistresses died in childbirth at the age of nineteen, and it is not implausible that Bluebeard, with his storied wealth, carriages of gold, and parade of wives, bears more than a passing resemblance to the Sun King. The tales in Perrault's collection became his most significant legacy, for the stories from French popular tradition made their way into court circles, where they became a source of delight and pleasure for sophisticated audiences before they retreated to the nursery.

Perrault's "Bluebeard" begins by highlighting the attractions of wealth and beauty: "There once lived a man who had fine houses, both in the city and in the country, dinner services of gold and silver, chairs covered with tapestries, and coaches covered with gold." But the man himself is "ugly and frightful," and his vast wealth cannot compensate for his appearance and the fact that he has a past ("He had already married several women, and no one knew what had become of them"). Still, one young woman is so dazzled by his ostentatious display of wealth that she agrees to marriage.[22]

What comes next is what folklorists call a "test of obedience," and it is one that Bluebeard's wife utterly fails. Called out of town for business, Bluebeard gives his wife license to entertain and throw parties while he is away. Handing her the keys to various chambers and storerooms, he gives her one last key, which opens "the small room at the end of the long corridor on the lower floor," a location that becomes all the more enticing for its remoteness. "Open anything you want. Go anywhere you wish. But I absolutely forbid you to enter that little room, and if you so much as open it a crack, there will be no limit to my anger." Here we have J. R. R. Tolkien's "Eternal Temptation"—the "locked door" with an explicit injunction about opening it. Who could possibly resist? And what could possibly go wrong? It is more than likely to the credit of all humans that we have an incorrigible urge to defy orders and prohibitions issued without any

Gustave Doré, illustration for "Bluebeard," 1862

explanatory context, especially when there is the added temptation of a key dangling right before our eyes. Those who put fairy tales between the covers of a book did not see it that way.

In Perrault's rendition of the tale, Bluebeard's wife loses no time getting to the room forbidden to her. All the while that her nosy female companions are rummaging through closets, admiring themselves in full-length mirrors, and declaring their envy of the wealth on display, Bluebeard's wife is so "tormented" by curiosity that she nearly breaks her neck racing down a staircase to open the door to the forbidden chamber. For a moment, she reflects on the harm that could come to her for a flagrant act of "disobedience," but she quickly succumbs to temptation and opens the door. Here is what she sees: "The floor was covered with clotted blood and . . . the blood reflected the bodies of several women hung up on the walls (these were all the women Bluebeard had married and then murdered one after another)."

Living in an age when men, inspired by their monarch, thought nothing of collecting mistresses, Perrault was quick to judge Bluebeard's wife and her friends, indicting these daughters of Eve for their envy, greed, curiosity, and disobedience. He seems less willing to denounce a man who has cut the throats of his wives. To be sure, it may seem redundant to comment on Bluebeard's character once the corpses of his wives come to light, but, unless we take the view that this is a story of "dangerous curiosity and justifiable homicide" (as does one nineteenth-century British playwright), the repeated references to the unchecked curiosity of Bluebeard's wife seem more than odd. What is at stake in this story, Perrault suggests, is the inquisitive instinct of the wife rather than the homicidal deeds of the husband. Fatima, as she is sometimes called in European versions of the story, has turned investigator, logically and shrewdly training all her instincts on detection and discovery.

The homicidal history of Bluebeard takes a back seat to his wife's curiosity (why is she so nosy about her husband's past?) and her act of disobedience (why does she not listen to her husband?). "Bloody key as sign of disobedience"—that is the motif singled out for many years by folklorists as the defining feature of the tale. The bloodstained key points to a double transgression, one that is not just moral but sexual as well. For one critic it was a sign of "marital infidelity"; for another it marked the heroine's "irreversible loss of her virginity"; for a third it stood as a sign of "defloration."[23] And so, like Eve, Bluebeard's wife is vilified for her inquisitive nature. What does her in is what Augustine described as the "lust of the eyes." By associating curiosity with original sin, Augustine turns an intellectual instinct into a sexual vice, cementing the connection between (female) curiosity and sexual desire.

Curiosity was reviled by the ancients, who saw in it a form of aimlessness linked to snooping and prying, unlike the more honorable "wonder," which was the true wellspring of wisdom, philosophy, and knowledge. The trait was forever giving women a bad name. Again and again, inquisitiveness and an excessive desire for knowledge are linked to women, as if to announce to the world that women's real frailty lies in the inability to resist the urge to know more: "Curiosity, thy name is woman." The inquisitive woman also becomes the compassionate woman, deeply invested in getting to the bottom of things and also restoring fairness to the world through concern and attentiveness, often to those who are unseen and unheard, the social outcasts and marginalized misfits of the world.

## "Literature Is a Fond and Faithful Spouse": Louisa May Alcott's Little Women

Where could women's curiosity go to resist being sexualized and to remain pure and unadulterated, as it were? *Alice's Adventures in Wonderland*, published just three years before *Little Women*, comes to mind, but Lewis Carroll, whose attraction to little girls is well documented, made sure that Alice remained a complete innocent, untainted by the desire for much else but sweets. The real resistance was located in a form of fiction invented, almost single-handedly, by Louisa May Alcott, when she accepted a dare from her literary editor, Thomas Niles. She was to write a girls' book, something that required her to do little more than reanimate her childhood and describe, imaginatively and inventively, the domestic world of four sisters as well as their ambitions—literary, artistic, spiritual, and domestic. The March girls set the stage for a host of other aspiring artists and writers who will appear in the pages that follow, from L. M. Montgomery's Anne of Green Gables to Hannah Horvath in *Girls*.

Henry James wrote, with some envy, that Alcott had "a private understanding with the youngsters she depicts, at the expense of their pastors and masters."[24] In other words, the author of *What Maisie Knew* (a novel that takes us inside the mind of the child of divorced parents) worried that Alcott was conspiring with children against adults, as Roald Dahl once claimed he had done while writing books for children. Alcott turned her back on a robust literary tradition that had made as its goal the spiritual uplift of children and the taming of their unruly instincts. Children's literature, with many strokes of Alcott's pen, turned into something *for* children rather than for their own good.

Louisa May Alcott loathed the idea of writing about girls: "I plod away, though I don't enjoy this sort of thing. Never liked girls, nor knew many, except my sisters, but our queer plans and experiences may prove interesting, though I doubt it."[25] Abigail (Abba) Alcott, the real-life "Marmee" to the four Alcott girls, described childhood activities that closely resembled what enlivens the domestic world of *Little Women*: "In the good old times, when 'Little Women' worked and played together, the big garret was the scene of many dramatic reveals. After a long day of teaching, sewing, and 'helping mother,' the greatest delight of the girls was to transform themselves . . . and ascend into a world of fantasy and romance."[26] "The story would write itself, Louisa knew," one biographer claims.[27] In two and a half months Alcott wrote 402 pages of the work that would become *Little Women*. Was she sanguine about the commercial prospects for the volume? Not at all, nor was her publisher. But when her editor gave the manuscript to his niece, Lilly Almy, the girl fell in love with the characters, could not put the manuscript down, and laughed until tears came to her eyes. Still, no one could have predicted the soaring success of *Little Women, or Meg, Jo, Beth and Amy*, published in Boston by Roberts Brothers in the fall of 1868. The 2,000 copies, printed and bound in purple, green, and terra-cotta cloth, sold out before the end of October, and another 4,500 copies of the book rolled off the presses before the year was out.

Alcott began work on the second volume of *Little Women* on November 2, vowing to write "like a steam engine," a chapter a day. By November 17, she had thirteen chapters in hand (presumably she rested on Sundays), and spent her birthday, later that month on November 29, alone and "writing hard." For her, writing was serious manual labor as well as intellectual work, but also something of an addiction. It is telling that, when her right hand was crippled from overuse of a steel pen, she taught herself to write with her left hand. Driving the passion for writing was not just the dream of literary fame but also the need to "do good" by supporting her family.

Jo March, the dominant figure in the quartet of March sisters, also aspires to make a name for herself. Jo loves to tell stories. An avid reader who enthusiastically quotes Isaac Watts, John Bunyan, and Harriet Beecher Stowe, she also stages plays with pathos and high drama and produces a newspaper inspired by *The Pickwick Papers*. She longs for nothing more than "a stable full of Arabian steeds, rooms piled with books, and . . . a magic inkstand, so that my works should be as famous as Laurie's music."[28] Striving for immortality, she wants to do "something heroic, or wonderful,—that won't be forgotten after I'm dead." Though well aware that she may be building castles in the air (that is the title of the chapter in which Jo articulates her aspirations), she adds, "I think I shall write books, and get rich and famous."[29] But Jo's ambition to become a writer runs afoul of her charitable activities (she sets up a school) and domestic arrangements (her husband rebukes her for writing "trash"). Telling stories is decoupled from social and cultural work and suddenly self-aggrandizing ambitions cannot coexist with philanthropic ventures, which require self-effacing modesty.

The conflict between literary ambitions on the one hand and altruistic instincts and domestic bliss on the other is mirrored in the life of Jo's creator. Louisa May Alcott, ever compassionate, benevolent, and self-sacrificing, applied for a position as a military nurse in 1862, on the day that she turned thirty, the earliest possible age for enlisting. Cleaning and dressing wounds led to a typhoid infection that compromised her health for the rest of her life. After the war, she wrote almost in defiance of her many physical ailments ranging from sore gums to bandaged limbs: "As I wrote Little Women with one arm in a sling, my head tied up & one foot in misery perhaps pain has a good effect upon my works."[30] Magically, she managed to merge writing with good deeds, churning out magazine fiction to support not just her parents but also her sisters and their families. "I dread debt more than the devil," she reported, and it could be said that the writing addiction and the impulse to keep poverty at bay fed on each other. Writing was Alcott's "bread and butter," and it was also a way of enacting the main theme of *Little Women*: hard work and self-effacing generosity are cardinal virtues in the story of the March sisters and their pilgrimage through life. Louisa May Alcott later became the guardian of her sister's daughter and a "father" to two nephews, and she was also the principal wage earner in the extended family for some time, making everyone financially secure by the time she reached the age of forty.

As noted, *Little Women* can be read as autofiction, a form of writing about the self in an account that is made up but with strong autobiographical features. Remarkably, Alcott used a life story—domestic, self-contained, and lively yet also anything but "heroic" or "wonderful"—to ensure that she would not be "forgotten," going down in history as the heroine of her own story. Alcott went far beyond the domestic. The March sisters have varying ambitions. They are all readers, using books as portals to other worlds that stretch their imaginations and enable them to dream, imagine, and invent. Meg, Jo, Beth, and Amy are all shaped by the stories they read, and Louisa May Alcott created a literary universe built by the fictional works she had read, with authors ranging from Bunyan and Brontë to Shakespeare and Dickens. Writing in the shadow cast by John Bunyan's *Pilgrim's Progress*, with its somber and sobering quest for redemption, Alcott inserted herself into a literary tradition but also inaugurated a new genre by writing a counter-narrative that replaced the faith-driven hero of Bunyan's work with four girls, each able to find a calling, all forging four very different identities.

Beyond that, *Little Women* is, in more than one sense, Louisa May Alcott's brainchild. We imagine authors to be creators, godlike in their power to construct entire worlds from words and to produce literary progeny. But from God on down, it has been men who have created (hence the awkwardness of the term "authoress," obsolete today because it has been displaced by the seemingly gender-neutral term "author"), and it has been women's destiny to procreate. What happens, as Louisa May Alcott asks in an essay called "Happy Women," when women choose to join the class of "superior women, who from various causes, remain single, and devote themselves to some earnest work; espousing philanthropy, art, literature, music, medicine"? Can they remain "as faithful to and as happy in their choice as married women with husbands and homes"? Alcott proceeds to marshal powerful examples of those who do, among them a woman who has followed her instincts and decided to remain a "chronic old maid." Here is her description of a woman who is seen as a social anomaly:

> Filial and fraternal love must satisfy her, and grateful that such ties are possible, she lives for them and is content. Literature is a fond and faithful spouse, and the little family that has sprung up around her . . . is a profitable source of satisfaction to her maternal heart. . . . Not lonely . . . not idle, for necessity, stern, yet kindly teacher, has taught her the worth of work; not unhappy, for love and labor, like good angels, walk at either hand.

Literature as the spouse who will always remain "fond and faithful"! And what else is the "little family" that has issued forth but literary progeny? Louisa May Alcott is more than likely the real-life old maid described in "Happy Women." She is, in any case, one of that number, a spinster par excellence, who gives birth to *Little Women*, a work marked by many literary forebears. With a touch of regret, Alcott once wrote that her stories were like offspring: "I sell my children, and though they feed me, they don't love me as Anna's do" (Anna was the author's older sister and the inspiration for Meg of *Little Women*). But through her literary issue, Alcott was able to "cherish" the talent she possessed, "using it faithfully for the good of others," and turning her life story into a "beautiful success." Writing came to rhyme with doing good.

In 1979, during the high tide of second-wave feminism, with its harsh critique of male-centered ideologies, Sandra Gilbert and Susan Gubar published a volume of literary criticism with a title alluding to Bertha Mason, the captive "monster" in Charlotte Brontë's *Jane Eyre*. *The Madwoman in the Attic* documented in detail the degree to which Western culture defines the Author as "a father, a progenitor, a procreator, an aesthetic patriarch whose pen is an instrument of generative power." Everything that happens in the stories that constitute the literary canon can be seen as Athena is to Zeus, a brainchild of a male writer. The "man of letters" becomes not just authoritative and influential but also heroic, a spiritual trailblazer and patriarchal leader.[31]

If Western religion installs a male God as the creator of all things, and the culture surrounding it assimilates that model for all creative efforts, where does that leave women? That is the question Gilbert and Gubar spend several hundred pages answering. Can women also produce brainchildren or are they limited to biological procreation? Louisa May Alcott charted one path for the female writer, giving us the unprecedented story of the birth of the artist as a young woman, setting her tale in a time that is hostile to the notion of women making a living from writing. Strongwilled Josephine March becomes not just a woman who asserts her right to self-expression and professional self-actualization but also a role model for the real-life readers who come after her (just like her author, Louisa May Alcott).

To measure Jo's impact on girl readers, we can turn to another literary success story: the British Harry Potter series. Its author, J. K. Rowling, tells us: "My favorite literary heroine is Jo March. It is hard to overstate what she meant to a small, plain girl called Jo, who had a hot temper and a burning ambition to be a writer." Or listen to Ursula Le Guin, who writes: "I know that Jo March must have had real influence upon me when I was a young scribbler. . . . She is as close as a sister and common as grass."[32] Yet there are limits to Jo March's breakthrough, as there were to Alcott's. Had Alcott become what her mother Abigail called a "beast of burden"? Some worried that Alcott had remade girlhood in the figure of Jo but was unable to reinvent what it meant to be a grown woman.[33]

Marriage to a flesh-and-blood "fond and faithful spouse" puts an end to Jo's ambitions to become a great writer. In a chapter called "Harvest Time," Jo has not yet given up the hope of writing a good book, "but I can wait," she tells herself. Jo settles into the more traditional role of mother and teacher, not only raising a family but also founding a school. "You should be ashamed to write popular stories for money," Professor Bhaer tells Jo in a book written by a woman to earn money. And, in a second ironic twist, an author who renounced marriage and devoted herself to a literary career writes a book about abandoning writing and embracing the pleasures of marriage. To be sure, Alcott would have preferred turning Jo into a "literary spinster," but so many "enthusiastic young ladies" clamored for marriage to Laurie that, "out of perversity," the author made a "funny match" for her. Unfortunately, the joke is on Jo, and it does not land without some of the same pain and humiliation Louisa May Alcott suffered as she navigated her way to professional success and literary spinsterhood.

## Orphan Anne's Imagination

Although some forty years separate Lucy Maud Montgomery's *Anne of Green Gables* (1908) from *Little Women*, Jo and Anne have much in common, despite their dramatically different family circumstances. The Canadian writer knew the work of Louisa May Alcott well, and no doubt found inspiration for Anne in the figure of Jo March. But Montgomery's Anne Shirley is an orphan, without steady support from loving parents, warmhearted siblings, and generous neighbors who care for her, guide her, and keep her from becoming bored. Montgomery's novel chronicles the endless escapades and scrapes of a spirited orphan, adopted by middle-aged siblings, showing how she wins the hearts of her adoptive parents and creates with them a true family. Anne, like Jo before her, has an oversized imagination, and she finds in writing an expressive outlet for her inventiveness.

"Anne is as real to me as if I had given her birth," Montgomery wrote, revealing that her character, like Jo March, is drawn from life.[34] After Montgomery's mother died of tuberculosis, her father packed her off to live with her strict maternal grandparents while he moved to Saskatchewan and remarried. Both Alcott and Montgomery adopt a transparently autobiographical style that contrasts sharply with the detached narrative voice found in the works of authors like Jane Austen and the Brontë sisters. Their coming-of-age works hint at the possibility of an identity as a professional writer in ways unusual for novels of the time.

Like Jo, Anne abandons her dreams of becoming an author, and in the sequels that followed the first book, her writing voice is muted. Still, many later readers understood that Anne Shirley was standing before a door that had not existed before *Little Women* was published, and now the door opened a crack wider. If Jo and Anne give in to the twin tugs of heterosexual marriage and domesticity, they still reveal the joy that girls can derive from creativity and self-expression. And the lives of their authors predict new possibilities of professional success, even if their personal lives, Montgomery's in particular, included some turbulence.

Montgomery's marriage to Ewan Macdonald, a Presbyterian minister, was, by her own account, loveless. Her husband suffered from severe bouts of depression, stemming from what he himself diagnosed as "religious melancholia," a fear that he would not be among the Elect chosen to enter heaven. Montgomery had her own mental health to worry about ("I have lost my mind by spells"), but still she became the main source of financial support for her husband and two sons. Later in life, after achieving literary celebrity and financial success, she fell into a deep depressive state. Utterly dejected by the prospect of a second world war and the possible conscription of her younger son, she wrote: "My position is too awful to endure. . . . What an end to a life in which I tried always to do my best in spite of many mistakes."[35] The official cause of her death was listed as a coronary thrombosis, but it is more than likely that Montgomery deliberately overdosed on medications for mood disorders.

*Anne of Green Gables* was rejected by four publishers before being accepted by L. C. Page, a publishing company in Boston. It quickly became a bestselling book. Like Alcott, Montgomery became something of a literary celebrity, yet her work never entered the official canon of works written in English. I recall once asking colleagues in Harvard's Department of English, as well as in the Program in American Studies, whether *Little Women*, a work that exists in 320 editions today in English alone, was ever taught in any courses, and the response was always a mildly amused, quizzical look, followed by a quick and definitive no. I quickly reasoned that it made no sense to follow up with the same question about *Anne of Green Gables*. What ranked high on the list of nineteenth-century American novels included in the curriculum? *The Scarlet Letter*, written by Nathaniel Hawthorne, Louisa May Alcott's friend and neighbor who famously explored with morbid attentiveness the shameful consequences of adultery. Anne and Jo could not form a more striking contrast with Hawthorne's Hester Prynne, yet both *Little Women* and the Anne of Green Gables series are dismissed as children's literature and trivialized as popular culture lacking liter-

Anne Shirley of *Anne with an E*, 2017
*Courtesy of Photofest*

ary merit. Recall how Hawthorne denounced popular women writers as a "damned mob of scribbling women!"—though he may have made an exception for Louisa May Alcott, whom he described as "gifted and agreeable" even if her commercial success occasionally rankled him.[36]

Today, Anne of Green Gables continues to have a strong following— even the crusty Mark Twain conceded that she was "the dearest and most lovable child in fiction since the immortal Alice."[37] Montgomery's book has been translated into thirty-six languages and inspired a silent movie, more than half a dozen television shows, cartoons, musicals, and so on. Its contribution to the Canadian tourism industry on Prince Edward Island is not at all negligible. Who would have imagined that Anne's story would be carried to the front by members of the Polish Resistance, turned into a television series in Sri Lanka, and included in the Japanese school curriculum of the 1950s?[38] Anne won the hearts not only of Marilla and Matthew Cuthbert but of readers all over the world.

When Lucy Maud Montgomery published *Anne of Green Gables*, she put reading, imagination, make-believe, talk, and writing on trial. In the relentless push-pull between Anne Shirley and Marilla Cuthbert, we discern the social pressures to which girls are relentlessly subjected as they grow up. Everything about Anne is designed to please readers of Montgomery's novel: her "beauty-loving eyes," her talkative nature, her lively imagination, and her love of books as well as of the outdoors. But Anne's compulsive conversational energy fails to find favor with Marilla. "You talk entirely too much for a little girl," she tells Anne, who thereafter holds her tongue "so obediently and thoroughly that her continued silence made Marilla rather nervous."[39] Marilla's contempt for talk extends to the printed word as well, and she feels nothing but disdain for young readers and writers. Resolutely unimaginative and austere, she denounces the "story-writing business" to which Anne and her friends subscribe as a "pack of nonsense" and declares that "reading stories is bad enough but writing them is worse."

As for imagination, the gift that makes Anne so winning and likeable and augurs well for her future—it is turned into a liability. The "wicked nonsense" of Anne's imagination transforms a spruce grove into a Haunted Wood filled with ghosts, skeletons, and headless men. Countless other acts of inspired fancy create an imaginative overload. When Marilla resolves to "cure" Anne of her imagination with a forced march through the woods at night, Anne repents and regrets "the license which she had given to her imagination." She resolves to be content with the "commonplace" from then on. Even play and pantomime become taboo after Anne, taking the role of the dead Elaine in Tennyson's "The Lady of Shalott," runs into a "dangerous plight" as she drifts down a river in a dramatic staging of the poem with her friends.

Domestic order, efficiency, and cleanliness are forever disrupted and undermined by Anne's inventive disposition. *Anne of Green Gables* runs the risk of turning into an endless series of chapters illustrating the perils of imagination even as it cannot help but celebrate that faculty by turning the heroine into the indisputable figure of the reader's sympathetic identification. Each chapter reads like a self-contained episode, with Anne's imagination running wild and getting her in trouble (she will burn anything in the oven because she becomes distracted by stories) while slightly depressed grown-ups are at first shocked and then delighted by her childlike innocence and spontaneity.[40] Still, the insistent positioning of imagination and all the attendant activities associated with it (daydreaming, reading, acting, playing, and writing) as imperiling the self and inflicting pain on others suggests that outgrowing an outsize imagination may not be such a terrible thing after all. It will, after all, finally end all those "irresistible temptations" to daydream, braid ribbons in your hair, or try to dye it black. Imagination is fine so long as it stays in childhood.

If nineteenth-century classic books about boys (Robert Louis Stevenson's *Treasure Island*, Mark Twain's *Huckleberry Finn*, Rudyard Kipling's *Captains Courageous*) take us from home on a series of adventures that go from bad (home) to worse (danger) until resolution and rescue are found, books about girls (Kate Douglas Wiggin's *Rebecca of Sunnybrook Farm*, Eleanor H. Porter's *Pollyanna*, Johanna Spyri's *Heidi*) begin at home and stay there, also often hinting at a backstory so disturbing that it is only partially elaborated. The sentimental and domestic rule supreme, driving out dark, sinister elements. Submitting to the straitjacket of a "feminine aesthetic," Montgomery prefers sentimental domesticity to the pulse-pumping excitement of adventures, quests, and journeys, with a narrative that has ornamental, effeminate elements embedded in the social world of the ordinary and everyday, presided over by women.[41] There are the "puffy sleeves" that Anne craves to have on her dresses, and then there is also the constant cooking and cleaning at Green Gables.

What we have in Montgomery's novel is a stay-at-home narrative that charts a gradual rapprochement between curmudgeonly adults in need of redemption and orphans in need of love and protection. That rapprochement risks sliding into complete assimilation into the world of adults (Anne will grow up, after all), though by no means the bleak one that Marilla once inhabited. Anne contemplates her future in the last pages of the novel, recognizing that, with Matthew's death, her horizons have "closed in": "But if the path set before her feet was to be narrow she knew that flowers of quiet happiness would bloom along it. The joys of sincere work and worthy aspiration and congenial friendship were to be hers; nothing could rob her of her birthright of fancy or her ideal world of dreams. And there was always the bend in the road." No one can kill off Anne's imagination, not even the author of her story, for whom the character took on a life of her own. Work and friendship become central to Anne's life, though, like Alcott, Montgomery gave in to readers who preferred the romance of marriage to the life of a spinster, one of Louisa May Alcott's "happy women" who embrace the romance of writing and good deeds.

Montgomery delayed Anne's marriage to Gilbert as long as possible, and she never abandoned the notion that friendship would be central in Anne's life, even after marriage. But writing does not seem to be in Anne's future. If it is, it will be in diminished form. "I felt so ashamed I wanted to give up altogether, but Miss Stacy said I could learn to write well if only I trained myself to be my own severest critic." So much for *The Lurid Mystery of the Haunted Hall*, a story inspired by Anne's reading of sensation fiction. Her writing club soon dissolves, and "an occasional bit of fiction" for magazines becomes her destiny, with the domestic and sentimental prevailing over mystery, romance, and melodrama.

*Anne of Green Gables* celebrates imagination yet is also committed to demonstrating the inevitable diminishing of that capacity and the importance of curbing it as you grow up. The publication of the work coincided with a moment when U.S. educators were just beginning to extol imagination and fantasy as important cognitive tools. "Fairy tale outranks arithmetic, grammar, geography, manuals of science; for without the aid of the imagination none of these books is really comprehensible," Hamilton Wright Mabie intoned in the preface to a 1905 volume entitled *Fairy Tales Every Child Should Know*. He argued that fairy tales should be brought into the orbit of the educational curriculum, "for the child has not only a faculty of observation and aptitude for work, he has also the great gift of imagination."[42] Just a year earlier the stage play *Peter Pan, or the Boy Who Wouldn't Grow Up* had its premiere at the Duke of York's Theatre in London, where both adults and children were enthusiastically clapping, on a nightly basis, to keep Tinkerbell alive, with the result that fantasy and imagination began making a powerful comeback on both sides of the Atlantic.

For the better part of the twentieth century, fostering the imagination was a high priority on the educational agenda. "Do you know what the imagination is, Susan?" Kris Kringle asks a child in the 1947 film *Miracle on 34th Street*. "That's when you see things that aren't really there," she pipes up. "Well, not exactly," says Kris with a smile. "No—to me the imagination is a place all by itself. A very wonderful country. You've heard of the British Nation and the French Nation? . . . Well, this is the Imagination. And once you get there you can do almost anything you want."[43] Imagination is also, of course, precisely the term used by the Walt Disney Company to promote its animated films and products. Through what is now termed "Imagineering," a new portal to the world of wonderlore opened up in the twentieth century. In *Anne of Green Gables*, L. M. Montgomery revealed how strongly she felt about the joys of an expansive imagination, yet the story of Anne Shirley reveals deep anxieties about the antisocial side to imagination, how it can isolate a child and turn her into something of a misfit, out of tune and out of step with the pressures and exigencies of the real world. Anne's brief infatuation with stories and writing turns out to be something she must outgrow as quickly as the plain brown dresses sewn for her by Marilla.

## A Tree Grows in Brooklyn, along with Empathy and Imagination

"You must not forget the Kris Kringle." These are the words of Mary Rommely, an Irish immigrant grandmother in Betty Smith's 1943 *A Tree Grows in Brooklyn*. She is giving her daughter advice about how best to raise her children, one of whom is the novel's heroine, Francie Nolan. And she urges her daughter to also tell legends, "fairy tales of the old country," and stories about "the great ghosts that haunted your father's people." But Francie's mother has reservations about telling her children "foolish lies." Still, Mary Rommely insists and offers a powerful counterargument that resonates with what Kris Kringle (living in almost the same neighborhood) declared in *Miracle on 34th Street* just a few years after the publication of Smith's novel. Uneducated and illiterate, she makes a plea for wonders and marvels: "The child must have a valuable thing which is called imagination. The child must have a secret world in which live things that never were. It is necessary that she *believe*. She must start out by believing in things not of this world. Then when the world becomes too ugly for living in, the child can reach back and live in her imagination. . . . Only by having these things in my mind can I live beyond what I *have* to live for."[44]

Living in the imagination is exactly what Francie does, "sitting on the gutter curb for hours," as her piano teacher, Miss Tynmore, observes. "What do you think of then?" she asks the quiet child. "Nothing. I just tell myself stories." Francie, impoverished and isolated, learns to make something from nothing. "Little girl, you'll be a story writer when you grow up," Miss Tynmore predicts.

A story writer is exactly what Betty Smith herself became, and *A Tree Grows in Brooklyn* is as close to autofiction as *Little Women* and *Anne of Green Gables*. At the age of fourteen, Smith's mother insisted that she quit school to help support her family. After that, Betty Wehner (her maiden name), like Francie, struggled to piece together a formal education over a period of many years, working nights and finishing high school only after she was married with two daughters. "I like to think of her as feminist back in the 1920s and '30s before the movement even developed," her daughter Mary later wrote about her. There was her mother, Betty Smith, in the midst of the Great Depression, a divorced woman with two daughters to raise. And how did she propose to support them? To make a living, she took bit parts in theater productions and turned to writing for a living, producing sketches, essays, plays (70 one-act plays alone), and anything that paid, knocking out copy in the early hours of the morning before the two girls left for school.

It is hardly surprising to find that Francie, like her author, discovers in writing a social mission. Giving up the pleasures of expressive sensationalism, she draws on real-life experience: "poverty, starvation and drunkenness," subjects that displease her English teacher, Miss Garnder. Those topics, this new teacher intones, are "ugly," and Francie is ordered to stop writing "those sordid little stories" and encouraged to write in a mode that is "pretty" and "cute." With a wonderful sense for drama and a reprise of Jo March's burning of her *Weekly Volcano* stories, Francie sets fire to her prose and chants "I am burning ugliness" as the flames rise high. Betty Smith's novel reminds readers of how women were discouraged from taking up social causes in their writing and guided toward the domestic and sentimental. At the same time, their writing was judged to be inferior in literary terms, precisely because of its subject matter. This curious double bind can be traced from Jo March to Anne Shirley and on to Francie Nolan, girls who are all criticized for daring to write in new, "unfeminine" ways.

What inspires Francie to turn her attention to subjects like poverty? Her own hardscrabble background, of course, explains much. But throughout the novel, as the perspective changes from Francie to her mother and back again, we discover that coming-of-age for Francie also means learning to be tolerant and to cultivate empathy. In the middle of the novel, we read an electrifying account about a young woman named Joanna who bears a child "out of wedlock" and is stoned by her women neighbors. "'Bitch! You bitch!' screamed the stringy one hysterically. Then acting on an instinct which was strong even in Christ's day, she picked a stone out of the gutter and threw it at Joanna." How does Francie react as witness to this atrocity? She is overwhelmed by pain: "A wave of hurt broke over Francie. . . . The hurt waves swept over her. . . . She was now getting her lesson from Joanna but it was not the kind of lesson her mother meant." "Let Joanna be a lesson to you," Francie's mother had said. The lesson turns into a tutorial about being "less cruel" and feeling empathy for others as well as compassion for their circumstances.

As in many other works that follow the pattern of the bildungsroman, in this case a girl's coming-of-age story, there is a powerful inflection point, a moment in which the heroine walks in someone else's shoes, feels their pain, or gets inside their skin. That form of social awareness has its origins less in parental instruction than in the reading experience. When Francie learns to read, the power of imagination is accelerated and intensified. One day, Francie turns a page and "magic" happens. "She looked at the word, and the picture of a gray mouse scampered through her mind. She looked further and when she saw 'horse,' she heard him pawing the ground and saw the sun glint on his glossy coat. The word 'running' hit her suddenly and she breathed hard as though running herself. The barrier between the individual sound of each letter and the whole meaning of the word was removed." Imagination builds a solid bridge between the mental conceptions of things and their real-world embodiment. With the power to move from the signifier (the word for a thing) to the mental concept of the thing and its real-world embodiment, Francie will never "be lonely." At the same time, she is anointed as a writer precisely because she can visualize and animate the lives of others.

A creative faculty of the mind, imagination is used to think, fantasize, and remember, among other things. The term "imagination" comes from the Latin *imaginare*, meaning "to picture oneself." There is a self-reflexive quality to that faculty, and it becomes evident when Francie returns to her childhood home and sees "a little girl sitting on a fire escape with a book in her lap and a bag of candy at hand." What does Francie do when she sees this "slender little thing of ten" but wave and call out "Hello, Francie."

Cover for the Armed Services edition of *A Tree Grows in Brooklyn*. *North Caro-
lina Collection, Wilson Special Collections Library, UNC–Chapel Hill*

"My name *ain't* Francie . . . and you know it too," the girl named Florry
shouts back. But in vain. Francie is able to picture herself as she was in
times past, reading as a ten-year-old, a bag of candy by her side. Through
imagination and its power to conjure up images and memories, Francie is
able to go back and remember who she once was. The past is always present, and it is reembodied and reenacted by successive generations.

The writers who invented Jo March, Anne Shirley, and Francie Nolan
were on a social mission to provide fictional role models who care about
the world. Recall how deeply care is embedded in the notion of curiosity, and it quickly becomes evident how our curious heroines are not just
adventurous rebels but also kind and compassionate. Francie's longing
to become a writer will not be subdued. Even when her Mama tells her
brother Neeley that Cornelius John Nolan is "a good name for a surgeon"
and does not tell her daughter that Mary Frances Katherine Nolan is a
"good name for a writer," she remains unstoppable. Like the tree that
grows in Brooklyn, her passion "lives" and nothing can "destroy" it. In

the end, we hear her thoughts about a future as a writer: "She knew God a little better, now. She was sure that He wouldn't care at all if she started to write again. Well maybe she'd try again someday."

## Writing and Trauma:
## Anne Frank's The Diary of a Young Girl

Alcott, Montgomery, and Smith—all experienced the trauma of war. The Civil War is kept at arm's length in *Little Women*, but Alcott herself served as a military nurse and suffered her entire life from the effects of the illness (and the mercury in the medicine used to cure it) contracted while she was on duty. Montgomery wrote the Anne series during World War I, and, in the aftermath of war, her life began to fall apart, with a preacher husband falling into a deep depression for his role in urging young men to enlist and then with the loss of her best friend during the global pandemic of 1919. Betty Smith published *A Tree Grows in Brooklyn* in 1943, just two years after the United States declared war on Japan and entered World War II. Her book became one of the Armed Services Editions given to soldiers on their way to war, and Smith evidently received more fan mail from soldiers than from civilians. All three women endured hardships. But two stayed reasonably safe on the home front, while the third suffered hardships to be sure, but not of the magnitude of soldiers and civilians caught in combat zones.

Around the time that Betty Smith was putting the finishing touches on *A Tree Grows in Brooklyn*, Anne Frank, living in comfortable circumstances with her family in the city of Amsterdam, was forced to go into hiding with her parents and sister to avoid arrest and deportation. Dutch forces had surrendered to the Nazis on May 15, 1940, just a day after the bombing of Rotterdam. The Netherlands remained under German occupation until the end of the war. No one who reads *Het Achterhuis* (*The Secret Annex* is the title Anne gave to the diary entries she wrote while in hiding) can avoid the long shadow cast by the circumstances of Anne Frank's death: the raid on the secret annex on the morning of August 4, 1944, by a member of the German SS and three members of the Dutch secret police, the interrogations at the Reich Security Offices, the transport to the Westerbork refugee camp, the subsequent deportation to Auschwitz and then on to Bergen-Belsen, where Anne Frank died of typhus.

We know Anne Frank through the diary entries she wrote, first in a small autograph book bound in red, gray, and tan checkered cloth with a small lock, then in school exercise books. In her first diary entries, dated June 1942, she begins by describing the joys of finding birthday gifts— among other things, a blouse, a game, a puzzle, a jar of cold cream, and roses—then quickly moves on to catty profiles of her classmates, and ends with an inventory of the many restrictions placed on the Dutch Jewish community. This is a book that challenges us to square the banalities of ordinary life with the unthinkable. Less than a month after those initial accounts, on July 8, Anne writes about how "so much has happened it's as if the whole world had suddenly turned upside down." The entry for the day ends with the Franks closing the door to the place that had been their home: "The stripped beds, the breakfast things on the table, the pound of meat for the cat in the kitchen—all of these created the impression that we'd left in a hurry. . . . We just wanted to get out of there, to get away and reach our destination in safety. Nothing else mattered." That safety was vouchsafed the family for two years and a month. Then they were rounded up, more than likely betrayed by a warehouse worker in the *Achterhuis*, hired after a trusted employee became too ill to continue working.[45]

Anne Frank's diary entries begin with a burst of enthusiasm about the prospect of having a confidante at last. "I hope you will be a great source of comfort and support," she writes on her birthday, the day on which she discovered the book on a table with her other gifts. At first the diary (later with its imaginary correspondent "Kitty") becomes the intimate friend whom she was longing to make, unable to find one in her sister, in her mother, or, earlier, in school chums. But with time, Anne Frank begins to see in her writing a mission. On March 29, 1944, she listened to a broadcast featuring Gerrit Bolkestein, Holland's exiled minister for education, art, and science, in which he urged residents of the country to collect "ordinary documents—a diary, letters . . . simple everyday material" for an archive that would detail the sufferings of civilians during the Nazi occupation.

Anne began redrafting her diary with an eye to posterity, hoping to provide a picture of what it was like to be in hiding by documenting what her family endured and how they had survived, even though she felt some skepticism about her work ever reaching the public eye. On 324 loose sheets of colored paper, she revised entries even as she continued to provide updates. She dreamed that her diary could someday appear in print, and she had even chosen a title (*The Secret Annex*) that promised to convey a sense of mystery and intrigue. It was, incidentally, her American publisher who decided, for promotional purposes, to call Anne Frank's work *The Diary of a Young Girl*.

One of Anne Frank's early loves was Hollywood, and she reverently pasted pictures of movie stars on a wall in her room. But she soon aspired to a different kind of fame, the immortality that could come from making a name for herself through writing. Yet she also clearly understood the value of writing as an expressive outlet. "If I don't have the talent to write books or newspaper articles," she declared, "I can always write for myself. . . . I want to go on living even after my death! And that's why I'm so grateful to God for having given me this gift, which I can use to develop myself and to express all that's inside me!"[46] How different from the immortality earned on the battlefield by figures like Achilles. The diary "kept her company and it kept her sane," Philip Roth noted.[47] A self-described chatterbox who spoke her mind, Anne found herself clamming up at times to avoid cutting, judgmental remarks from her elders. The diary gave her a chance to "talk back" with impunity.

"One of the most compelling figures to emerge from World War II wasn't a military hero or a world leader," Katerina Papathanasiou wrote in 2019.[48] Anne Frank became almost as well known as the Allied leaders of that war, though few would have thought to refer to her as a heroine, seeing her more as a victim, martyr, or saint. The historian Ian Buruma called her the "Jewish Saint Ursula" and "a Dutch Joan of Arc."[49] Philip Roth saw genius in her writing and referred to her, in *The Ghost Writer* (his reimagining of Anne Frank's life), as being "like some impassioned little sister of Kafka's." But, like so many women writers before her—all of them older if not necessarily wiser—Anne Frank became heroic by using words and stories not just as a therapeutic outlet for herself but also as a public platform for securing justice.

Anne's diary entries are full of acts of heroism, small and large. Anne is willing to let the eccentric Mr. Dussel share her room, looking on it as nothing more than one of many willingly made "sacrifices for a good cause." She worries about those "we can no longer help." Counting herself lucky to be able to buy food, she complains about the selfishness of those living in the tight quarters of the annex but never about the forced circumstances of the family's living arrangements. There are rats in the food supply, toilets that malfunction, burglars who threaten the security of the hideaway, the constant sound of gunfire, sirens, and planes, and, from the window of the annex, the sight of people being dragged away by police. And yet, though Anne admits fear, she never allows herself to shut down or to give in to the darkness that surrounds her. The diary reveals how she was able to preserve decency, integrity, and hope, despite living in a regime determined to exterminate her along with the elderly, the ailing, and all those who failed the test of Aryan purity.

Long classified as "merely" a book assigned to high school students, *The Diary of a Young Girl* is rarely credited for its literary genius. How many teenagers would have been capable of writing a compelling memoir or of thinking reflectively as Anne Frank did? She writes with the confessional verve of Saint Augustine, exhibits a Du Boisean understanding of double consciousness in describing the out-of-body experience of observing herself, and displays the unforgiving stoic candor of Kafka. Certainly there are many literary prodigies who wrote works that quickly entered the canon, but they are rare. Lord Byron published two volumes of poetry in his teens. Mary Shelley completed *Frankenstein; or, The Modern Prometheus* (1818) when she was eighteen. Arthur Rimbaud wrote almost all his poetry while still a teenager. Daisy Ashford famously wrote *The Young Visitors* (1919) at age nine. S. E. Hinton published *The*

*Outsiders* (1968) when she was nineteen. These are the notable exceptions, and most of these authors did not start writing something at age thirteen that would eventually be published.

According to a 1996 survey that appears on the Anne Frank Museum website, half of U.S. high school students had been assigned *The Diary of a Young Girl*. Today that number has declined, but readers continue to discover Anne's voice and how she used her storytelling gifts to document the atrocities of the Nazi era and also to report about the heroism of the helpers who sheltered her family members and kept them alive. But it is, above all, the diary that has kept Anne alive in our imaginations even after the arrests at 263 Prinsengracht, not just, of course, the diary but also the details of Anne's life in the camps with her sister and mother. It is impossible to read about the Franks at Auschwitz and Bergen-Belsen without tearing up: Edith starving because she passed on every bit of her rations to her daughters; Anne hauling rocks and digging up sod as part of the pointless labor assignments in the camps; children under fifteen sent directly to the gas chambers; Anne meeting up with former classmates who describe her as bald, emaciated, and shivering; Anne, "delirious, terrible, burning up," dying most likely in a typhus epidemic.

In a remarkable volume about Anne Frank's book, her life, and her afterlife, the American novelist Francine Prose recalls the hours in which she read the diary for the first time as a child, immersed in it until day faded into night. Fifty years later, she reads the diary with her students at Bard College: "And for those few hours during which my students and I talked about her diary, it seemed to me that her spirit—or, in any case, her voice—had been there with us, fully present and utterly alive, audible in yet another slowly darkening room."[50] It's unlikely that Anne Frank ever really believed that writing would bring her immortality, but the words in her diary turned out to be prophetic: "I want to go on living even after my death."

## Harriet the Spy Becomes Less Cruel and Scout Discovers Empathy

Just a decade after Anne Frank's diary appeared in print in the United States, Louise Fitzhugh published a novel about a girl obsessed with writing in her diary. It seems almost sacrilegious, at the least disrespectful, to invoke Anne Frank's diary work in the same breath with Harriet M. Welsch's compulsive writing in Fitzhugh's 1964 *Harriet the Spy*. Like an addict, Harriet is forever reaching for her notebook, unable to "go anywhere without it," scribbling "furiously."

What does Harriet write? Certainly nothing that is evidence of precocious genius. Her notebooks are filled with crude adolescent insults, along the lines of "CARRIE ANDREWS IS CONSIDERABLY FATTER THIS YEAR" or "LAURA PETERS IS THINNER AND UGLIER. I THINK SHE COULD USE SOME BRACES ON HER TEETH." And "PINKY WHITEHEAD WILL NEVER CHANGE. DOES HIS MOTHER HATE HIM? IF I HAD HIM I'D HATE HIM."[51] But Harriet's entries bear an eerie resemblance to what is recorded on the second day of Anne Frank's diary: "J. R. . . . is a detestable, sneaky, stuck-up, two faced gossip who thinks she's so grown up." Or "Betty Bloemendaal looks kind of poor, and I think she probably is." "E. S. talks so much it isn't funny. . . . They say she can't stand me, but I don't care, since I don't like her much either." Both of these gifted girls find their voices, discovering the value of self-critical reflection and learning about the significance of generosity and kindness.

"I grew up reading this series of books called 'Harriet the Spy,' and I just thought they were the neatest things. . . . I sort of modeled my early life after Harriet the Spy," Lindsay Moran told a CNN reporter in an interview about her career at the CIA.[52] Moran was obsessed with the investigative energy and scriptomania of Harriet M. Welsch, who lives in New York City with her parents. Harriet is obsessed with recording her misanthropic observations, on a daily basis, about the people she observes—the stock boy Joe Curry, the socialite Mrs. Agatha K. Plumber, and the cat owner Harrison Withers, among others. Her ambitious plans to become a writer backfire when classmates find one of her notebooks and read the many vicious pronouncements—savagely cruel in many cases—about how they look and what they say.

What we might otherwise find admirable in an eleven-year-old protagonist (the ambition to become a writer) becomes a liability in light of the pain and humiliation inflicted on others once Harriet's notebooks go public. Harriet may not set out to be a bully, but her cutting remarks wound friends and classmates, all young and vulnerable. The novel about her misadventures in espionage has vanished from lists of recommended books for the young drawn up today. But back in 2004, Anita Silvey, an expert on children's literature, included it in her list of one hundred best books for children, in large part because it was a volume that resonated powerfully with young readers.[53] They had no trouble connecting with Harriet's sense of being a social misfit. And they could not but admire how she managed to find a safe place to compensate for her loneliness— safe only until it was not. Here was a traumatized child (Ole Golly, the woman who is her de facto mother, abruptly quits her position as Harriet's nanny) who becomes both detective and writer, a loner yet also a snoop who copes with her social isolation through a form of writing that, admittedly, borders on a social pathology. But Harriet finds religion, and it comes in the prosocial form of empathy.

The philosopher Richard Rorty tells us that some books help us become independent and self-sufficient, and then there are others that help us become less cruel. He divides the latter category into books that enable us to discover the evils of social institutions (Harriet Beecher Stowe's *Uncle Tom's Cabin* would be a good example) and those that enable us to see our own failings (Charles Dickens's *Bleak House* belongs to that category).[54] *Harriet the Spy* falls squarely into the class of books that help us become less cruel by letting us see the effects of our own actions on others.

The therapist recruited by Harriet's parents (we are on the Upper East Side in New York City) to help their daughter work through the trauma of separation from her beloved nanny has some insights into the mind of the young writer in training. Harriet eavesdrops on the telephone conversation between her father and the "Doctor," catching only fragments of what her father says. "Well, Dr. Wagner, let me ask you this . . . yes, yes, I know she's a very intelligent child. . . . Yes, well, we're well aware that she has a lot of curiosity. . . . Yes, a sign of intelligence, yes, quite right. . . . Yes, I think she just might make a writer."

The curious child of Fitzhugh's novel suffers from what could also be diagnosed as a raging case of "incuriosity."[55] In fact, Harriet becomes something of a monster of incuriosity, exhibiting a lack of interest in anything that does not relate to her own personal obsession, and unable to understand the pain she has inflicted on others. To be sure, we can attribute the failure to empathize in part to her age and to the trauma of separation from a mother figure, but her private pursuit of self-fulfillment and autonomy through writing is grounded in cruelty to virtually everyone in her real-life orbit.

What rescues Harriet from turning into a monster of incuriosity? Undeterred by the social ostracism of her friends and classmates, and even by a letter from Ole Golly urging her to apologize, she continues to write stinging prose: "FRANCA DEI SANTI HAS ONE OF THE DUMBEST FACES YOU COULD EVER HOPE TO SEE. . . . SHE IS ABOUT OUR AGE AND GOES TO A PUBLIC SCHOOL WHERE SHE IS ALWAYS FLUNKING THINGS LIKE SHOP THAT WE DON'T HAVE. . . . SHE DOESN'T HAVE A GOOD TIME AT HOME BECAUSE EVERYONE KNOWS HOW DUMB SHE IS AND DOESN'T TALK TO HER."

Is there redemption for Harriet? Does she learn anything at all, beyond following Ole Golly's advice to apologize and to conceal the contempt she feels for others with "little lies"? In the novel's last chapter, Harriet watches her two friends, Janie and Sport, from a distance, and it is then that she can finally get in touch, not with her feelings, but with theirs. "She made herself walk in Sport's shoes, feeling the holes in his socks rubbing against his ankles. She pretended she had an itchy nose when Janie put one abstracted hand up to scratch. She felt what it would feel like to have freckles and yellow hair like Janie, then funny ears and skinny shoulders like Sport." This may not yet be empathy, but it is a transformative moment for Harriet, turning her from callous observer in search of autonomy and fame into someone who can walk in someone else's shoes.

Like *Harriet the Spy*, *To Kill a Mockingbird* (1960) lets us see the world through the eyes of a girl, though in this case Scout tells the story of her childhood as an adult. Scout slips back with ease into the consciousness of her experiencing self, then seamlessly moves back to the older and wiser adult, who adds information and clarifies the child's account. The double consciousness and double identity on display (the young Scout and the older and wiser narrating self) explains much about the audience the book found. *To Kill a Mockingbird* is a crossover book, appealing as much to adults as to the young, perhaps more so to adults. Harper Lee enabled grown-ups to return to childhood and immerse themselves in all the felt perils of that time—the keen sense of injustice in the world, the hypocrisy of adults, and a sense of acute defenselessness. But we can also immerse ourselves in the pleasures of childhood, aided by small Proustian nudges that help us remember what it was like to be as unknowing yet also as sensitive to the tremors in the world as Scout is.

*To Kill a Mockingbird* takes us inside a child's mind, but it also self-reflexively sends a powerful message about the importance of perspective, identification, and empathy. "You never really understand a person until you consider things from his point of view . . . until you climb into his skin and walk around in it," Atticus tells Scout. And then there is the golden moment near the end of the novel, when Scout's voice shifts into the third person and, standing on Boo Radley's porch ("I had never seen our neighborhood from this angle"), she describes the events in her story from Boo Radley's point of view. Suddenly we realize that she has internalized her father's wisdom and is standing in the shoes of her neighbor. In some ways, *To Kill a Mockingbird* is the book that inaugurated a turn toward empathy as the highest social good in what the publishing trade now calls books for young adult audiences. It is the exact opposite of the cruelty we witness in Harriet's notebooks.[56]

We know that Scout's conversion experience, seeing things from a new angle through the eyes of another, changes her, for what does she do but tell a powerful story about race and injustice in the Deep South during the Great Depression. Her story is now in a book, and she has written herself into a history, a history that reminds us of the production of meaning through storytelling. As for Harriet, it is something of a challenge to speculate on the effects of Ole Golly's advice on her after her notebook is made public. But as Harriet the Spy continues to pursue her dream of becoming a writer, it is hard not to imagine that she will allow her innate curiosity to conquer incuriosity and that compassion will vanquish compulsion and cruelty.

## Saying Their Name: Angie Thomas's The Hate U Give

*To Kill a Mockingbird* was the book that opened the eyes of many readers in the United States to anti-Black racism and racial injustice. It is a landmark work in its advocacy of understanding and empathy. But, ironically, that empathy is trained not on Tom Robinson, an innocent Black man falsely accused of rape and shot by the police while trying to escape imprisonment, but on Boo Radley, a man who remains free after murdering another man for physically assaulting two children.

It took Toni Morrison to readjust our perspective on novels like *To Kill a Mockingbird*, a book that ranks high among those assigned to high school students in the United States. In 1990, writing about whiteness and the literary imagination, she referred to the "strategic use of black characters to define the goals and enhance the qualities of white characters."[57] This riskless way of constructing heroism is deeply problematic for many reasons, and it remains a stubbornly persistent problem in our collective literary and cinematic imagination, with a stereotype that has devolved into what Spike Lee called the "Magical Negro"—a humble, low-status figure who selflessly helps white people secure their personal salvation. What the filmmaker had in mind were characters ranging from Jim in Mark Twain's *The Adventures of Huckleberry Finn* and Uncle Remus in Disney's *Song of the South* to Red in *The Shawshank Redemption* and John Coffey in *The Green Mile*. They generously build the platform for the white hero's redemption in self-effacing acts that are rarely acknowledged as heroic.

"An Empathetic, Nuanced Portrait of a Teen's Political Awakening." That was the headline given to Richard Brody's *New Yorker* review of the film *The Hate U Give*. Interestingly, the young adult book on which it was based, Angie Thomas's *The Hate U Give* (2017), received far less media coverage than the film. Empathy becomes the controlling affect, according to the reviewer of the film, as if suddenly, out of the blue, audiences can finally feel what those affected by police brutality can feel.

What took so long? is the question that comes to mind. And why did we have to wait such a long time for a Black girl as heroine in YA fiction? To be sure, there are some other examples, and they are forty years apart: Mildred Taylor's *Roll of Thunder, Hear My Cry* (1976) and Jacqueline Woodson's *Brown Girl Dreaming* (2014). Thomas's book hit a nerve with readers, young and old, sounding full chords in ways that few YA novels have. *The Hate U Give* draws readers into the complexities of the Black Lives Matter movement with a fictional memoir that captures the truth of a historical moment. Its emotionally charged personal perspective on Black communities and political action connects with the #SayTheirNames movement and the effort to remember victims, protest their murders, and demand an end to police violence.

The novel begins with the piercing screams of Starr Carter, a Black teenager, who has just witnessed the shooting of her friend Khalil by a white officer. "Officer One-Fifteen" mistook Khalil's hairbrush for a gun. "No, no, no, is all I can say," Starr writes in her first-person account of the events of that night. Caught between threats from local drug dealers to keep silent and the pleas of an activist lawyer to speak out and testify, Starr struggles to find her voice and to speak up, both in the courtroom and at a public protest unleashed by the failure to indict Officer Brian Cruise Jr. in the shooting death of Khalil Harris.

Just Us for Justice represents Starr pro bono, and its attorney, Ms. Ofrah, urges Starr to speak out: "You matter and your voice matters," she tells Starr. What Starr discovers in the aftermath of the shooting is the importance of breaking silence: "What's the point of having a voice if you're gonna be silent in those moments you shouldn't be."[58] An unwilling heroine who feels "un-brave" much of the time, she summons "the tiny brave part" of herself and speaks, telling the story as it happened to the grand jury. Her testimony fails to make a difference, but at a protest rally that turns violent, ending in destructive fires and looting, Starr deploys her "biggest weapon" and speaks out. "Forget trigger happy," she thinks to herself, "speaker happy is more my thing," affirming the truism about pens being mightier than swords.

The novel ends with the promise of rebuilding and making things right. After telling her story in the present tense, plunging us in medias res, into the thick of things, Starr begins to speak in the cadences of the bards, griots, and storytellers, reaching back to tell the story of Khalil and memorialize her friend, endowing him with the immortality once conferred on heroes from the ancient past. She is to Khalil as Homer was to Achilles. "Once upon a time there was a hazel-eyed boy with dimples. I called him Khalil. The world called him a thug. He lived, but not nearly long enough, and for the rest of my life I'll remember how he died. Fairy tale? No. But I am not giving up on a better ending." And with that she recites the names of victims of police shootings, moving backward in time to "that little boy in 1955 who nobody recognized at first—Emmett." Starr invokes Emmett Till, the fourteen-year-old African American boy from Chicago who was lynched in Mississippi in 1955 and whose brutal murder made him a powerful catalyst for action in the civil rights movement. And she closes her memoir with a promise: "I'll never be quiet."

"My biggest literary influences are rappers," Angie Thomas declared in an interview published in *Time* magazine. The neighborhood in which she grew up did not have successful doctors and lawyers, or writers for that matter, but the rappers were doing well, and she could connect with their lyrics. (She used Tupac Shakur's album *Thug Life* as the inspiration for her title *The Hate U Give*.) When she was a teenager, *Twilight* and *The Hunger Games* were the two big franchises in books and films for young audiences, but Thomas was not able to relate to either one. She was in touch not only with rappers but also with #BlackLivesMatter, which, like #MeToo, spawned a movement. It had been back in 2013 that Alicia Garza, Patrisse Khan-Cullors, and Opal Tometi created a hashtag that led to recognition of the struggles of Black people in the face of police brutality.

Thomas gives a remarkably even-handed account of deeply internalized biases on both sides of the racial divide, and her call for activism, "to keep fighting the good fight," is meant not as a call to arms but as an appeal for conversation, with words as tools rather than guns as weapons. If Thomas, who came close to committing suicide as a bullied adolescent, insists that she is more interested in "instilling empathy" in her readers than in imposing on them a "political agenda," she also shows that with empathy comes political awakening.[59] Her portrait of Starr Carter's resilience and strength, how she moves from intimidated silence to spirited speech, suggests that this coming-of-age story is about more than feelings and caring. Its vivid portrayal of the two worlds Starr Carter straddles—one in her run-down, gang-ridden neighborhood, one at her posh school—turns it into a clarion call for social justice. Growing up in a culture that had relied on oral traditions to transmit wisdom from one generation to the next and that had also developed a literary style that spoke from the heart in the vernacular, Angie Thomas used her voice to convey why the lives of her characters matter and what we can all do to combat state-sanctioned violence against Black Americans. When Starr Carter finally speaks out, everyone in her social orbit is animated and transformed by her words.

# CHAPTER 5

# DETECTIVE WORK

## From Nancy Drew to Wonder Woman

*I came to believe that being a private detective
was the work I was meant to do.*

—SHIRLEY JACKSON

*I doubt that a writer can be a hero. I
doubt that a hero can be a writer.*

—VIRGINIA WOOLF, "Professions for Women"

WHEN BILL MOYERS recalled his conversations with Joseph Campbell at George Lucas's Skywalker Ranch and later at the Museum of Natural History in New York, he spoke of Campbell's great erudition. But what really impressed him about the American guru of mythological wisdom was that he was a "man with a thousand stories." Those stories, from cultures all over the world, captured not just the meaning of life but also the "rapture" of being alive. Rapture takes different forms for men and for women. The ecstasies of the woman's journey take her down a path from maiden to mother, a "big change, involving many dangers." Both Campbell and Moyers believed that women could become true heroes by giving birth. Childbirth was the equivalent of the hero's ordeal. "What is a woman? A woman is a vehicle of life. . . . Woman is what it is all about—the giving of birth and the giving of nourishment." Boys, by contrast, deprived of the opportunity to give birth, turn into "servants of something greater" once they grow up.[1]

More than two decades earlier, Betty Friedan had dismantled and undone the myth of what she called the "Happy Housewife Heroine." *The Feminine Mystique*, published in 1963, was the book that dared to address the problem with no name and that launched a major social movement, reaching into the lives of its readers and transforming them in ways that childbirth had not.[2] The real-life women of postwar U.S. culture, Friedan declared, kept having babies "because the feminine mystique says there is no other way for a woman to be a heroine." In stories printed in women's magazines of the 1950s, Friedan discovered, only one in a hundred included a heroine with a job, and the feature articles had titles along the lines of "Have Babies While You're Young," "Are You Training Your Daughter to Become a Wife?," and "Cooking to Me Is Poetry." One of the titles Friedan mentions rang a bell with me as I read through that sad list, and I feel sure that I read it back in the day: "Why GI's Prefer Those German Girls." And the answer was of course the cult of *Kinder, Küche, und Kirche* (Children, Kitchen, and Church) that continued to flourish in postwar Germany and was embodied in the German *Hausfrau*.

In 1962, just one year before the publication of *The Feminine Mystique*, Helen Gurley Brown, later the longtime editor of *Cosmopolitan* magazine, published *Sex and the Single Girl*, a book that communicated, with breathless prose, the pleasures of looking your best, having affairs, and snagging the man of your dreams (among other things, keeping a spray atomizer on your desk to make sure you always looked fresh at the office was considered obligatory).[3] Brown advised her readers to cook well ("it will serve you faithfully"), get rid of baby fat (it belongs on babies), live alone (even if it meant renting a space above a garage), and "lay a trap" for the "glittery life." Unconstrained by husband and children, the Cosmo Girl was sexually active, supremely self-confident, and ready to pounce. She was "a potent amalgam of Ragged Dick, Sammy Glick and Holly Golightly," Margalit Fox wrote in the *New York Times* obituary for Helen Gurley Brown, adding that the Cosmo Girl always had a good time whether wearing her fabulous clothes or taking them off.[4]

Recall the terms of Achilles' Choice, when Thetis, his mother, confronts her son, the man who will become the hero of the Trojan War, with a decision. He can choose to abandon the battle, have children, and die a happy old man, or continue fighting, become famous, and earn immortality. The choice is between *nostos* (home) and *kleos* (glory).

Women in the postwar era faced a similar divide in the road, since "having it all" seemed an impossible goal. But for them, as Campbell told Moyers, marriages can fall apart, especially once the children leave the house: "Daddy will fall in love with some nubile girl and run off, and Mother will be left with an empty house and heart, and will have to work it out on her own, in her own way."[5] That meant that *nostos* might in fact not be the best option. But how could women win immortality at a time when they could not possibly go to war? As we have seen, writing, becoming a woman of letters, finding a voice and using it to deliver social justice, became the path to glory. But in contemporary popular culture, that writing is often carried out in tandem with a hunt that demands the focused determination of a bloodhound.

The trope of the "aspiring writer" can be found in many TV series, from the struggles of Rory Gilmore to become a reporter in *Gilmore Girls* (2000–2007) to the bitter triumph of Guinevere Beck, who lands a book deal in the first season of *You* (2017) before dying at the hands of her boyfriend. Beginning with *Sex and the City*, which aired from 1998 to 2004, and up to *Girls*, airing from 2012 to 2017, a writing career was something like the holy grail for girls and women, as it had been for Jo March, Anne Shirley, and Francie Nolan. For Carrie Bradshaw, in *Sex and the City*, that career took a back seat to finding Mr. Right, who manifests himself as Mr. Big (Helen Gurley Brown would have approved). For Hannah Horvath, in *Girls*, self-actualization takes a different form, as she pursues becoming a writer and unintentionally also ends up with a baby.

Before turning to teen detectives and women sleuths, it is worth taking a look at what makes Carrie and Hannah run. The two have discarded all the trappings of the Feminine Mystique, yet they remain to double duty bound, developing a professional identity as writers while also seeking a romantic connection. Carrie simpers for Mr. Big, flirts with Berger, and has a fling with a jazz soloist, while Hannah gets serious with Adam, indulges in a "sexcapade" with a pal's underage stepbrother, and has a fling with a surfboarding instructor named Paul-Louis. They are both on the prowl but also bent on self-actualization. What we see in the near decade that separates them is a turn toward investigative work in the service of social justice, a mission shared with the private eyes and sleuths who appear in this chapter. These are women of action, and they lead up to a long-awaited superheroine who can finally take her place among action figures ranging from Superman and Batman to Spider-Man and Thor.

## "Once upon a Time in a City Far Away": Carrie Bradshaw and Hannah Horvath

Even those critical of *Sex and the City* as a featherweight television production will concede that the series channeled and also reshaped our cultural understanding of courtship, dating, and marriage, especially when it came to sex and single women. The women in *Sex and the City* were grown-ups, but more like gal-pals or girls, in the best senses of those terms, adventurous and uninhibited, ready to do all and tell all. In some ways they seem to have stepped out from the pages of Louisa May Alcott's "Happy Women," this time as modern bachelorettes instead of nineteenth-century spinsters ("Why do we get stuck with old maid and spinster and men get to be bachelors and playboys?" an irate Miranda asks her friends).[6] They may not have been exactly happy, but they rarely sank into what Freud called neurotic misery (since this is New York City, psychoanalysis is right there to help out). Instead they navigated what the founding father of psychoanalysis called untreatable forms of ordinary human unhappiness.

Scrambling to meet deadlines, suffering anxiety attacks when a hard drive fails, and feted at book parties, Carrie Bradshaw, played by Sarah Jessica Parker, gives us the portrait of a young woman as writer. But with each passing season, we are drawn into what looks more and more like a roller-coaster ride of fairy tale–themed romance, until it becomes something of a relief when Carrie finally hits the jackpot and gets her happily-ever-after with a certain prince named Mr. Big. It is he who rescues Carrie from a failed relocation to Paris with a faux version of Mr. Right, and brings her back to New York City, where she is doomed to marry and languish in two predictably soulless movie sequels. Being a thirty-something single writer in New York City may have its upside, but the consolations of a sex-and-relationships column cannot provide the satisfactions of marriage to a wealthy, attractive, and elusive bachelor who wanders, Odysseus-like, from one port to the next until he finally docks at the right one.

All the more astonishing, then, to discover that the young Carrie Bradshaw, in *The Carrie Diaries*, the fictional prequel or origin story to the HBO series, moves in a different direction, discovering in writing pleasures and satisfactions that compensate for the disappointments of romance. Like many who came before her, Candace Bushnell, author

Carrie Bradshaw of *Sex and the City*
*Courtesy of Photofest*

of the bestselling anthology on which the television series was based, saw the craft of writing as an expressive form, a type of autofiction that enabled her to process the ebb and flow of daily life. "I write entirely to find out what I'm thinking, what I'm looking at, what I see and what it means," Joan Didion had written back in 1976.[7] Both the series and the book on which it is based give us a dose of real life, direct and unembellished, with little literary artifice. In autofiction, attention is focused on the narrator's status as writer, and the writing of a book becomes the goal etched on the book itself.[8]

Candace Bushnell herself began writing as a child, and the two back-stories she wrote for *Sex and the City*—targeted at teen readers—were partly autobiographical. *The Carrie Diaries*, published in 2010, and *Summer and the City*, published a year later, are reminders that Carrie started young as a writer. "I've been writing since I was six. I have a pretty big imagination," she tells us, emphasizing the powerful link in fiction for girls between imagination—the power to visualize things, real and counterfactual—and writing.[9] As a child, her role models were the "lady writers" pictured in the author photos of her grandmother's romance novels. But soon she learns to suppress the "secret excitement" she feels about writing that kind of fiction, and turns to the "real" in order to establish her credentials.

What she discovers in the course of her efforts to enroll in a writing program is, once again—just like Jo, Anne, and Francie—the need to tame the imagination, to take up topics drawn from her own social domain. Writing for *The Nutmeg*, her school newspaper, she discovers the power of using her voice to change the culture of her school—to address, what else but the toxicity of high school cliques. Tellingly, for her second assignment, an article entitled "The Queen Bee," she uses a gender-neutral pseudonym, "veiling her identity to ensure that her work will be taken seriously."[10] Her mission is not to become prom queen but to critique the entire concept of the prom queen.

What is permitted the young Carrie Bradshaw is not permitted to her older and wiser self. The teenager can struggle and flourish with her writing (as she does in *The Carrie Diaries*), but the thirty-something woman of *Sex and the City* must train her sights on finding a suitable romantic partner. "I have always been a firm believer that men, marriage and children are not the 'answer' for all women," Candace Bushnell declared in an interview printed as an appendix to *The Carrie Diaries*, sounding all the while like Betty Friedan addressing the younger crowd, at a time when she was channeling Helen Gurley Brown for the adult-themed *Sex and the City*.

The young Carrie's efforts to define herself are carried out against a backdrop of revealing archetypes. When a personal crisis unfolds, "odd thoughts" come to her mind, among them: "In life, there are only four kinds of girls: The girl who played with fire. The girl who opened Pandora's Box. The girl who gave Adam the apple. And the girl whose best friend stole her boyfriend."[11] (The girl who played with fire, a female analogue to Prometheus, is more than likely a reference to Stieg Larsson's 2006 novel of that title, the second novel in his Millennium trilogy.) That series of "archetypes," with a new one that, once again, vilifies women, is a reminder of how we focus on the dark side of women's actions. The origin story for *Sex and the City*, more than the adult-focused TV show and movies, is a powerful reminder that our cultural stories about women from times past continue to resonate with us today in negative ways, and that the only way to loosen their tight grip on us is to craft new stories—transforming "the girl whose best friend stole her boyfriend" into "the girl who became a writer."

The series *Girls* features Hannah Horvath, played by Lena Dunham, as a twenty-something making her way from post-college narcissistic aimlessness to a form of self-awareness and social responsibility as she struggles to find her voice and become a published writer. She and her circle of three girlfriends mirror, magnify, and distort the quartet from *Sex and the City*. We are in the funhouse, looking at Carrie, Samantha, Miranda, and Charlotte through the curved mirror of millennial sensibilities.

In some ways, we are all writers, or at least potentially so, and Hannah is supremely aware of that fact when asked about her "real job" in New York, which involves casual labor in a coffee shop. "I'm a writer," she nonetheless insists. "And that's how you make money?" her interlocutor presses on. "No, I don't have any money," Hannah responds, having just been cut off financially by her parents. "Do you have an agent?" is the next question. "No, I don't have an agent," the defeated Hannah responds.

Hannah's first success at monetizing her craft comes in the form of an e-book anthology of her essays, with an editor who is elated that she suffers from "mental illness"—"That's something we can work with!" When that project collapses after the suicide of the editor, Hannah enrolls in the Iowa Writers' Workshop, only to find that she is not suited for ventures that require social interactions and collaboration. Her leap to self-actualization comes when she is interviewing an acclaimed author named Chuck Palmer and declares, while asking about the sexual assault charges brought against him by several women, "I'm a writer, you know, and I mean I may not be a rich writer or a famous writer . . . but I am a writer, and as such I think I'm obligated to use my voice to talk about things that are meaningful to me."

Hannah's odyssey takes her from extreme navel-gazing to a sense of purpose for her writing. The girl of Girls becomes the It Girl, turning into a woman writer of the #MeToo era, letting go of the excitement of imaginative fiction and turning to essayistic social critique. Hannah's New York Times op-ed in the Modern Love section and a storytelling performance at Housing Works reveal how she has found her mission in writing that disavows fiction and turns to the essay as a form of social engagement. Still, in a brilliant twist, the final season gives us an episode that shows Hannah watching her ex-boyfriend's film about their relationship, turning the entire series into an infinite loop about picturing yourself being pictured. And we end with a snappy reminder that narcissism is a key feature of every writer's personal profile. Never mind that in real life Lena Dunham found her calling in the medium of film.

Hannah's turn from fiction to journalism has its own logic in a culture that was processing the rage and resentment brought on by news about decades of sexual exploitation and social suppression. Conducting her own investigative inquiry with the serial predator Chuck Palmer, she models the more subtle forms taken by that exploitation and begins to show, paradoxically, that imaginative works of fiction and film can be as compelling as the real-life stories that inspired them. We have documentaries (*Predator*), movies inspired by real-life events (*The Morning Show*), books (*Catch and Kill*), and podcasts (*Chasing Cosby*) about power imbalances and gender inequality. Lena Dunham joins the ever-growing ranks of writers and filmmakers who use their imaginations to take up the ethical issues of the #MeToo movement and explore the emotional consequences of power imbalances between genders.[12] *Girls* reminds us that detective work is always part of the cultural calculus in the work carried out by writers of fiction.

## Detectives, Private Eyes, and Female Dicks

The cult of the writer, as we have seen, led almost directly from *Little Women* through fiction for girls to screen fantasies about topical writing as professional work. But epistemophilia, the love of knowledge that has its origins in our innate curiosity, has a second dimension that merits exploring. Are there women less bent on the search for self-actualization and enlightenment than on advocacy and the kind of social work associated with inquiring minds? Reading may enlarge the world, as it does for the many young writer-heroines in our fictions, but writing has a deeply private and personal dimension that shrinks the universe down to a solitary mind wrestling with emotion, interiority, and existential crisis. It is hard not to associate the loneliness of the long-suffering writer with a poet like Emily Dickinson, seated at her tiny desk in Amherst, Massachusetts, writing verse on sheets later hand-sewn into fascicles. But words on the page, printed or written by hand, like the stories that circulated in the form of gossip, mattered even more back then, precisely because they were a way of getting out the word at a time when speaking in public was rarely an option for most women.

Unlike the writer who traffics in words on the page, often in private spaces, detectives have a job that requires investigative action in the public arena—the inspection of the crime scene, the search for clues, the interrogation of suspects. But detectives are, for good reason, called *private* eyes, for as much as they scan crime scenes and search for suspects, they also try hard to fly under the radar, keeping a low profile to maximize their ability to collect information. The first female detective in British literature was a Mrs. Gladden ("the name I assume most frequently in my business"), whose serial adventures were published in 1864 by James Redding Ware, who used the pseudonym Andrew Forrester.[13] Mrs. Gladden credits her sleuthing skills to her unobtrusiveness—she can easily pick up local gossip, masquerade as a servant, and trade on the assumption that, as a woman, she could not possibly be capable of solving a crime.

The female detective is something of a breakthrough figure. Driven by curiosity and determined to find justice, she is often both insider and oddball, a woman who operates in the public sphere even as she is often desperately trying to cover her tracks or elude detection herself. In some ways she fits right in with the foundational figures of the detective novel, those brooding geniuses known as "armchair detectives" for their reclusive nature and sharp intelligence. Edgar Allan Poe's Chevalier C. Auguste Dupin and Sir Arthur Conan Doyle's Sherlock Holmes made their literary debuts nearly fifty years apart, the one in 1841, the other in 1887. Both sleuths work by ratiocination, more introspective and reflective than adventurous and gregarious. They reason out their solutions in the company of admiring interlocutors, sycophantic sidekicks who are more like codependents than associates. "I am lost without my Boswell," Holmes proclaims in "A Scandal in Bohemia." Both Dr. Watson and Dupin's unnamed companion are deeply deferential and always impressed by the investigative virtuosity of their confidants.

Women sleuths, by contrast to Dupin and Holmes, tend to be loners, navigating the process of solving a crime on their own. There is no supportive subordinate to extol their feats of logic and fact-finding finesse. To be sure, the friends of Nancy Drew in Carolyn Keene's series are in awe of her sleuthing skills, but mainly at a safe remove—Nancy carries out most of her work as a solo private eye. Agatha Christie's Jane Marple is also characterized by a high degree of autonomy. She lives alone, she thinks on her own, and her success is not dependent on having an interlocutor who is a sounding board and sympathetic listener. Adept at problem-solving and deriving pleasure from investigative work (with almost a "lust" for it), Miss Marple is unfettered by the bonds of kinship. She is a lone wolf and therefore also absolved of choosing between marriage and career or between romance and crime-solving, as so often happens with a younger generation of investigators.[14]

In many ways, detective work seems like the perfect profession for women in the first part of the twentieth century, for they could operate clandestinely, be intellectually adventurous, and break rules at a time when most options were closed to them. Many of their male precursors were already eccentric figures: Poe's Auguste Dupin goes out only at night and admits no visitors to his lodgings, while the violin-playing Sherlock Holmes is addicted to cocaine. And the often remarked kinship between lawbreakers and law enforcers ("Criminals and detectives could be as closely befriended as Sherlock Holmes and Watson," Walter Benjamin tells us in a philosophical meditation on crime fiction) becomes all the stronger when rebels with a cause, women who are willing to cross social boundaries, take up sleuthing. Even when the conflict dividing the two sets of figures is clearly demarcated, with one a champion of law and order, fighting for the common good, and the other representing wrongdoing, evil, and disorder, there is still a sense that they are mutually enabling accomplices rather than pure adversaries.

Where are the woman detectives? They should be ubiquitous, for, after all, women are nosy, gossipy snoops, always eavesdropping, prying, and rarely minding their own business. The term "female dick" may be oxymoronically jarring, but women, with their eagerness to meddle, are all in a sense private eyes. The term "private eye," is said, by the way, to have been based on a Pinkerton agency logo that featured the words "We Never Sleep" printed under a painted eye. The earliest use of the term, as documented by the *Oxford English Dictionary*, was in Raymond Chandler's "Bay City Blues," published in 1937 in a magazine called *Dime Detective*: "But we don't use any private eyes in here. So sorry."[15] Yet eight years earlier it had appeared in the 1930 *Nancy Drew: The Mystery at Lilac Inn*, when Nancy Drew is gruffly told, "Try to figure this one out, Miss Private Eye!" right before she is given a shove and dragged down to a river.[16] It is deeply symptomatic that Nancy Drew, still a heroine today for many young readers, was overlooked when it came to defining the term that defined her.

## The Mysteries of Nancy Drew, "Best of All Girl Detectives"

Nancy Drew, the sixteen-year-old girl detective (later turned into an eighteen-year-old), and Miss Marple, the septuagenarian sleuth, both made their first public appearances in 1930, the younger in *The Secret of the Old Clock* and the elder in *The Murder at the Vicarage*. A look at the origins of the younger detective will shed light on the adventures not only of her British elder but of the many female investigators who follow in her footsteps as crime solvers.

Edward Stratemeyer, one of the most prolific writers in the world and the creator of *The Bobbsey Twins*, *Tom Swift*, and other book series for children, also invented the character of Nancy Drew. He felt confident that the amateur girl detective would become as commercially success-ful as his Hardy Boys. After he pitched the new series to the publish-ing house of Grosset & Dunlap, the firm decided to take a conservative approach and negotiated with an unknown journalist named Mildred Wirt to write the first volumes for flat fees ranging from $125 to $250 (reduced to $75 during the Great Depression). *The Secret of the Old Clock*, the first book in the series, was published under the pseudonym Car-olyn Keene.

Over the years, the books about Nancy and her detective skills have been translated into forty-five languages, with sales so astronomically high that it is no longer possible to track them. "Nancy is the greatest phenomenon among all the fifty-centers. She is a best seller. How she crashed a Valhalla that had been rigidly restricted to the male of her spe-cies is a mystery," one expert on the series wondered.[17] Intelligent, fearless, stylish, and strong, Nancy Drew is flanked by two sidekicks, the tomboy George and the girly girl Bess, whose roles seem limited to making the adventurous and glamorous Nancy look even better than she already is on the page.

Is it an accident that so many of our female Supreme Court justices cite the Nancy Drew series as a source of encouragement and inspiration? Sandra Day O'Connor, Ruth Bader Ginsburg, and Sonia Sotomayor have all professed their love for the teen investigator, finding themselves, as did O'Connor, "totally absorbed" by the series.[18] The girl gumshoe was evidently also a role model for Hillary Clinton.[19] It seems more than likely that part of the appeal for these accomplished women was not just that Nancy solves mysteries but that she is committed to serving justice—that is what Nancy does supremely well.[20]

In the Nancy Drew series, we discover the dark side to the pastoral world of River Heights, a town that is sometimes described as rural, sometimes as urban, sometimes as suburban, depending on which book in the series you are reading. That's where Nancy resides with her widower father, Carson Drew, and a housekeeper named Hannah Gruen. The cozy villages of British murder mysteries may have high body counts, but the world of Nancy Drew, by contrast, is plagued by unusually high robbery rates. There are close calls but few corpses. What motivates Nancy goes beyond the return of stolen property. While she is committed to seeking justice, she also embodies the ethics of care described by Carol Gilligan in her landmark study of women's developmental paths and how those paths differ from those of their male counterparts.[21] "You are always putting yourself out to do a kindness for somebody or other who simply doesn't count in your life at all," Nancy's pal George declares in *The Sign of the Twisted Candles*.[22]

Gilligan's *In a Different Voice* argued that women, who see themselves embedded in a social network, approach ethical problems differently than their male counterparts. While women are oriented to an ethics of care, focused on connection, relationship, and conflicting responsibilities, men tend to think in terms of an ethics of justice, with codified structures of competing rights. For Gilligan, the terms "web" and "hierarchy," while not perfect analytical categories, capture two disparate visions about care and justice. Gilligan later argued that these divisions were less gender based than thematic, and that the contrasting feminine and masculine voices are connected to two modes of thought as much as to two genders.

Nancy Drew's insistence on affirming the principles of the legal systems in place (her father is, after all, a lawyer) turns out not to conflict at all with securing and strengthening a communal web of relationships. She disrupts Gilligan's binaries, suggesting that it is possible to secure law and order, but never at the expense of others. Whether rescuing a friend from turbulent waters, restoring stolen goods to an impoverished child, saving the inhabitants of a burning house, or freeing a boy from cruel exploitation, Nancy manages to model heroic behavior, risking her neck in a series of perilous adventures that reveal her commitment to serving justice and restoring goods and reputations, even while speaking "sweetly" and "kindly."[23]

Why, then, was Nancy Drew banned from libraries? I recall vividly that the volumes were absent from the shelves of the otherwise well-stocked local library in the Chicago suburb where I grew up. When I decided to include the Nancy Drew books in my research for this volume, I found myself furtively reading the series in the Farnsworth Room at Harvard's Lamont Library, with its "extracurricular reading," a collection that, as the placard in the room announced, did not pretend to offer "the best reading." It was just a place to browse, "where an hour may be passed with pleasure." The New York Public Library system did not carry the Nancy Drew books until the mid-1970s. They were considered "worthless, sordid, sensational, trashy, and harmful," a menace to "good reading," as one Canadian librarian put it. Under the right supervision, "this trash will find its way to the furnace, where it belongs."[24] Like the Hardy Boys books, which were denounced as working on a boy's brain "in as deadly a fashion as liquor will attack a man's brain," they were "not written but manufactured."[25] "I wish I could label each one of these books: 'Explosives! Guaranteed to Blow Your Boy's Brains Out,'" grumbled the chief librarian of the Boy Scouts.[26] Metaphors of toxicity abound in describing book series for girls and boys: "Much of the looseness of morals and of the contempt for social conventions for which the rising generation is blamed is due to the reading of this poisonous sort of fiction."[27]

The charge of bad writing, along with adult anxieties about flat prose,

failed to diminish the appeal of Nancy Drew herself to adolescent readers. She thrilled them with her adventurous spirit and inspired them
with her courage and kindness. One of the more explicit critiques worried that series books glorify characters who have broken with "the traditions and conventions which society has found essential to its highest
goals."[28] Guilty as charged, many young readers would respond, for, once
Nancy becomes a detective, she also acquires agency in ways that allow
her to make a break with dependency on the adults around her. In a volume like *The Mystery at Lilac Inn*, for example, Carson Drew is astonish-
ingly cavalier when it comes to Nancy's many brushes with death. Unlike
real-life parents or caregivers, the adults never act on concerns about her
safety, nor do they limit her movements in any way.

Many critics have pondered the mystery of Nancy Drew's charm and
charisma, both for the residents in her hometown of River Heights and
for her readers. The blue roadster explains much, as does Nancy's physical
endurance and attractive appearance. Nancy can change tires in a thun-
derstorm, fix motorboats in the dark—she carries heavy loads with confidence. "Three capable, muscular, brainy girls such as we are shouldn't
need any help," she tells her pals in *The Clue in the Diary*.[29] "Unusually
pretty," with "fair" skin, "friendly blue eyes," and "golden curly hair,"
Nancy has a winning way with all those who enter her orbit.[30] But these
attributes pale by comparison with Nancy's powers of what Edgar Allan
Poe, author of, arguably, the first detective story in the United States,
"The Murders in the Rue Morgue," called *ratiocination*. In the very first
book in the series, Nancy gazes at the "disorder" around her and searches
her mind for an "explanation." "What could it mean?" she asks herself.[31]
Even under the most extreme circumstances, as when she is locked in the
closet of an abandoned house and left to suffocate and starve, Nancy is
levelheaded and unflappable. "I'm only wasting my strength this way. I
must try to think logically," she tells herself in *The Secret of the Old Clock*.[32]

Decoding mysteries, sorting out the truth, finding meaning—those
are all things we do when we read. Nancy's sleuthing activities mirror,
externalize, and enact exactly what young readers do when they pick
up *The Secret of the Old Clock* or *The Hidden Staircase*, working right

alongside Nancy to unscramble enigmas and solve riddles. Beyond that, the Nancy Drew books offer compact allegories of loss and restoration, returning objects of value to the deserving and punishing the undeserving. As morality plays, the plots often turn on a single "lost" object, stolen goods that are restored to their legitimate owners. The universe is set right again.

Issues of ownership and legitimacy are not surprising in a series that was ghostwritten by members of a literary syndicate.[33] Ironically, the Nancy Drew books were fronted by a male entrepreneur who farmed out the writing of individual volumes to women authors. Edward Stratemeyer, the undisputed wizard of series books, grew up in New Jersey, the son of German immigrants. He worked in his father's tobacco shop, using its basement to operate his own printing press and distributing stories such as "The Newsboy's Adventure." Before long, he embarked on a career that led to the writing and production of over thirteen hundred dime novels, serials, and Westerns. The breakthrough for him came when Horatio Alger Jr., suffering from failing health ("in a state of nervous breakdown," as he put it), wrote to Stratemeyer, asking him to complete two stories. After Alger's death in 1899, Stratemeyer "completed" eleven of his books even as he was writing the Rover Boys, a series that met with tremendous commercial success.

By 1900, Stratemeyer, though by no means suffering writer's block, decided to spend less time writing and more time recruiting authors for what became known as the Stratemeyer Syndicate. He would work with publishers and authors, developing a series with the publishing house and then creating characters and plot outlines for the hired ghostwriters. Between 1905 and 1985, the Syndicate produced over a thousand volumes that included a number of literary franchises.

If the Nancy Drew series gives us individual heroics, with a self-reliant girl possessing an astounding skill set, it is shadowed by the tension between the authentic and the fraudulent, with a host of doubles, impersonators, and identity thieves.[34] Dual authorship had a built-in rivalry between a public face (Carolyn Keene, a.k.a. Edward Stratemeyer) and a secret ghostwriter (Mildred Wirt Benson), and the books themselves reproduce that rivalry by putting their heroine on the trail of counterfeiters and thieves, those who appropriate property that rightfully belongs to others. In *The Secret of the Old Clock*, there is a bogus will and the genuine article, which Nancy discovers and uses to ensure that the rightful beneficiaries get their inheritance. In *The Bungalow Mystery*, an identity thief is jailed and the true heir wins back the estate to which he is entitled.

Is it possible that Mildred Wirt Benson somehow wrote her own struggle with authorial identity into the series (consciously or not), turning Nancy into a sleuth who uncovers, among other things, true identities, the genuine article, the real thing? Benson herself was the first woman to receive a graduate degree in journalism from the University of Iowa. She was a champion swimmer who played golf and flew planes (taking up flying at the age of sixty), in addition to writing a newspaper column and books with her as named author.[35] And her intense interest in pre-Columbian archaeology is a reminder that writing mysteries and digging up artifacts from the past are oddly compatible pursuits.

Benson had no real reverence for authorship, considering herself as doing piecework more than anything else: "I didn't analyze it," she writes about the plots assigned to her. "It was just a job to do. Some things I liked and some things I did not like. It was a day's work. . . . One year I wrote 13 full-length books and held down a job besides."[36] Since Stratemeyer drafted the plots, perhaps he too is implicated, with an unconscious sense of guilt or shame that revealed itself in stories that turn on fraud. The Nancy Drew books offer up two cases to be solved: the manifest crime, offense, or robbery that serves as a challenge to the girl sleuth and her readers, and also the mystery of authorship and the question: Who invented the Nancy Drew books and the wonders of that world? By plotting mysteries, Mildred Wirt Benson inscribed the loss of her identity as author into a series that bears the name of Carolyn Keene and was masterminded by Edward Stratemeyer, head of a syndicate, a man who masqueraded as a woman.

In the proposal for the series, which was to feature a girl detective, Stratemeyer wrote, "I have called the line the 'Stella Strong Stories,' but they might also be called the 'Diana Dare Stories,' 'Nan Nelson Stories' or 'Helen Hale Stories.' "[37] A later proposal adds specifics: "Stella Strong, a girl of sixteen, is the daughter of a District Attorney of many years standing. He is a widower and often talks over his affairs with Stella and the girl was present during many interviews her father had with noted detectives and at the solving of many intricate mysteries. Then, quite unexpectedly, Stella plunged into some mysteries of her own. . . . An up-to-date American girl at her best, bright, clever, resourceful, and full of energy."[38] Mildred Wirt was commissioned to write the first volume, along with the next two in the founding first three books of the series (with thirty books in all). Her recollection of Stratemeyer's reaction (though contested by some scholars) reveals a decision to take ownership of the sleuth, for she did not stand down when given advice: "Mr. Stratemeyer expressed bitter disappointment when he received the first manuscript, *The Secret of the Old Clock*, saying the heroine was much too flip and would never be well received."[39]

Readers did not seem to mind a "flip" girl detective, and Nancy Drew lives on today, not just in books and reboots of the books, but also in video games, films, and merchandise. Her appeal is summed up by one critic as residing in "the image, however abstract, of a young woman who is able to forget the 'distinction of sex'—at least so far as that distinction is rewritten as limitation."[40] Laura Lippman, bestselling author of the crime fiction series featuring "accidental PI" Tess Monaghan, revealed why she was partial to the Nancy Drew books. The books validated curiosity, seeing it as a virtue rather than a vice.[41] Capable and caring, Nancy not only manages to make stalled trucks start up again but can also nurse ailing elders back to health.

Figures like Elsa in Disney's *Frozen* franchise and Katniss Everdeen in the Hunger Games trilogy, but especially Hermione in the Harry Potter series, are all reminders of the powerful afterlife of Nancy Drew in cultural productions for children. Hermione (and is it any coincidence that her name is linked with Hermes, god of speech and cunning?) uses spells and incantations to navigate the mysteries of Hogwarts, with its trap doors, secret rooms, enigmatic maps, and magical wardrobes. From "oculus reparo" (a charm for mending glasses) and "alohomora" (for unlocking doors) to "wingardium leviosa" (the levitation charm) to "petrificus totalus" (the full body-bind curse), Hermione, model student yet also rulebreaker, is ready to break and enter, eavesdrop, and steal in order to discover solutions to the challenges facing the adventurous trio she forms with Harry and Ron. Beyond that, she exceeds Nancy's passion for justice by becoming a social activist who founds the Society for the Promotion of Elfish Welfare (SPEW), an organization designed to advocate for the rights of an oppressed group. It is no coincidence that, like the spinsters of detective fiction and the old wives before them, she is also labeled a nosy "know-it-all."

## Spinsters Seeking Justice

Spinsters and old maids are on the decline. Type those terms into Google Ngram and you will find that the term "spinster" was on the rise until the 1930s, spiking in 1934, with a falling off after that. "Old maid" peaked in 1898, and since then has been steadily vanishing, with a small spike in 2004, perhaps only to broadcast how out-of-date the term had become. Yoking youth with senescence, the term "old maid" suggests someone who is never the right age and can never assume full-fledged autonomy. Today, "singles" and "bachelorettes" have supplanted spinsters and old maids.

For a time, "spinster" was the term given to women (or, occasionally but rarely, men, as the *Oxford English Dictionary* tells us) who engage in spinning as an occupation. From the seventeenth century onward, the word was used as a legal designation for unmarried women, until it finally became a casually used descriptor for women once fertile but now beyond the age of bearing children. The *OED* records a use of the term in 1882 that suggests a spectacularly condescending attitude toward these women: "Providence is wonderfully kind to plain little spinsters with a knack of making themselves useful." In other words, staying unmarried meant that you could be useful to others (usually as a caretaker of aging parents and the children of siblings), though that did not mean that you could actually make something of yourself.

The term "spinster" resonates powerfully with notions of spinning and solitude, and also with the spookiness of self-imposed seclusion and sinister designs. Like many who were educated in the United States in the 1960s and 1970s, my personal understanding of spinsters was shaped by their literary representation. Novels taught me the horrors of spinster-hood, especially of women left at the altar. Here is Charles Dickens's Miss Havisham in *Great Expectations*, in all her alarming morbidity:

> I saw that the bride within the bridal dress had withered like the dress, and like the flowers, and had no brightness left but the brightness of her sunken eyes. I saw that the dress had been put upon the rounded figure of a young woman, and that the figure upon which it now hung loose had shrunk to skin and bone. Once, I had been taken to see some ghastly waxwork at the Fair, representing I know not what impos-sible personage lying in state. Once, I had been taken to one of our old marsh churches to see a skeleton in the ashes of a rich dress that had been dug out of a vault under the church pavement. Now, waxwork and skeleton seemed to have dark eyes that moved and looked at me. I should have cried out, if I could.[42]

Miss Havisham belongs to the living dead, inhabiting a house infested with spiders and mice. Here is what Pip, the youthful hero of the novel, sees when he enters the dining room of her house:

> The most prominent object was a long table with a tablecloth spread on it, as if a feast had been in preparation when the house and the clocks all stopped together. [A] center-piece of some kind was in the middle of this cloth; it was so heavily overhung with cobwebs that its form was quite indistinguishable; and, as I looked along the yel-low expanse out of which I remember its seeming to grow, like a black fungus, I saw speckle-legged spiders with blotchy bodies run-

ning home to it, and running out from it, as if some circumstances of the greatest public importance had just transpired in the spider community.

Spinsters seem doomed to consort with spiders. Both operate in solitude, busily spinning their webs, threads, and yarns, creating death traps for their prey. The young boy Pip turns into something of a stray fly, lured into Miss Havisham's infested mansion. Pip's great expectations and Miss Havisham's lost illusions work together to produce two compel-

Harry Furniss, "Miss Havisham" for
Charles Dickens's *Great Expectations*, 1910

ling accounts of romance gone wrong. The novel writes large the spine-tingling horrors of the spinster and of her intrigues.

Paradoxically, spinsters are highly visible beings yet also impercep-tible presences. Visible as objects of scorn, pity, revulsion, and derision, they are also invisible in having little social purchase. Seen as superflu-ous, and designated as UFs (Unnecessary Females) in the era after World War I, when there were 1,098 women to every 1,000 men, the spinster came under constant fire for her lack of productive labor and reproduc-tive capability.[43]

It was in England that spinsters made a comeback, now as sleuths who rivaled hard-boiled private eyes in their shrewd deployment of detec-tive skills. How that happened is a mystery in itself worth unraveling. In 1930, a group of British writers, among them Agatha Christie, Dorothy L. Sayers, Hugh Walpole, and G. K. Chesterton, set up the Detection Club, whose members held regular dinner meetings in London. Those who joined had to swear the following oath: "Do you promise that your detectives shall well and truly detect the crimes presented to them using those wits which it may please you to bestow upon them and not placing reliance on nor making use of Divine Revelation, Feminine Intuition, Mumbo Jumbo, Jiggery-Pokery, Coincidence, or Act of God?"[44] Note that the majority of the writers in the Detection Club published their work in the so-called golden age of detective fiction, inventing "whodunits," mys-teries designed to "arouse curiosity," as Ronald Knox put it. Knox, who was a priest as well as a writer of detective fiction, formulated the "Ten Commandments" of detective stories, and these normative features are tarnished by ethnic slurs and condescending remarks about intuition and deviations from an established form.

1. The criminal must be mentioned in the early part of the story, but must not be anyone whose thoughts the reader has been allowed to know.

2. All supernatural or preternatural agencies are ruled out as a matter of course.

3. Not more than one secret room or passage is allowable.

4. No hitherto undiscovered poisons may be used, nor any appliance which will need a long scientific explanation at the end.

5. No Chinaman must figure in the story. [Charlie Chan had made his first appearance in 1925 in Earl Derr Biggers's *House without a Key*.]

6. No accident must ever help the detective, nor must he ever have an unaccountable intuition which proves to be right.

7. The detective himself must not commit the crime.

8. The detective is bound to declare any clues which he may discover.

9. The "sidekick" of the detective, the Watson, must not conceal from the reader any thoughts which pass through his mind: his intelligence must be slightly, but very slightly, below that of the average reader.

10. Twin brothers, and doubles generally, must not appear unless we have been duly prepared for them.[45]

The Golden Age of Murder, as some call it, was bookended by two world wars, providing comfort in the form of cozy mysteries (or "cozies" as they were called, in contrast to darker, "hard-boiled" detective fiction more graphic in its depiction of violence). Offering sensation bundled with distraction, these volumes also served to reduce one anxiety by amplifying another.[46]

Today we may be charmed by figures like Agatha Christie's Miss Marple, Dorothy L. Sayers's Harriet Vane, or Jessica Fletcher in the series *Murder, She Wrote*, but the priests of high culture had a different view about these lady detectives and the mystery writers who created them. America's eminent twentieth-century literary critic Edmund Wilson, never a fan of popular culture, famously (and mirthlessly) wrote in the *New Yorker* about his indifference to the detective novel in a series of articles, one of which mocked an Agatha Christie title: "Who Cares Who Killed Roger Ackroyd?" The entire genre, he declared, is nothing more than "a habit-forming drug," and its readers are victims of a "form of narcotic." The coup de grâce comes in his own resolve to avoid all detective fiction, but Agatha Christie's volumes in particular: "So I have read also the new Agatha Christie, *Death Comes as the End*, and I confess that I have been had by Mrs. Christie. I did not guess who the murderer was, I was incited to keep on and find out, and when I did finally find out, I was surprised. Yet I did not care for Agatha Christie and I hope never to read another of her books."[47]

But Wilson has remained in the minority. Jane Marple's colossal appeal can be documented not just in sales figures but also in the powerful literary and cinematic afterlife of the spinster detective. She makes appearances on stage, screen, and television and also stands as godmother to woman detectives ranging from Amanda Cross's Kate Fansler to P. D. James's Cordelia Gray.

But before Miss Marple there was Miss Climpson, Alexandra Katherine Climpson to be precise, a middle-aged "spinster" in the employ of Lord Peter Wimsey, Dorothy L. Sayers's renowned British aristocrat and amateur detective. In the 1927 murder mystery *Unnatural Death*, she is introduced in a chapter entitled "A Use for Spinsters." The epigraph to that chapter cites an "authority" named Gilbert Frankau on how women are disproportionately represented in the populations of England and Wales, where "there are two million more females than males."[48] Lord Peter congratulates himself on employing one of the many "spinsters" in England and wonders out loud if one day there will be a statue erected to him, "the Man who Made Thousands of Superfluous Women Happy."

Although Miss Climpson herself is no gossip, she is an expert inquiry agent, blending in with local gossips as they knit and carry out needlework. "People want questions asked," Lord Peter declares to his friend Detective-Inspector Charles Parker. "Whom do they send? A man with large flat feet and a note-book—the sort of man whose private life is conducted in a series of inarticulate grunts." Lord Peter is no fool, and his strategy is to send "a lady with a long, woolly jumper on knitting-needles and jingly things round her neck." She can ask all sorts of questions, and "nobody is surprised. Nobody is alarmed." Miss Climpson does the legwork for Lord Peter, and her contributions to crime-solving are not at all negligible. Hers is also not a risk-free profession, as becomes evident before the case closes. In *Strong Poison*, written three years after *An Unnatural Death*, she uncovers the key piece of evidence to solving a murder case that landed the mystery writer Harriet Vane (later to become Lord Peter's wife) in jail.

Agatha Christie transformed the status of the spinster sleuth, turning her supporting role into that of lead actor. Now she has become a feisty, self-sufficient, free-spirited figure who can solve cases without a team of subordinates. Artfully contrived artlessness best characterizes Agatha Christie's Miss Marple, the gossipy old lady who knits and gardens, minding her own business while also getting in everyone else's business. "She was inquisitive," she tells herself at one moment, conforming to the stereotype of the busybody in ways that provide her with "camouflage" as a detective. "You could much more easily send an elderly lady with a habit of snooping and being inquisitive, of talking too much, of wanting to find out about things, and it would seem perfectly natural," she reflects.[49]

Miss Marple's skills run along the lines of what we today call the interpersonal, and she herself gives us a powerful refutation of the idea that gossiping and "talking scandal" are worthless. And she mounts a defense of "superfluous women," rebutting her nephew's condescending description of such women as having "a lot of time on their hands." As it turns out, *"people"* are their chief interest: "And so you see they get to be what one might call *experts*."[50] That idle talk and gossip can serve as conduits of vital information becomes evident from Miss Marple's investigative methods. "Everything's talked about," a detective observes in *The Mirror Crack'd*. "It always comes to one's ears sooner or later."[51] Snooping and eavesdropping—all the activities associated with dowagers and matrons—enable Miss Marple to put together the pieces of a puzzle that solves a mystery. A newsie as well as a gossip, Miss Marple is found at the beginning of *Nemesis* reading the paper, scanning the front page, then turning to births, marriages, and deaths. In some ways, of course, all these activities could also be seen as the province of writers, those who take command of a universe and are able to probe its hidden spaces, divine the motives of its actors, and restore order in a world that has undergone some kind of upheaval. The interpretive energy of Miss Marple is, of course, also mirrored in the hermeneutic drive of readers, who struggle to make sense of the rupture in the social order that a murder produces.

The dithering old maid becomes a daunting embodiment of Nemesis, a clear-sighted, sober, impartial agent of justice in a world driven by passions that can turn toxic and murderous. At one point Miss Marple wears a hat with a bird's wing, an unmistakable allusion to the winged Greek goddess who often also carried a whip or a dagger and came to be known as the daughter of justice and the sister of the Moirai, or Fates. What is the last novel in which Miss Marple is featured but *Nemesis*, a work in which knitting, one of the spinster's signature sidelines (along

Albrecht Dürer, *Nemesis (The Great Fortune)*,
1501–2. *Metropolitan Museum of Art*

with gossiping and gardening), takes on mythical significance. Inspector Neele in *A Pocket Full of Rye* makes the following observation about the amateur sleuth: "He was thinking to himself that Miss Marple was very unlike the popular idea of the avenging fury. And yet, he thought that was perhaps exactly what she was."[52] Knitting joins spinning, weaving, and creating tapestries and textiles as an activity that goes hand in hand with dispensing justice.

Nemesis and knitting are repeatedly linked in the Miss Marple mysteries in ways that cannot but bring to mind Madame Defarge's knitting on "with the steadfastness of Fate" as she becomes an instrument for securing retributive justice in Charles Dickens's *A Tale of Two Cities.* "I *could* be ruthless if there was due cause," Miss Marple explains to her housekeeper. In reply to a question about what constitutes due cause, she declares, "In the cause of justice."[53] And what is the moniker she gives herself but "Nemesis," with one client "amused" that she describes herself with that particular word. Mr. Rafiel, the man who hires Miss Marple for her "natural genius" in the area of "investigation," buttresses the connection between knitting and serving justice when he tries valiantly to uncouple the two activities: "I envisage you sitting in a chair . . . and you will spend your time mainly in knitting. . . . If you prefer to continue knitting, that is your decision. If you prefer to serve the cause of justice, I hope that you may at least find it interesting."[54]

All of Miss Marple's pastimes—knitting, gardening, gossiping, and eavesdropping—mingle comfortably with ratiocination, and the lady detective, unlike her male counterparts, does not sit and smoke or take late-night strolls to fire up her neurons. The domestic field of "trivial" pursuits is not at all separate from higher-order thought. "You know my method," Holmes tells Watson, inadvertently connecting his methods with those of Miss Marple: "It is founded upon the observance of trifles."[55] Like the spinster, who traffics in the trivial, the detective too reveals how the devil of detection is in the details, the little things that often go unnoticed but become symbolically central. Just as the extraneous detail grows in significance, taking on explanatory power, so the marginalized spinster, barely visible, is endowed with mythical weight.

In a sense Agatha Christie can be seen as the Queen of Crime who advanced opportunities for elderly women (in a culture that mocked them for being feeble, foolish, and irrelevant). Miss Marple, as two critics point out, "subverts the 'spinster' category by which society seeks to diminish and trivialize her."[56] Yet in a touch of irony, it is the formidable Miss Marple who also safeguards and secures a social order that views the spinster as a figure of contempt or tolerates her as an amusing, pitiful fixture in the social landscape. Saint Mary Mead, the idyllic village in which murder occurs with astonishing regularity, never really changes: "The new world was the same as the old. The houses were different . . . the clothes were different, the voices were different, but the human beings were the same as they always had been." Even the conversations, we learn, "were the same."[57] As in the Nancy Drew series, the restoration of reputations, inheritances, and the social order is what is at stake, even for the oddballs, misfits, and eccentrics at the margins.

The conservative streak in Miss Marple will come as no surprise to those who have read Agatha Christie's autobiography. "I was a married woman," she wrote, "and *that* was my occupation. As a sideline, I wrote books." Those are modest words from one of the world's most prolific authors, a woman who wrote nearly one hundred novels and as many short stories in addition to two autobiographical works. Never mind that her sales are calculated in the billions. Domestic chores did not disrupt Christie's writing routines; rather, they were in a symbiotic relationship with creating a first draft: "The best time to plan a book is while you are doing the dishes."[58] That the boredom of household practices might foster a vivid imagination in thrall to mystery and murder may also have a certain logic to it.

In the course of the twentieth century, the female detective morphs from the 1930s teen sleuth, spinster detective, and undercover agent into a dutiful wife in the 1940s (who helps unravel mysteries to save the man she loves), and finally into an expert investigator from the 1980s onward, with TV cops Cagney and Lacey, fiction writer Jessica Fletcher, and hard-boiled agents like Clarice Starling and V. I. Warshawski.[59] The female investigator is finally freed of the obligation to hew to a small set of stereotypes and, no longer constrained by the marriage imperative, she can become ageless, as it were, as well as polymorphously inquisitive. Suddenly her private life shrinks in unexpected ways. It becomes as inconsequential as the inner life of Raymond Chandler's Philip Marlowe, who famously walks the "mean streets" and is not only "the hero" but also "everything."[60]

## Privileged and Disadvantaged: Kate Fansler and Blanche White

Carolyn Heilbrun, a professor of English at Columbia University who wrote detective novels under the pseudonym of Amanda Cross, explained to her readers that writing detective fiction was for her a form of self-actualization and also of self-creation, enabling her to produce a new identity rather than replicating what once was and always will be. "I was recreating myself," she wrote about her experiment in writing detective novels. "Women come to writing . . . simultaneously with self-creation."[61] Her Kate Fansler is also a literature professor, and she moonlights as a sleuth, solving mysteries using the same skill set she employs to read texts critically for her day job. Reading is, after all, in many ways a process of detection, with authors (reliable and unreliable) leading us across narrative terrain.[62] No coincidence, it could be added, that the compulsive knitting of Kate Fansler's literary antecedents has now been replaced by entanglements with texts. In addition, the challenges facing Professor Fansler are often literary in nature, as the title *The James Joyce Murder* (1967) suggests, with its chapters named after stories found in Joyce's *Dubliners*. And solving the mystery of a female professor found dead in the men's room of the English department at Harvard University in *Death in a Tenured Position* (1981) creates plenty of opportunities for literary banter about authors ranging from George Herbert and Charlotte Brontë to George Eliot and Henry James.

The Kate Fansler series is in many ways prophetic, constructed by a feminist professor who wrote eloquently and at length about gender discrimination in her home department and who also envisioned a future that would be different for both her women students in the English department at Columbia University as well as for her literary progeny. Here is Heilbrun's description of her detective heroine, borrowed in some ways from Joseph Campbell's playbook, but with gender roles reversed:

> Without children, unmarried, unconstrained by the opinion of others, rich and beautiful, the newly created Kate Fansler now appears to me a figure out of never-never land. That she seems less a fantasy figure these days—when she is mainly criticized for drinking and smoking too much, and for having married—says more about the changing mores, and my talents as prophet, than about my intentions at the time. I wanted to give her everything and see what she could do with it. Of course, she set out on a quest (the male plot), she became a knight (the male role), she rescued a (male) princess.[63]

With the rise of the female detective novel also came attention to crisis situations that had not been part of the traditional fabric of the detective narrative that largely depicted men. Unemployment, poverty, and domestic violence, subjects almost always avoided by the male detective writer, become the province of figures like Cordelia Gray in P. D. James's *An Unsuitable Job for a Woman* (1972), as they were for Francie in *A Tree Grows in Brooklyn*. Cordelia is a "lonely, courageous and unprivileged private eye," and she inherits an "unsuccessful and seedy detective agency" after the suicide of its proprietor.[64] Caring more about friendship than about finding a fellow, these woman detectives see romance as a threat to their hard-won independence and are often more passionate about pursuing a lead than about keeping a date. The search for justice takes a new turn, with a focus on "making things right" and restoring reputations.

In a similar vein, Barbara Neely's Blanche White series, in which Blanche takes on "emancipatory projects" that have not traditionally been in the purview of the detectives in crime fiction, marks a second sea change in woman detectives.[65] As a Black woman, Blanche does what Miss Marple does so well and hides in plain sight, the perfect location for gathering clues and information. A domestic worker, she remains, through her race and her social status, doubly invisible to her employers and those around them. To ensure that no one in her orbit suspects anything, she also plays dumb: "Putting on a dumb act was something many black people considered unacceptable, but she sometimes found it a useful place to hide. She also got a lot of secret pleasure from fooling people who assumed they were smarter than she was by virtue of the way she looked and made her living."[66]

"Night Girl." "Ink Spot." "Tar Baby." Those are the nicknames Blanche's cousins use to tease her about her skin color (she is just a shade darker than they are). What was once humiliating turns into a source of power for Blanche, who becomes Night Girl, "slipping out of the house late at night to roam around her neighborhood unseen." Suddenly she becomes "special," "wondrous," and "powerful," capable of gathering knowledge in ways that endow her with what others think of as second sight. Wearing a cloak of invisibility empowers Blanche, as do her patient listening skills. She knows storytellers can't be rushed: "Their rhythm, the silences between their words, and their intonation were as important to the telling of the tale as the words they spoke."

If Blanche is as curious and caring as her white counterparts in detective fiction, she faces challenges unfamiliar to figures like Kate Fansler or even Cordelia Gray. For her, race is a fundamental fact of life, and it puts her at odds with representatives of the law (*Blanche on the Lam* begins with a jailbreak) and adds social responsibilities unknown to the solitary, loner types that make up the ranks of sleuths and private eyes (Blanche is partial caretaker for her dead sister's two children). And it adds a sense of obligation to the community to which she belongs. In the end, she refuses to accept the "hush money," or "aggravation pay," that might enable her to live comfortably, preferring instead that justice be served and that she hold sacred the memory of Nate, a victim of the crazed murderer Blanche faces down.

## Wonder Woman

Female sleuths seem to be a breed apart. By nature reclusive, they often live alone, and though they investigate the murders of the rich and famous, they themselves are nearly always of low social status. Into this landscape leaps a figure who became an instant celebrity, glamorous, enigmatic, and endowed with attributes that made her, what else but a superhero. She too is a crime solver (and she also has a shy, retiring side, a disguise that links her to the spinster sleuth and to Alcott's happy spinsters), but she uses far more than her wits to outmaneuver those on the wrong side of the law.

Wonder Woman! Who could have imagined that U.S. culture of the 1940s would produce a stubborn genius with the audacity to dream up a woman who could perform "sensational feats" in a "fast-moving world." The first issue of *Wonder Woman* begins with an image of Diana sprinting through the air wearing boots with stiletto heels and dressed in a blue skirt emblazoned with white stars, topped by a red bustier decorated with a golden eagle. "At last," we read, "in a world torn by the hatreds and wars of men, appears a *woman* to whom the problems and feats of men are mere child's play."[67] That image and those words capture perfectly William Moulton Marston's fantasies about the power of women to protect and to save.

Dr. William Moulton Marston, lawyer, psychologist, screenwriter, and inventor, was possibly the only person—certainly one of the few men—possessed of the kind of imagination that could invent Wonder Woman. His radical politics, eccentric beliefs, and unorthodox marital arrangements made him something of an anomaly, and a wonder, for his own time. A member of the class of 1915 at Harvard University, Marston collected two additional degrees, one in law and one in philosophy, and, equipped with those degrees, he dreamed up a new mythology, improbably female centered at a time when the United States was preparing to enter a deadly world war, fought in the main by men, that led to the loss of seventy-five million lives. At the home front, women were drawn into the labor force in unprecedented numbers, taking on roles that were vital, if not as obviously heroic (in the conventional sense of the term) as those of the soldiers traveling overseas.

Marston was an intellectual iconoclast, well ahead of his time in many ways. His *Emotions of Normal People*, published in 1928, more than a decade before America entered World War II, began as a work of psychological theorizing but moved into the mode of a political manifesto declaring that women would soon dominate men and teach them that "love (real love, not 'sex appetite') constitutes . . . the ultimate end of all activity." Recruiting "Love Leaders" to reeducate men would revolutionize the world and create a more compassionate social order, one in which masculine modes of violence, aggression, and force would no longer dominate. Women could take the lead, he later declared: "Someday, I sincerely hope, women will demand and create love schools and universities."[68] Less than a decade later, in 1937 and still four years before the involvement of the United States in hostilities, Marston spoke at the Harvard Club of New York to declare that in a matter of a thousand years women would rule the country politically and economically. Quoting Marston, the *Washington Post* wrote that "women have twice the emotional development . . . that man has. And as they develop as much ability for worldly success as they already have the ability for love, they will clearly come to rule business and the Nation and the world."[69]

After a string of failed enterprises and adjunct academic posts, Marston finally hit upon the idea of using a comic book to promote the idea that the "blood-curdling masculinity" of the superheroes in DC Comics ought to give way to a heroine who combines the "force, strength, and power" of Superman or Batman with a woman's capacity for love, tenderness, and generosity. And, like magic, Wonder Woman, agent of peace and justice, was born, materializing just in the nick of time, right before the Japanese attack on Pearl Harbor: "She appears as though from nowhere to avenge an injustice or right a wrong! As lovely as Aphrodite—as wise as Athena—with the speed of Mercury and the strength of Hercules—she is known only as *Wonder Woman*, but who she is, or whence she came, nobody knows!"[70]

Marston invented his own mythology, constructing a backstory for

Wonder Woman that begins in a utopian world called Paradise Island. "Introducing Wonder Woman" was a nine-page origin story that appeared in the fall of 1941.[71] With a few swift strokes and concise word balloons, it filled readers in on the culture in which Princess Diana grew up and evolved to become Wonder Woman. "In Amazonia," Hippolyte tells her daughter, Diana, "women ruled and all was well. Then, one day, Hercules, the strongest man in the world, stung by taunts that he couldn't conquer the Amazon women, selected his strongest and fiercest warriors and landed on our shores. I challenged him to personal combat—because I knew that with my MAGIC GIRDLE, given to me by Aphrodite, Goddess of Love, I could not lose." It is more than odd that what gives Hippolyte the strength to defeat Hercules is a magic *girdle*. I recall as a child reading the Wonder Woman comics and cringing at the idea of this superheroine wearing so constricting a garment. In fact, or rather in the Greek sources, Hippolyte wears what the Greeks called a *zōstēr*, or war belt.[72] And defeat Hercules she does, though only to be outmaneuvered by him in ways that require more help from Aphrodite and that lead eventually to a home on Paradise Island.

In Amazonia, women isolate themselves from the world of men, rule themselves, and "all is well" under the benevolent guidance of Aphrodite. By contrast, in the world of men, Ares serves as patron deity, and his subjects "rule with the sword." In a word, we have a situation that mirrors the split in the United States between isolationists on the one hand, demanding that the United States avoid foreign entanglements and stay out of the war, and interventionists, who favored military support for European allies. What unfolds in Marston's work is an impassioned plea favoring intervention even from those who are strong advocates of peace.

Captain Steven Trevor, a U.S. Army officer, crashes his plane on the shores of Amazonia. Aphrodite urges the Amazons to take Captain Trevor back to his homeland so that he and his new allies can "help fight the forces of hate and oppression." And Athena chimes in, with a call to send the "strongest and wisest Amazon—the finest of your wonder women!" Hippolyte's daughter Princess Diana is sent to America to preserve "liberty and freedom," for America is "the last citadel of democracy, and of equal rights for women." For a change, it is Wonder Woman and not Superman who is here to save the day.

Once Princess Diana lands her invisible plane in America, she takes Captain Trevor to an army hospital and reunites with him at the headquarters of U.S. military intelligence. There she disguises herself as Diana Prince (get it?), a secretary with glasses and hair pulled back in a bun, prim, proper, and professional as she takes dictation (almost giving herself away when she instinctively uses Greek letters). Turning into a cartoon version of the female trickster, Wonder Woman is dedicated to bringing justice into the world. Part of her strategic plan is to use an alias and to adopt a profession that requires her to be adept at writing, if only in the form of transcription. In addition to fighting off thugs and engag-

*Wonder Woman*, 2017. *Courtesy of Photofest*

ing in high-speed car chases, she is also a compassionate nurse and, of course, an efficient secretary ("Diana types with the speed of lightning!"). She does all that and, remarkably, also undoes gender stereotypes in ways that were unimaginable in her time and still challenging to process today.

Wonder Woman fights evil and injustice at all levels by organizing strikes, boycotting products, and leading political rallies. She ends the excesses of profiteering on the part of a milk trust that has been raising the price of its product and starving American children. She becomes a labor activist who works to double the salaries of underpaid clerks at Bullfinch's Department Stores. "Blistering blazes!" Trevor Jones declares at one point. "Why will that beautiful gal always invite trouble? If she'd only married *me*, she'd be at home cooking my dinner right now."

In 1942 Marston wrote, in ways that today sound somewhat quaint but still carry real force, about the importance of providing women with opportunities for "self-expression in some constructive field: to work, not at home with cook-stove and scrubbing brush, but outside, independently, in the world of men and affairs."[73] That the two women Marston loved (one of whom he married) were suffragists explains much about the origins of Wonder Woman. His wife, Sadie Elizabeth Holloway, and his "mistress," Olive Byrne (a niece of Margaret Sanger, one of the pioneering figures in the women's movement), advocated birth control and were feminists long before feminism became a dirty word in the 1970s. Marston himself belonged to the "sufs" at Harvard College. More than likely, he attended rousing lectures at Harvard by Florence Kelley, the social and political reformer who fought against sweatshops and for a minimum wage with an eight-hour workday, and by Emmeline Pankhurst, the leader of the suffragette movement in the United Kingdom who helped earn women the right to vote.

The *Wonder Woman* franchise was to Marston's mind a brilliant way to harness the cultural authority of America's "most popular mental vitamin" (comic books) to disseminate his theories about the power not just of love but also of justice. In fact, the love of justice—avenging injustices and righting wrongs—is what makes Wonder Woman so powerful a force in the pantheon of superheroes. Wonder Woman, as Marston's biographer, Jill Lepore, tells us, is the most popular female superhero of all and has outlasted many of her male counterparts. "She had golden bracelets; she could stop bullets. She had a magic lasso; anyone she roped had to tell the truth. . . . Her gods were female, and so were her curses. 'Great Hera!' she cried. 'Suffering Sappho!' she swore. She was meant to be the strongest, smartest, bravest woman the world had ever seen."[74]

Comic-book superheroes operate in a medium that functions much like folklore, taking the pulse of a culture and tapping into its unconscious fantasies and fears. With whirlwind energy and operatic passion, they stage clashes between good and evil, heroes and villains, the virtuous and the corrupt. It is up to the superheroes to rescue, heal, restore, and make things right. Children are rarely given opportunities for adventure and high drama, and comic books can provide all the pleasures and excitement denied them, along with what psychologists who see value in reading the genre describe as cathartic release, a safe outlet for passions that might otherwise run amok.[75]

Some begged to differ. On May 8, 1940, Sterling North, the literary editor of the *Chicago Daily News*, denounced "sex-horror serials" (by that he meant comic books) as a "national disgrace" and bemoaned their toxic effects on the coming generation, making it "even more ferocious" than the current one. By 1955, after the U.S. Congress had held three days of hearings on whether comic books were contributing to higher rates of violent crime in teens, an interim report on comic books and juvenile delinquency voiced concerns about how the medium offers "short courses in murder, mayhem, robbery, rape, cannibalism, carnage, necrophilia, sex, sadism, masochism, and virtually every other form of crime, degeneracy, bestiality, and horror."[76]

The *New Republic* worried that "Superman, handsome as Apollo, strong as Hercules, chivalrous as Launcelot, swift as Hermes, embodies all the traditional attributes of a Hero God," a god that had been embraced by Nazi Germany. "Are Comics Fascist?" *Time* magazine fretted.[77] Marston, by creating a superheroine, deftly ducked the charge of buying into Nazi ideologies about the superman, or *Übermensch*.

The advisory board of DC (Detective Comics) and AA (All-

American) Comics responded swiftly to the growing moral panic about superheroes with instructions on how writers and artists could clean up their act. They produced a long checklist of "thou shalt nots," among them: "We must never show a coffin, least of all with a corpse in it." "No blood or bloody daggers." "No skeletons or skulls." "We must not roast anybody alive." "No character is permitted to say 'What the . . . ?' " "We must not chop limbs off characters." William Marston took a more positive approach. He argued that Superman and Wonder Woman did nothing more than pursue our two greatest national aspirations, "to develop unbeatable national might, and to use this great power, when we get it, to protect innocent, peace-loving people from destructive, ruthless evil."[78] In many ways, Wonder Woman was his stealth contribution to the war effort.

With sales off the charts, the publisher decided to energize the readership base for comics with two questionnaires, the first listing six superheroes and asking which one ought to be a member of the Justice Society: Wonder Woman, Mr. Terrific, Little Boy Blue, the Wildcat, the Gay Ghost (later renamed the Grim Ghost), or the Black Pirate? Wonder Woman won that 1942 poll, and she triumphed in a second survey that asked, "Should WONDER WOMAN be allowed, even though a woman, to become a member of the Justice Society?" The publisher was surprised to discover the enthusiasm for what he called "the encroachment of a female into what was a strictly masculine domain."[79] Who will be surprised when Wonder Woman, who fights for democracy, justice, and equality and can perform superhuman feats, is named the society's secretary? Recording words *and* performing deeds (for a change), she is— Praise Aphrodite!—to double duty bound.

# CHAPTER 6

# TO DOUBLE DUTY BOUND

## Tricksters and Other Girls on Fire

*If men see the trickster element in women*
*at all, they limit their view to the conniving*
*sorceress, the wily seductress.*

—MARILYN JURICH, *Scheherazade's Sisters*

*"You opened Pandora's box over there!"*
*"Now I'm Pandora? What'd they do*
*to her? Chain her to a rock?"*
*"That was Prometheus."*

—ELIZABETH AND HANK IN *Madam Secretary*

## New Mythologies

Joseph Campbell fretted about the disappearance of the gods, the loss of sacred spaces, and the contraction of belief systems in the modern era. "The old-time religion belongs to another age, another people, another set of human values, another universe," he lamented in conversation with Bill Moyers.[1] We can no longer rely on biblical wisdom, for it is dated, belonging to the first century BCE. And we can't go back, he insisted. He worried also about the risk that the next generation would turn inward, seeking transcendent meaning in psychedelic drugs, narcotics, and other controlled substances. How do you keep myth alive and relevant in what Campbell viewed as an era of secularization and disenchantment? For him, the new saviors would emerge from the world of art. Storytellers, filmmakers, poets, and artists, he believed, could reinvigorate the mythological universe and bring meaning and substance back into ordinary life, creating ontologically rich sites that could serve as proxies for foundational religious beliefs.

But not just any artist would do. "There's an old romantic idea in German, *das Volk dichtet*," Campbell observed. That phrase implies that "ideas and poetry" emerge from the bottom up, from the common people. Campbell vigorously denied that particular dictum, insisting that new mythologies emerge from "an elite experience." The gifted artist, the singular genius, may interact with the folk, "but the first impulse in the shaping of a folk tradition comes from above, not from below."[2] When it came to the sacred precincts of myth, Campbell was in favor of ensuring that the high priests of culture remained in power.

Campbell's disdain for the "folk" extended to popular culture in general as well as to anything that belonged to the culture of childhood. He dismissed fairy tales, for example, as pure entertainment, lacking the weightiness of myth. For that reason he was also oblivious to much of what was in the very air he breathed. How could he have missed Wonder Woman, who made it into print during the war years, just when he was starting work on *The Hero with a Thousand Faces*? It was right under his nose, in his very neighborhood, and it must have been part of the cultural baggage that young women were bringing with them to Sarah Lawrence when he was teaching there. To be sure, Wonder Woman was in many ways an anomaly, a comic book that was sui generis and that interested adults only insofar as it was a bad influence on the children they were raising. It was thought, at the time, that a medium we now elevate by using the term "graphic novel" rather than "comics" belonged to the domain of pure entertainment rather than to the serious business of myth and religion.

When it came to movies, however, Campbell was willing to allow a little wiggle room. "There is something magical about films," he stated, and movie actors can turn into "real" heroes, for they have a double presence, on the silver screen and in the flesh. (Campbell was, of course, writing well before the era of devices that stream content.) When asked whether John Wayne had become a mythical figure, he affirmed that the actor, a role model for his fans, had moved into "the sphere of being mythologized." Shane, Rambo, and Douglas Fairbanks were all names that came up in conversation with Bill Moyers, and Campbell was eager to affirm that all three transcend celebrity status, with features that can be found in the thousand faces of heroes. They are "educators toward life."[3]

What was playing at the movies in the 1940s when Campbell was writing *The Hero with a Thousand Faces*? *All the King's Men*, a film that traced the political fortunes of Willie Stark, a populist governor in the Deep South, had won the award for Best Picture in 1949, when Campbell's book was published. The year before, it was *Hamlet*, starring Laurence Olivier. And then there was *Gentleman's Agreement* (1947), about a journalist taking on a Jewish identity; *The Best Years of Our Lives* (1946), about veterans returning to civilian life; and *The Lost Weekend* (1945), about an alcoholic writer. The early 1940s featured *Casablanca* (1942), with its doomed romantic couple and men as heroic Resistance fighters, but there was also *Rebecca* (1940) and *Gaslight* (1944), with their homicidal husbands and terrified women. *Mrs. Miniver* (1942) and *Madame Curie* (1943) give us cinematic heroines, but they stand as exceptions in a field of nearly sixty nominated pictures that include *Citizen Kane*, *The Maltese Falcon*, *Battleground*, and other dramas of men beleaguered.

How do the Academy Awards of 2020 stack up against those of the 1940s? At first glance, little has changed, with films like Martin Scorsese's *The Irishman*, Todd Phillips's *Joker*, Fernando Meirelles's *The Two Popes*, and Pedro Almodóvar's *Pain and Glory* vying for Best Picture. But Greta Gerwig's *Little Women* and Noah Baumbach's *Marriage Story* have been squeezed in, between the war drama *1917* and Quentin Tarantino's *Once upon a Time in Hollywood*, perhaps a hint that the landscape is a shade different. The Academy Awards turn out to be something of a lagging indicator, or perhaps the Academy is just a deeply conservative institution still unprepared to nominate films with female directors and leads.

Today there are a host of heroines on-screen—flip, fast-talking, gender fluid, brainy, sinewy, chain-smoking, and brash—and they are not about to go away. Appearing on a spectrum that takes us from crazed crusaders through single-minded avengers to strapping warrior women, they fight battles, first with words, but soon with weapons as well. Predictably, Hollywood also gives us a perversion of the heroine who has taken so long to emerge, with screen fantasies, scripted and directed mainly by men, that show women dressed to kill rather than crusading for a cause.

## Tricksters, Male and Female

Hero worship comes easily to every culture, and today we continue to idolize heroes and heroines, neglecting their equally admirable partners in combating villains. These are the mythical figures known as tricksters—antiheroes, outsiders, misfits, interlopers, and, yes, losers—clever, self-serving, amoral, and determined to survive in a cutthroat culture (hello, Scheherazade) rather than to sacrifice themselves to a higher cause (goodbye, Jesus). Many have access to some kind of magical power: superhuman strength, shapeshifting, or spellcasting. Opportunistic and stealthy, they will lie, steal, and cheat, refusing to play by the rules or to become part of a corrupt system riddled with contradictions that do things like transform predatory hypercapitalists into kindhearted philanthropists. Undermining the system, overturning authority, and revitalizing their culture, these mischief makers paradoxically emerge as cultural heroes, champions of those who are marginalized and oppressed. They are the agents of renewal and change.

"All the regularly discussed figures are male," Lewis Hyde tells us in *Trickster Makes This World*, his magisterial study of the culture-building feats of tricksters, originally published in 1998. Who will fail to hear a distant echo of Joseph Campbell's voice telling his readers that there are no models in the mythological universe for women's quests? The stars in the trickster firmament range from the Greek Hermes and Nordic Loki to the Native American Coyote and African Hare. Tricky women exist, Hyde concedes, but when they make trouble, their subversive antics and disruptive tactics fall short of the "elaborated career of deceit" that marks the lives of those cultural heroes we know by the name of trickster.[4]

There may be good reasons for the absence of female tricksters in what Hyde aptly describes as the patriarchal mythological imagination. The male trickster is never found at home, sitting by the hearth, brooding over impossible chores and dreaming of rescue. Driven by hunger and appetite, he is always on the road, mobile and mercurial in ways unimaginable for women in most cultures. As a boundary-crosser and traveler, trickster is adept at finding ways to gratify his multiple appetites—chiefly for food and sex, but for spiritual satisfactions as well. He is even capable of procreation, as the Winnebago trickster named Wakdjunkaga reveals when he changes into a woman to marry the son of a chief and bear three sons. But that trickster, like Hermes (who is sometimes depicted as a hermaphrodite), remains resolutely masculine and macho, with nothing more than the magical capacity to turn into a woman.[5]

It may well be that tricksters are, by their very nature, *male*, heavy-duty patriarchal constructs, say, in the tradition of Anansi or Hermes, designed to define the addictions, appetites, and desires of manly men. (Hermes is, of course, less of an inveterate sex addict, since most of the womanizing in the Greek mythological universe was left to Zeus.) As the product of mythological systems constructed by male bards, poets, priests, and philosophers, trickster's powers may simply have been reserved for male agents.[6] But who is to say that the female trickster never carried out her own clandestine operations, functioning in furtive ways and covering her tracks to ensure that her powers remain undetected?

Few in the past would have described Penelope, a symbol of hard-core fidelity, as a "trickster," but Margaret Atwood construed her differently, as a knowing agent of power. Perhaps the female trickster has played her own survival game and endured simply by staying invisible and confounding the traditional approach we adopt when we try to make sense of our cultural stories. And now, in cultures that grant women forms of mobility and subversive agency unknown in earlier ages (yet still purposefully unavailable in many regions of the world today), she can join up with the more visible postmodern female counterparts brought to us courtesy of the Hollywood Dream Factory, where fantasies about power and playfulness can run wild. It is time to trace the covert operations of a set of female tricksters—girls gone wild in ways that challenge cultural stereotypes. They may not have "fully elaborated" careers but still they remind us that there is a female version of the mythical male trickster, one with its own set of defining features.

But first an important caveat. What if some of these female tricksters are an invention of defensive fantasies, possibly mounted as resistance to the encroachments of women on male-dominated territories? Certainly, it is possible to make the case that a film like David Slade's *Hard Candy* (2005), a recycling of "Little Red Riding Hood" starring a female predator stalking her pedophile male quarry, captures male anxieties about women exacting revenge for a history of rapacious behavior. Or that Alex Garland's *Ex Machina* (2014) reveals just how threatening women can be when they turn professional and are suddenly endowed with a higher intelligence, turning on men in vicious ways, not just slapping them or displacing them, but now killing them off. Do these directors, along with their teams of screenwriters, producers, casting directors, and so on, have their finger on the pulse of the culture, reflecting back to audiences their fantasies and fears, or are they struggling with their own personal demons, embodying them on-screen to haunt our imaginations? The answer varies, of course, with each film, and we can endlessly debate exactly where a movie will land on the spectrum that takes us from the culturally symptomatic to what is up close and personal.

A look at data from the film industry is a reminder to keep asking "Who is telling the story and why?" A 2016 study sponsored by the Annenberg Foundation found that roughly two-thirds of speaking or named characters in films made between 2007 and 2015 were male and only one-third female. Only 32 percent featured a female lead or co-lead. Of the one hundred top-grossing films of 2019, 92.5 percent of the directors were men, 7.5 percent women. Women fared better as writers (12 percent) and as producers (22 percent) but worse as composers (less than 1 percent).[7] In 2019, of the one hundred top-grossing films, 10.7 percent were directed by women. Kathryn Bigelow is the only woman to ever win the Academy Award for Best Director (was it coincidence that the film, *The Hurt Locker*, was a war thriller with a nearly all-male cast?).[8] The Annenberg study gives us all the more reason to look closely at new archetypes that have emerged and at who is constructing them. In many ways, we are in an exploratory phase, for no one has yet written a rule book along the lines of *The Hero with a Thousand Faces* for the heroine's journey and quest or considered how the trickster factors into the cultural logic of new media. How do these new cinematic tricksters represent a deviation from earlier norms and how do they move the needle in ways obvious but also imperceptible in our understanding of female heroism?

It is not hard to rattle off female stereotypes in movies from the past century. There is the femme fatale (*Double Indemnity* and *The Maltese Falcon*), the prostitute with a heart of gold (*Irma la Douce* and *Pretty Woman*), the sassy Black woman (*Monster-in-Law* and *Waiting to Exhale*), the terrified Final Girl of Horror (*Halloween* and *The Texas Chainsaw Massacre*), and so on. Monstrous and power hungry or marginalized and powerless, these characters are masters of seduction and also of suffering. Recall Hitchcock's declaration during the filming of *The Birds*, when its star, Tippi Hedren, was subjected to vicious daily assaults from birds that were in turn protected by the ASPCA: "I always believe in following the advice of the playwright Sardou. He said 'Torture the women.'" The only real problem, he added, was that we don't torture women enough. (The French dramatist Victorien Sardou had put that theory into practice in his five-act play *La Tosca*, later adapted for Puccini's 1900 opera of that name, which gives Tosca more to endure than is imaginable.) From *The Perils of Pauline* through *Gaslight* to *Rosemary's Baby*, glammed-up women have screamed, shrieked, and cowered in terror while men plot to torment them.

Are we flying blind in the twenty-first century? Are there no models for the woman's quest, as Campbell asserted near the end of his life, when he pointed out that women were only now moving into arenas of action that had formerly been reserved for men alone? "We are the 'ancestors' of an age to come," Campbell reminded us. That's what makes us the inventors of new mythical models that will guide generations to come. And he advocated creating those new models with compassion rather than passion, in ways that would promote growth and strength rather than power. To his credit, what he wanted was not just new wine in old wineskins, but a new, headier wine in fresh wineskins.[9] The film industry, now decentralized, dispersed, and operating in multiple production sites ranging from Hollywood to Bollywood and beyond, has constructed many of those new models (with help from blockbuster novels), and it has reversed course in astonishing ways, creating a new pantheon of female heroines.

## Crazed Crusaders

When Lisbeth Salander, the girl with the dragon tattoo in Stieg Larsson's Millennium trilogy, encounters a man who regards her as "legal" prey, we quickly realize exactly what sets this skinny hacker apart from heroines of the past. And it is not just her tattoos, spiked quills of black hair, and Doc Marten boots. Salander invites Advokat Bjurman into the lair of her bedroom and leads him to the bed, "not the other way around." Her next move is to fire seventy-five thousand volts from a Taser into his armpit and push him down on the bed with "all her strength." In a stark reversal of Sardou's imperative to torture the women, Salander ties up Bjurman and tattoos a series of colorful epithets onto his torso. A sadistic sexual predator is transformed in an instant into her abject victim. This is the woman who will solve the brutal murders (all of young women) committed by a serial killer in a corrupt culture of shady industrialists, Nazi sympathizers, and sexually perverse civil servants.[10]

Stieg Larsson's Millennium trilogy gave us one of the first in a parade of twenty-first-century female tricksters, women who are quick-witted, fleet-footed, and resolutely brave. "Tiny as a sparrow," "fierce as an eagle," "a bruised animal"—it is not by chance that reviewers of Hollywood's version of the first installment to the trilogy, *The Girl with the Dragon Tattoo*, used animal metaphors to capture Lisbeth's nature. She has exactly the same ravenous appetite, along with the predatory instincts, of animal tricksters (Coyote, Anansi, Raven, Rabbit). Female tricksters are always famished (bulimic binges are their update on the mythical figure's insatiable appetite), and also driven by mysterious cravings that make them appealingly enigmatic. Surrounded by predators, they quickly develop survival skills, crossing boundaries, challenging property rights, and outsmarting all those who see them as easy prey. But, unlike their male analogues, they are not just self-serving, cleverly resourceful, and determined to survive. They're also committed to social causes and political change, though not without running into the uncomfortable paradox of finding that a social crusade against violence can beget more violence.

Lisbeth, as fans of Stieg Larsson's Millennium trilogy will recognize, is a woman on a mission. Unlike Scheherazade, she does not use the civilizing power of story to change her culture (although one could argue that Larsson tries to do just that by beginning his novel with statistics about the number of women in Sweden who have been threatened by a man). Instead Lisbeth aims to exact revenge for injuries done to her and to a sisterhood of female victims. It is worth noting that Larsson's trilogy was a long, belated apology for a dark secret of his own. At the age of fifteen, he witnessed the gang rape of a woman named Lisbeth and failed to intervene, an experience that haunted him and inspired a story that ended with symbolic retribution, vicarious and cathartic, at least for its author.

Lisbeth's humorlessness, her almost pathological lack of affect, makes her an unlikely candidate for the role of trickster. But like classic male tricksters, Lisbeth has a bottomless appetite—for food, as well as for sexual partners, both male and female. In the film directed by David Fincher, she stuffs herself with french fries while hunched over her Mac laptop and chain-smokes her way through the investigation. Her "high metabolism," she claims, keeps her looking skinny. Although she is described as an "anorexic spook" by one of the novel's villains, she is endlessly gorging herself with something like "three big open rye-bread sandwiches with cheese, caviar, and a hard-boiled egg" or "half a dozen thick sandwiches on rye bread with cheese and liver sausage and dill pickles." Constantly brewing coffee, she shovels down Billys Pan Pizza as if eating her last meal. Consuming "every kind of junk food," she may not have body dysmorphia but she clearly has some kind of eating disorder.

Gluttony is writ large in the Millennium trilogy, and sexual appetite as well, with Salander presented as what one critic describes as a "popular culture fantasy—adolescent-looking yet sexually experienced." In fact, the depictions of Salander as both victim of rape and partner in consensual sadomasochistic erotic practices are so explicit as to arouse the suspicion of creating a spectacle designed to play into the voyeuristic desires of readers. "Misogynist violence is appalling," one critic notes archly; "now here's some more."[11] The same could be said for the graphic display of women's mutilated corpses in crime-scene photos that are regularly inserted into scenes of investigative work to add cinematic dash to the otherwise dull images of open laptops, scattered files, and ashtrays full of cigarette butts.

That Lisbeth's physical strength, as well as her technological savvy and varied appetites, is modeled on male figures becomes evident when we learn about her superhuman strength. She is nimble and muscular enough to defeat school bullies as a child and later, as an adult, she beats

*The Girl with the Dragon Tattoo*, 2011
*Courtesy of Photofest*

up thugs twice her size in physical combat. In the second novel of the trilogy, we discover that Lisbeth was trained as a boxer and was once a serious competitor in contests with men. Whether roaming bars, lighting up, or roaring off on a motorcycle, she mimics male behavior throughout the film version of *The Girl with the Dragon Tattoo* rather than shaping a unique female identity. Her appeal derives in large part from the ability to serve as an ironic double of the classic male trickster, masquerading, performing, and imitating in ways that offer both serious reenactment and gender-bending parody.

"She's different," Lisbeth's boss, Dragan Armansky, tells a client in the Fincher film, who responds by asking, "In what way?" The answer: "Every way." "Out of place" is an understatement to describe Lisbeth's first appearance in the film, as she marches, with robotic purposiveness, into what looks like a soulless conference room for corporate headquarters, with two men in suits awaiting her arrival. "I find it's much better if she works from home," Armansky declares dryly before she enters the room. Lisbeth looks oddly waiflike even with her black mohawk, multiple piercings, and motorcycle getup. "Different" captures precisely the reaction of critics and viewers, who were unprepared for a punked-out, feral hacker who rights wrongs using a form of hard-wired intelligence never seen before in a female lead. When Lisbeth embarks on her revenge saga, she is relentlessly focused on uncovering the identity of a serial killer who has left a trail of corpses—all young Jewish women, with their shared biblical names as the only clue.

Lisbeth possesses what her author described as "sheer magic." As noted, when we first see her in the book, it is through the eyes of her employer, Dragan Armansky, and he describes her as one of those "flat-chested girls who might be mistaken for skinny boys at a distance" and as a "foreign creature." Like Hermes before her, she wears a cloak (his is described as one of shamelessness). Sweden's National Board of Health and Welfare has declared her to be "introverted, socially inhibited, lacking empathy, ego-fixated," as well as exhibiting "psychopathic and asocial behavior." She has difficulty "cooperating" and is "incapable of assimilating learning." She may exhibit the classic traits of Asperger's syndrome, but she is also cunning and moves about the world with the nimbleness of a spider on its web. Her athletic prowess is given visual expression in the film as she navigates her way through a world filled with electronic trip wires. Her gymnastic agility aligns her once again with the impudent Hermes and his folkloric kin, whose clever antics disturb boundaries and challenge property rights. A master of the World Wide Web, Lisbeth has, like Anansi before her, her own network to administer, this time by cracking codes and hacking into systems.[12]

Hackers feed off the lightning speed of the internet, violating regulatory measures and legislative rulings. Detached from the world, socially backward, misanthropic with a serious bad attitude, and often living alone in dark, claustrophobic spaces, Lisbeth fits right in when it comes to uber-nerds.[13] Her seeming lack of emotional involvement masks a deep commitment to avenging rapists, murderers, and other women-hating men—and to do good. As compensation for agreeing to keep quiet about the discovery that the now-dead Martin Vanger carried on the family tradition of murdering young women, she demands donations to the National Organization for Women's Crisis Centers and Girls' Crisis Centers in Sweden, a bargain of convenience that could be turned against her as a crusader for social justice.

Property rights are always in crisis, constantly contested, with conflicts between agrarian economies and commercial exchanges dominating in the past and concerns about data privacy, security, and uninvited surveillance ruling today. Hermes, as god of commerce, came long ago to embody the spirit of capitalist enterprise in his association with artisans and merchants. But as cattle rustler and master of "stealth," he was also linked with agrarian interests as well as with robbers and thieves, working both sides of the street and therefore supremely well qualified to mediate disputes.[14] Our new conflicts about privacy and intellectual property, oddly, still stand under the star of Hermes. In a world that enforces boundaries by technological means, Lisbeth enjoys unparalleled freedom and mobility, mirroring computers, tapping telephones, and deactivating alarms, leaving collective forms of regulation powerless. An expert at lawlessness and (data) trespassing, as she describes herself, she leaves no traces behind and is able to outwit even top security consultants. Hers is a mercurial art, and she goes about her work with a genius that makes us wonder whether her stolen goods are not in fact earned gifts.

As it happens, Lisbeth is most often on the wrong side of the law but on the right side of justice. She may be diagnosed with Asperger's syndrome and she may be profoundly asocial, but her curiosity about the deaths of others (she loves "hunting skeletons") makes it clear that she does not share all the symptoms of those with attention deficit disorder. Like Bluebeard's wife, an unacknowledged female trickster, she also enjoys "digging into the lives of other people and exposing the secrets they were trying to hide." It is this deep investigative bent that sets her apart from Hermes, Coyote, and Hare. Lisbeth, much as she is wedded to a world of technology, cannot resist spying and trying to read the minds of others and understand their motivations.[15]

"I find it hard to think of an equivalent of Lisbeth Salander anywhere else in the worlds of crime novels or films," wrote Lasse Bergström, head of the Swedish firm that published Larsson's trilogy.[16] His reaction mirrored the response of Larsson's readers as well as many viewers of the film *The Girl with the Dragon Tattoo* (2011). And yet our culture seems to be creating, in films like David Slade's *Hard Candy* (with its seemingly vulnerable Little Red Riding Hood look-alike), heroines who take justice into their own hands and enact revenge fantasies against what Stieg Larsson called "men who hate women" (the manuscript for what is now a trilogy originally came in two parts, each with that title). Building on rape-revenge films of the 1970s and 1980s (*Lipstick, I Spit on Your Grave, Extremities*, etc.), *The Girl with the Dragon Tattoo* gives us a heroine whose identity exceeds her status as rape victim. Lisbeth is neither traumatized nor deranged by the abuse she has suffered. She accepts violence against women as the way of the world and acts efficiently to create a deterrent by exacting revenge for it. Combining the survival skills of the trickster, the cool intelligence of the boyish Final Girl, and the courage of rape victims who testify against their abusers, she becomes part of an action plot that is coded as an inviting crime/retaliation narrative, providing viewers with all the satisfactions of revenge enacted.

Stieg Larsson's literary inspiration for Lisbeth Salander came from an unlikely source: a popular children's book that was translated from the original Swedish into over seventy-five languages and became one of the top-selling books of children's literature. Larsson explicitly named Pippi Longstocking, the heroine of Astrid Lindgren's book of that title, as a model for Lisbeth. That Salander uses the nameplate "V. Kulla" (a not-so-veiled reference to Pippi Longstocking's home, Villa Villekulla) strengthens the connection, even if Salander denies any kinship bonds. "Somebody'd get a fat lip if they called me Pippi Longstocking," she asserts with characteristic pugnaciousness.[17]

Astrid Lindgren's Pippi Longstocking is "no ordinary girl."[18] With no adults supervising and limiting her activities, the world becomes a playground for her transgressive boundary-crossing. From the start, Pippi puts her trickster skills on display, lying "all day long" (as a result of dwelling too long in the Congo), reciting tall tales about adventures in exotic locales ranging from the "Cannibal Isles" to "Arabia." A hunter and "Thing-Finder," as well as a girl who loves riddles, she outriddles her enemies, defeating bullies, bandits, and strongmen. Pippi tells tall tales in order to outfox school officials and local authorities. A disruptive force, she succeeds, as skillfully as her mythical male counterparts, in uncovering the absurdity of social conventions and regulations in a culture that cannot countenance the idea of a girl who is autonomous, without parental supervision and without a legal guardian.

"Never Violence!" was the title of a speech Astrid Lindgren delivered on the occasion of receiving the Peace Prize of the German Book Trade, and it led to a landmark legislative ruling in Sweden prohibiting physical violence against children, the first law of its kind. In the 1978 Frankfurt address, Lindgren tells a moving story about a boy sent into the woods by his mother to fetch a birch rod, a switch she will use to punish him. Unable to find a rod, the boy returns home in tears and tells his mother, "I can't find a rod, but here's a stone you can throw at me."[19] A champion of children's rights and animal rights, as well as an early environmental activist, Lindgren cast her lot with the powerless and vulnerable, while also creating a heroine who models irreverent vitality, determination, and resilience for readers.

Larsson more than likely grew up not just with the Pippi Longstocking books but also with an awareness of Astrid Lindgren's crusade against violence. It is not hard to imagine how Sweden's most prominent fictional girl shaped his conception of a "dysfunctional girl with attention deficit disorder—someone who would have trouble fitting in," as he described Lisbeth. There are other, possibly less likely, prominent cultural figures that worked on his imagination. One might be found in the figure of Lex in Steven Spielberg's *Jurassic Park* (1993), a film that reminds us of how fictional and cinematic girls—brash and bold—are often in the vanguard, anticipating the liberties that will one day be embraced by their somewhat older, adult counterparts.

It is Lex who saves the day for the group of sightseers touring Jurassic Park, when they discover that some of the ferocious predators on the island have broken free and are on the rampage. She sits down at the computer, recognizes how it runs ("It's a UNIX system! I know this!"), and then pulls up a program called "3D File System Navigator" to restore security systems in Jurassic Park. Her name, of course, has already signaled her expertise in computer language and language systems in general. Interestingly, in Michael Crichton's *Jurassic Park* (the novel on which the film is based), it is Lex's brother Tim who manages, on his own, to get the security systems back online. He wards off dinosaurs, protecting Lex when the adults are either dead or have let the children down. In a stroke of crowd-pleasing genius, Lex becomes, in Spielberg's film, the computer geek, adept at coding and at command language, and it is she who saves the day.[20] In odd ways, perhaps because of its collective creative process that draws on a range of imaginative palettes and its willingness to be both cutting-edge and edgy despite the high financial stakes, Hollywood seems magically attuned to what is in the airwaves, anticipating what is to come rather than just recycling what is in the here and now.

Lex and her facility with languages did not appear out of thin air. When we turn to the fairy-tale repertoire, it becomes clear that *Jurassic*

*Park* is to some extent a reimagining of "Hansel and Gretel." Recall that the voracious velociraptors who turn on Lex and Tim are all female—this is Jurassic Park and the female dinosaurs have miraculously discovered how to reproduce ("Nature finds a way"). And the raptors mount their assault on the two siblings in a kitchen space, making it evident that we are watching some kind of weird sci-fi update of the Grimms' tale. Gretel saw her "moment in history" (that's how Anne Sexton described it) and shoved the cannibalistic witch into the oven. Lex diverts the raptors while struggling to crawl into a cabinet, and her mirror image on what looks for all the world like an oven leads one of the raptors to crash headlong into a hard surface. It is worth noting that Hansel and Gretel are able to return home on the back of a duck, thanks to the poetry in the spells Gretel chants. Like the mythical Hermes, the two children are adroit liars and arrant thieves who, like all tricksters, also traffic in enchantments.

That Spielberg was playing in *Jurassic Park* with gender role reversals becomes evident through the carefully orchestrated color coding in the film. For starters, Hammond, the naïve idealist, is always dressed in white, while Malcolm, the cynical realist, wears black. It seems, then, not coincidental that the paleontologist Alan Grant wears a blue shirt at the beginning of the film, while his collaborator Ellie Sattler wears a pink shirt. By the end of the film, his shirt is caked with mud, and Sattler's pink shirt is tossed aside to expose a blue undershirt beneath it.[21] Lex may not seem to be a close cousin of Lisbeth Salander—she is less adventurous, irreverent, and fearless than the girl with the dragon tattoo—but the two are in the vanguard of a movement that invests *girls* (Lisbeth is called exactly that in all three of the novels in Larsson's trilogy) with skills that were traditionally in the DNA of heroes, young and old. The stakes may not be high for Pippi Longstocking, but intelligence, craft, and a skill set that involves mastery of language (of one kind or another) become, for Lisbeth, Lex, and Gretel, matters of life and death. All survivors, they are all also crusaders, crazed by the perils in the world around them but triumphant in their focused response to the threats aimed at them and at those for whom they care.

## Artful Avengers

*Three Billboards outside Ebbing, Missouri* (2017), directed by Martin McDonagh, reminds us of just how unhinged our new female tricksters can be, with the character played by Frances McDormand swiftly turning from "mad mommy" to "Charles Bronson."[22] The film gives us an unlikely heroine: fifty-something Mildred Hayes, feckless and fidgety, recently divorced, a woman on the verge throughout the film and for good reason: her daughter was brutally raped and murdered, and no one has been arrested. Mildred, herself a survivor of spousal abuse, channels her anger into seeking justice. She begins the quest to identify and arrest her daughter's killer by renting three billboards. The words that appear on those billboards are: "Still No Arrests?" "How Come, Chief Willoughby?" and "Raped While Dying." Mildred embraces bold defiance in multiple ways, at first using words as weapons when she puts her high-wattage questions and statements of fact on public display. But soon she moves to more provocative strategies, producing injury and inflicting harm when she turns a drill on her dentist's thumbnail and then gut-punches teenagers in ways that make us wonder whether this is in fact the turn we want our new cultural heroines to take. And when the violence is played for laughs, it becomes all the more evident that justice stands in the shadow of vengeance. And that is the point at which we may want to ask who is behind the scenes, creating new sword-wielding female tricksters who undo the older models of word-wielding women.

"You're a badass, take-no-prisoners woman," a defeated husband tells his wife in Gillian Flynn's *Gone Girl* (2012), a multi-million-copy, bestselling novel turned into a film two years later. Directed by David Fincher, the film takes the idea of the avenger heroine to the point of near parody. In scenes of stylized violence, we watch a woman turning into an agent of the kind of homicidal rage ordinarily inflicted on women by men (as the data convincingly tell us). *Gone Girl* turns the tables, creating a crafty killer, a woman who is seductive, smart, and treacherous. Gone is the cowering victim and instead we have a lead who knows exactly how to find her version of justice—she has become a towering figure of revenge. Is *Gone Girl*, then, a feminist manifesto, with a woman rebelling against the cultural pressure to play the "cool girl" and "Amazing Amy," then getting even in ways cold-blooded and chilling, or is it a misogynist rant featuring a female psychopath who fakes her own death, lies about being raped, and kills to cover her tracks? In classic trickster fashion, Amy engages in self-serving deceptions, taking on the role of an amoral outlaw who sheds feminine stereotypes and takes control in ways that women have traditionally not. In what feels like a masterstroke of irony from an author who has tapped into the idea of heroines using storytelling and writing as forms of self-actualization, Amy keeps a diary, with entries that will be used to incriminate her husband in her staged murder. "She's telling the better story," her husband Nick tells his lawyer in the film version of *Gone Girl*. "She's telling the perfect story," the lawyer responds.[23] Amy may be a monster, but she is doing nothing more than defamiliarizing the cinematic stereotypes of psychopathic men, all the while masquerading as an abused female victim.

Many of these new tough girls are not at all inclined to temper justice with mercy (think Quentin Tarantino's 2003 *Kill Bill*), especially when they are on political missions. *Zero Dark Thirty* (2012) has Maya, a CIA officer obsessed with hunting down Osama bin Laden, who operates in a theater of global combat that offers entirely new terrain for female heroics. Maya may cringe while witnessing violent interrogations and torture, but her determination to find and punish terrorists never falters. *Homeland*'s Carrie Mathison, from the same era, is more complicated, but she, too, obsessed with a terrorist named Abu Nazir, shows a form of unforgiving single-mindedness that shades into pathology. Both Maya and Carrie continue the tradition of wielding language as a weapon. Maya turns an office window into a slate for issuing reprimands. Carrie creates a visual map of her manic thinking, papered with evidence and clues that eventually lead to Abu Nazir's capture.

Many of the female tricksters who have emerged in the late twentieth century and early twenty-first century are girls, and they are often modeled on figures from fairy tales. But now they have complemented their arsenals of verbal weapons with heavier artillery. Cinematic culture dotes on Little Red Riding Hood almost as much as Granny does, creating girls that turn into the monsters that once preyed on them. The revenge fantasy enacted in *Gone Girl* turns even darker in recent films, with heroines sporting hooded sweatshirts or red leather jackets, carrying a basket (containing weapons more likely than food) as they make their way to Granny's. In the 1990s, Little Red Riding Hood turns from vulnerable innocent into a ferocious *grrrl*.

Matthew Bright's *Freeway* (1996) takes us to the mean streets of Southern California, with an urban Red Riding Hood named Vanessa Lutz (does her last name scramble "slut"?). In her red leather jacket—packing heat in her basket—she makes her way to Granny's house. The Little Red Riding Hood tropes drop in ways that are fast and furious, and she is seen trying to elude a host of stalkers, among them a pedophile serial killer named Bob Wolverton. (His profession? What else but child psychologist.) In these woods, there is no rescuing huntsman, as becomes clear when Vanessa's boyfriend, Chopper Wood, is gunned down by rival gang members.

On the way to Grandmother's house, Vanessa's car breaks down, and the smooth-talking Wolverton, who camouflages his homicidal impulses using the guise of a benevolent therapeutic intervention, gives her a lift. Vanessa gains the upper hand, and, like James Thurber's feisty Red Riding Hood who pulls a pistol from her knickers when the wolf threatens her, she reaches for her revolver when Wolverton reveals his true intentions and identity (the dead giveaway that he is California's I-5 killer is that he cuts off her ponytail with a straight razor). Wolverton, critically injured and left mutilated after being shot by Vanessa, manages to make his way to Granny's trailer park, where he conceals himself by wearing a shower cap and capacious nightgown. Vanessa is no fool, and she wrestles the predator to the ground, knocking him out and delivering her final line, "You got a cigarette?" to horrified police officers, who arrive only once the danger is past. She becomes one cool and casual customer.

It would be reassuring to imagine that Matthew Bright's girl in red has become a cultural heroine, a survivor who manages, against the odds, to turn the tables on the adults who have victimized her, some of whom are psychopaths masquerading as social workers. Vanessa has been seen as the figure who points the way to a reversal of values, undermining a status quo that turns a blind eye to the sadistic impulses of prison guards, police officers, and social workers and fails to recognize the social injustices inflicted on marginalized groups.[24] But the foul-mouthed, proudly illiterate, gun-toting high school dropout who asks for a cigarette after slaying Wolverton is hardly a role model. Her retaliatory moves are instinctive and in the service of her own personal survival rather than fueled by righteous indignation at the social order. She may set things right by bringing Wolverton to justice, but they will remain awry so long as a grrrl's only recourse is to the tactics of the assailant.

Although David Slade did not set out to make a Little Red Riding Hood film, the story flashes out at us in his 2005 *Hard Candy* when we see, on the poster advertising it, a girl dressed in a red hoodie, messenger bag slung over her shoulder. She is positioned with her back to us, feet poised on a platform the size of a skateboard, right in the middle of an animal trap lined with jagged blades. "Absolutely terrifying!" shouts the banner over the image, and we are entitled to imagine that this film, too, will subject us to the horrors of watching an adolescent girl at the mercy of a homicidal maniac, a killer who remains ominously invisible on the poster.

In this updated spin on the fairy tale, the girl and the wolf have their first encounter online. Thonggrrrrll14 and Lensman319 flirt in a chat room and arrange a rendezvous. The names and numbers are telling: this Little Red Riding Hood is a flirtatious fourteen-year-old (underage and seductive), and her date will be with a photographer, a man who lives off a craft that suggests an investment in visual pleasure. And indeed the thirty-two-year-old Jeff will turn out to be not just a photographer of women but also a consumer of pornography, with a stash of incriminating images in a floor safe. Encoded in the names of these two adversaries are their gendered roles, with Thonggrrrrll14 named after a provocative article of clothing and Lensman319 gesturing at the notion of the male gaze.

Inspired by a newspaper account about Japanese girls luring businessmen to designated locations and then robbing them, *Hard Candy* initially takes us down the traditional path, setting up expectations that a young innocent stalked by an internet predator will also become his victim. But Hayley Stark, brilliantly played by Ellen Page, turns out to be less than innocent. Intent on avenging the murder of a friend, she sets out to torture Jeff in ways that are nearly unimaginable, leading him to believe that, after anesthetizing his groin area, she performed surgery, castrating him and disposing of his testicles in a plastic bag. Merciless, pitiless, and ruthless, Hayley responds coldly to Jeff's pleas to stop with references to his failure to feel any kind of compassion for his victims. To the bitter end, she occupies the role of avenger with the unforgiving harshness of the predator himself.

Like David Slade, the writers for the television series *Buffy the Vampire Slayer* decided to reboot "Little Red Riding Hood" in ways that go beyond mere adaptation. In Season 4, episode 4, called "Fear, Itself," Buffy dresses up on Halloween night as the girl in red. When she meets her friend Xander on the way to a festive gathering, he asks: "Hey, Red. What you got in the basket, little girl?" Buffy's answer is telling: "Weapons. . . . Just in case." When she finally encounters the monstrous Gachnar, a miniature beast who lacks the power to terrify, the camera pans to the sole of her foot as it is about to crush her antagonist. On a previous episode, Buffy had made the mistake of dressing in a princess costume, only to find herself falling victim to a spell that turned her into the character she was impersonating. Learning from past experience, she is now prepared—as a girl in red—for the beast in the woods.[25]

Joe Wright, the director of *Hanna* (2011), put these killer girls on steroids when he reinvented Little Red Riding Hood as a genetically modified teenage assassin, dressed in pelts when we first see her. Raised by her father in the wilderness, where she hunts moose and befriends wolf puppies, Hanna is trained by him in languages, survival skills, and martial arts. But she remains in the dark about civilization. Roughing it in a cabin in northern Finland, she is closer to nature than to culture. "Once upon a time there was a very special girl who lived in the woods with her father," the trailer to the film announces. Hanna may not dress in red, but she is immersed in fairy tales, caught repeatedly by the camera in the act of reading the volume of Grimms' fairy tales that was in her hands when her mother died. And, of course, the illustration on one of the pages we see is from "Little Red Riding Hood."

Hanna's mission is to shoot the CIA intelligence operative Marissa Wiegler (played by Cate Blanchett), who murdered her mother and is now intent on killing Hanna and her father. She visits not only Grandmother's house but also a place known as Wilhelm Grimm's house in Berlin, where a wolf dressed up as Grandmother lies in a bed.

Joe Wright explained in an interview the importance of the fairy-tale setting in the woods and how his plot maps onto fairy-tale encounters with evil. "These stories were told every day," he noted. "The Little Mermaid, Hansel and Gretel and Rapunzel were part of our lives, but they're violent and dark and cautionary tales and they go some way to attempt to prepare children for the obstacles that they may face in the wider world," he added.[26] Wright draws on not only fairy tales but also fantasy literature, with Hanna as a dark double of Alice in Wonderland, entering the real world and experiencing its electronic wonders, along with everything else, for the first time as a teenager. But his warrior heroine probably has more in common with Robert Ludlum's Jason Bourne than with Little Red Riding Hood.

*Hanna* is a reminder that fairy tales have taken a dark turn, with heroines who can outrun, outsmart, but above all outshoot their adversaries in action segments that move with the lightning speed of video-game sequences. The film is framed by two scenes of shooting. In the first, Hanna uses a bow and arrow to kill a moose; she then shoots it in the heart to put it out of its misery. The film closes with Hanna pointing a gun at Marissa Wiegler, shooting her in the heart, and repeating the words, this time without pity, that opened the film: "I just missed your heart." From where did Marissa, both wicked witch and cold-blooded wolf, emerge to meet Hanna? From the jaws of an amusement park wolf, of course. Both women run with the wolves in a film that mimics the action movie, that classic juggernaut of Hollywood cinema that features heroes on a journey. Are our new heroines nothing but a carbon

*Hanna,* 2011
*Courtesy of Photofest*

copy of Campbell's hero, fighting battles in dark places from which they emerge covered in blood but victorious? Are we installing a new model that mimics the old rather than creating an archetype that is in tune with the values we embrace today: empathy, care, and connection?

## Warrior Women

Fans swooned over Arya Stark's triumphant sleight-of-hand before slaying the Night King in the godswood with a Valyrian steel dagger in the finale to HBO's popular series *Game of Thrones*. Maisie Williams, the actress who portrayed Arya, was worried that fans would hate how the Battle of Winterfell was resolved and would believe that Arya did not really deserve to be the savior in the long-running series. But the show prepared viewers for the finale by presenting Arya first as the "distressed female" of classic horror, next turning her into a clever master of masquerade, and finally allowing her to morph into the winning survivor who looks death in the face and finds the strength to slay the monster. Even as she is terrorized and tortured, Arya, the Final Girl in *Game of Thrones*, rises to the challenges of the Evil that no one else was able to face down.

Television shows of the past decades have given us many pumped-up, tough-talking women: Diana Rigg as Emma Peel in *The Avengers*, Eartha Kitt as Catwoman in *Batman*, Lynda Carter in *Wonder Woman*, Lindsay Wagner in *The Bionic Woman*, and Angelina Jolie as Lara Croft. But *Game of Thrones* modeled an entirely new set of possibilities, not just with Arya but also with Lady Brienne of Tarth, a stoic, fierce swordfighter in armor. Then there is Sansa Stark, who evolves from disagreeable teen to capable leader of her people, and Queen Cersei (a clever homonym for Circe), traumatized, entitled, vindictive, and conniving. And who can forget that "beautiful evil" known as Daenerys Targaryen, survivor, liberator, and destroyer?

More than any other branch of the film industry, the Disney Company has mastered the fine art of picking up disturbances in the cultural airwaves and adapting the stories it tells on-screen to adjust to new social circumstances. Once upon a time in the world of Disney animation, men fought the battles and defeated the villains. Eric, the Prince Charming of *The Little Mermaid* (1989), rows out to sea at the end of the film to confront the flamboyant, power-hungry, sassy octopus-witch Ursula, who has usurped King Triton's crown and now has his authority ("The sea and all its spoils bow to my power"). Ursula, incidentally, was inspired in looks and behavior by drag legend Divine. "You monster," Ariel screams at her, and Ursula, who knows that Ariel can resort to little more than name-calling, answers back by calling her a little brat. While the Little Mermaid is helplessly caught in the vortex of a whirlpool, Eric mans a ship, commands it to move full speed ahead, and impales Ursula on its bow. Bolts of lightning course through her body as she deflates and sinks into the sea, clearing the way for Ariel and Eric to live happily ever after.

*Beauty and the Beast* (1991) gives us a final battle that pits the faux Prince Charming, Gaston, against Beast, who leaps from one parapet to the next to escape his rival's bullets and blows. Beast has all but eluded and defeated Gaston, but he makes the near-fatal mistake of sparing his rival's life. Beast is not a beast, after all, though his animal instincts and vigor give him an advantage in the film's final standoff. He may vanquish Gaston, but salvation comes from Beauty, who restores Beast's health and lifts the curse cast on him.

Recent animated Disney films tell a different story. Ever since Always-brand feminine products made a video advertisement, "Always #LikeAGirl," in 2014, girls have begun to run like the wind in our media productions. Always did a takedown of the phrase "like a girl," revealing that the phrase was designed to humiliate or insult rather than to show approval or give praise. Running like a girl meant that you were not really running at all, just engaging in ungainly giraffe-like motion forward. After the video went viral, #LikeAGirl power runs became the fashion in Hollywood, with Elsa in *Frozen* and *Frozen II*, along with Moana in the 2016 animated film of that title, leading the pack.

*Frozen* and its sequel, *Frozen II*, mark a recalibration of the norms in the Disney Princess franchise. Here are films that earn the highest possible marks on the famous Bechdel test, with two named female leads who talk about many things besides men.[27] Anna and Elsa may still have royal blood (they also have the spaghetti-thin figures of Barbie dolls along with the spooky eyes of Bratz dolls), but even with their pinched waists, alabaster plastic skin, and ski-jump noses they are strong enough to scale mountains, race through snowdrifts, survive tidal waves, and, on another level, face up to the truth that their elders were driven by greed.

In *Frozen II*, the dam built by Anna and Elsa's grandfather on the land of Indigenous peoples turns out to be part of a colonial scheme rather than a vaunted act of altruism. In this brave new world of Disney heroines, Anna manages to engineer the destruction of a dam that would have spelled the doom of the Enchanted Forest, and Elsa makes a solo power run into tsunami-like waves to tame the rebellious Nokk (a supernatural water horse) that will carry her to the rivers of ice. "Kissing won't save the forest," Elsa tells us, gesturing to earlier films like *Snow White and the Seven Dwarfs* and *Beauty and the Beast* and reminding us that times have changed. "Can you see how determined she is!" my five-year-old granddaughter blurted out with glee when we were watching Elsa dive into tidal waves and smash ice floes.

Who could have imagined that Disney would halt the juggernaut of fairy tale–themed animated films to make a movie that turns to Polynesian creation myths as its foundational narrative? Were they listening to complaints about White Saviors and Eurocentric mythical imaginations? *Moana* (2016) opens with a scene of an Indigenous people's storytelling: a grandmother telling young children the story of Te Fiti's transformation. Te Fiti, once the god of creation, has turned into Te Kā, a demon of destruction, after the demigod Maui extracted her heart with his magical fishhook. It will be Moana's mission to return Te Fiti's heart and thereby save her island from ecological devastation and restore its natural beauty. Suddenly Disney princesses can embark on heroic quests and travel down paths different from the one that takes them to the happily-ever-after of matrimony.

"You're no one's hero," Moana, who gives as good as she gets, defiantly tells Maui, who has been boasting about being "a hero to all." "You stole Te Fiti's heart," she tells him. "You cursed the world!" she shouts at the muscle-bound demigod who sports animated tattoos on his chest. Although Moana eventually gets some help from Maui in her rescue mission, she single-handedly doubles down in her efforts to defeat Te Kā and "save the world." Disney's effort to create a new type of heroine has met with as much controversy as praise. How dare a corporation claim Indigenous mythology as its property and masquerade its monetization of Polynesian traditions as cultural preservation? Disney colonized not only the mythology of the Pacific Islanders, but also its fabrics and its rituals, reducing the multivocal mythical universe of Pacific Islanders to a single, homogenized story branded as its own. The two codirectors of the film are even woven into the film on the fabric of a tapa, or barkcloth, that bears their images, as if to insert and solidify their ownership of the story with a visual signature and prop. Protests that accused Disney of "brownface" cultural appropriation in a range of costumes and pajamas were taken seriously and led to recalls of merchandise.[28]

Moana's quest resembles in some ways the journeys of Campbell's heroes, but with a crucial difference. Unlike Maui, who uses a magical fishhook that doubles as weapon and instrument of transformation (he is also a trickster), Moana is committed to matters of the heart that lead to healing, beauty, and ecological balance. Driven by compassion for her people and for the natural world, she is also propelled by natural curiosity (not greed and conquest) about the world beyond her reef and its wonders. Maui may once have been the hero to all—after all, he is the demigod credited with bringing fire to humans and pulling up the island with his fishhook—but his vanity, egotism, and lack of care have turned him into something of an oaf, charming but unattractively arrogant. Moana may still be a Disney princess—"If you wear a dress and have an animal sidekick, you're a princess," Maui jeers—but she has taken cues from the folkloric and mythical heroines who came before her as well as the heroes from times past. She power-swims like Elsa and learns to sail, yet preserves a sense of obligation to her people and an adventurous desire to escape the constraints of the domestic world.

Princesses may be fast disappearing from the Disney repertoire, but the resurgence of fairy tales in films oriented to young adult audiences has given us a new type of heroine, a warrior woman who has modeled herself on the hero archetype. Gone are the sleeping beauties, nice and narcotized, passively awaiting liberation and the arrival of a prince. Instead we may have a new archetypal heroine, shooting 'em up, bobbing and weaving, or, like Rey in *The Force Awakens*, wielding a light saber. But with a twist. These warrior women are also caring and compassionate, in touch with the natural world as well as with those who inhabit it.

Take Rupert Sanders's *Snow White and the Huntsman* (2012), in which the title figure, played by Kristen Stewart, is nothing like the charmingly goofy princess of Disney's live-action *Enchanted* or the spunky yet vulnerable Snow White in ABC's series *Once upon a Time*. This Snow White becomes a "pure and innocent" warrior princess, an angelic savior who channels Joan of Arc and Tolkien's Aragorn, as well as the four Pevensie siblings from C. S. Lewis's *The Chronicles of Narnia*, to save the kingdom of her late father (stabbed to death by the queen on their wedding night). When we first see her (as a child), she has rescued an injured bird and plans to help it heal. And when we last see her, she conquers a massive monster with pity.

In *Snow White and the Huntsman*, everyone is armed, and swords, scimitars, axes, snares, and shields feature as prominently in this film as they do in the Middle Earth of *The Hobbit*. Romance is edged out by the racing energy of horses speeding through dramatic landscapes and by expertly choreographed combat scenes. This is a Snow White designed to appeal to those who crave action in their entertainments.

Do we risk installing a disturbing new archetype of female heroism, one that emulates the muscle and agility of classic male heroes? When we look at Hollywood's refashioning of fairy-tale heroines in films ranging from *Hansel and Gretel: Witch Hunters* (2013) to *Maleficent* (2014), the slide from one extreme to another becomes evident. Suddenly the comatose beauty turns into a glamorous mutineer with an impressive arsenal of weapons at her disposal.

*Snow White and the Huntsman* takes us into a wilderness of environmental depredations and dynastic conflict. Charlize Theron's fair-haired wicked queen presides over subjects with ravaged faces in landscapes that resemble toxic oil spills; in her shape-shifting magic, she reconstitutes herself at one point from what looks like a flock of crows caught in an oil slick. Her rule has no doubt created the viscous black horrors that Snow White encounters in the denuded woods to which she flees. The film's raven-haired heroine, by contrast to the queen, soothes savage beasts with her compassionate face and, as a digitally miniaturized Bob Hoskins, playing one of the seven dwarfs, proclaims: "She will heal the land." Snow White is no passive, guiltless damsel. Her exquisite beauty, combined with charismatic leadership, enables her to defeat the evil queen and redeem the desolate landscape of the kingdom and its ailing inhabitants.

## Savvy Saviors: Hunger Games and Golden Compasses

Hollywood demands much of its new heroines (and the actresses who play them), requiring heavy lifting in the form of contoured features, sculpted bodies, and a disposition that displays courage without showing it off. If any heroine has it all, it is Katniss Everdeen in the *Hunger Games* films, a set of movies based on Suzanne Collins's bestselling trilogy of tales about a postindustrial, postapocalyptic wasteland that requires its inhabitants to revert to hunter-gatherer practices in order to survive. Collins, who began her career writing children's television shows, was bold enough to invent a new heroine, one that was never meant to exist. Living in the country of Panem, which, despite its name alluding to the Latin word for bread, is anything but bountiful, Katniss is another emaciated trickster, little more than "skin and bones."[29] To survive, she uses her bow and arrows, hunting game to support her family in ways that suggest some kind of kinship with Artemis, goddess of archery and the hunt.

Katniss not only possesses contraband weapons but, in true trickster fashion, is also a trespasser and poacher. In order to reach hunting territory with sufficient game, she must become a boundary-crosser, traversing a "high chain-link fence topped with barbed-wire loop," which is electrified for a good part of the day as a deterrent to poachers. The so-called Peacekeepers (or security forces) cannot outwit Katniss, whose sharp ears detect exactly when the electricity is turned off and who can find a loose stretch in the fence and surreptitiously slide under it. While training with Peeta, the other Tribute from Panem chosen by lottery to play in deadly games with only one survivor, Katniss learns how to build snares that will leave human competitors dangling and to camouflage herself with mud, clay, vines, and leaves. A master of ruses and stratagems, she wins the Hunger Games by outwitting not only her twenty-two opponents but also the Ministry itself.

Like Gretel, Pippi Longstocking, and Lisbeth Salander before her, Katniss gorges on rich food, yet her hunger never ceases. "I'm starving," she says, right after eating prodigious amounts of "goose liver and puffy bread." At one of the banquets, she "shovels" lamb stew into her mouth and takes big gulps of orange juice. At another she eats herself sick in an orgy of dining comparable to Hansel and Gretel's feast outside and inside the witch's house. Her fantasies about food resemble the inventories we find in both the Grimms' fairy tale and Salander's grocery lists: "The chicken in creamy orange sauce. The cakes and pudding. Bread with butter. Noodles in green sauce. The lamb and dried plum stew." Katniss admits to eating that stew "by the bucketful," even though "it doesn't show," in ways that point to classic bulimic behaviors. The emphasis on orality is not at all unusual, given the sociocultural climate of Panem, but it is a reminder of how the appetites of male tricksters are transformed and remade in their female counterparts, turning into disorders rather than signs of vitality. Katniss, like Gretel, moves from the primary orality manifested in a country where there are only two options: the famine conditions of the district in which she lives or the decadent feasts of the ruling class, who prove to be true bulimics, constantly vomiting in order to return to the trough with appetite renewed.

The presence of mockingjays reminds us that orality yields at times, even in Panem, to aurality. Mockingjays, we learn, are a hybrid of female mockingbirds and male jabberjays, genetically altered birds bred to memorize human conversations. Created by pure accident, mockingjays can replicate both human voices and bird whistles. They possess the gift of mimicking human songs: "And they could recreate songs. Not just a few notes, but whole songs with multiple verses." These magical avian creatures become an emblem of revolutionary possibility and of civic solidarity. But beyond that, they also keep poetry alive in Panem. Suzanne Collins described them as zoological doubles of Katniss:

> So here we have her arriving in the arena in the first book, not only equipped as someone who can keep herself alive in this environment—and then once she gets the bow and arrows, can be lethal—but she's also somebody who already thinks outside the box because they just haven't been paying attention to District 12. So in that way, too, Katniss is the mockingjay. She is the thing that should never have been created, that the Capitol never intended to happen. In the same way they just let the jabberjays go and thought, "We don't have to worry about them," they thought, "We don't have to worry about District 12." And this new creature evolved, which is the mockingjay, which is Katniss.[30]

Suzanne Collins, then, invented a heroine who "should never have been created," according to those in authority. She is sui generis, and although she did not appear out of thin air, she evolved in unexpected ways, suddenly emerging out of obscurity into celebrity through the Hunger Games.

Katniss has inherited the gift of song from her father. In response to the request of a fellow combatant, dying on the forest floor, Katniss produces a "mountain air," and, "almost eerily," the mockingjays take up the song. In a rare moment of utopian plenitude during the Hunger Games, Katniss sings a few notes from Rue's song and listens as the mockingjays repeat the melody: "Then the whole world comes alive with the sound." The "lovely, unearthly harmony" produced by the birds leads Katniss, "mesmerized by the beauty of the song," to close her eyes and listen. It will be her task not only to win the Hunger Games but also to restore beauty and civility to a land devastated by both natural disasters and human failures, a land that has created the Avox, a person whose tongue has been cut and who can no longer make sounds or speak. Collins, who alludes frequently to the ancient world with names (Seneca and Caesar) and with rituals (gladiatorial games and annual tributes), was no doubt familiar with the horrors of Philomela's punishment for speaking out.

Suzanne Collins's Katniss combines Lisbeth's survival skills with a passionate social mission, but she lacks the hipster sexual confidence and self-consciousness of her older Swedish counterpart. As many commentators have pointed out, she is modeled on Artemis, goddess of the hunt, carrying the same silver bow and arrows. Like the goddess, she too is protector of the young and volunteers to take her sister's place when her name is chosen at the Reaping. Virginal and unaware of her own sexual allure, she has been described as that "rare thing" in pop culture: "a complex female character with courage, brains and a quest of her own."[31] Lisbeth's emotional deficits and surplus sexual energy are balanced by Katniss's compassionate intensity and sexual innocence.

Like Gretel's exercises in dissimulation, Katniss's snares, ruses, and strategies lead her to poetry, to a display of how the melodious consolations of imagination are not imaginary consolations. Throughout the games, we learn about the value of wits—the "wits to survive"—as well as about the importance of "outsmarting" others, remaining nimble and agile in order to defeat those with superior physical strength. Peeta, too, knows how to "spin out lies," and the paired allies use their intelligence wisely to defeat the twenty-two other Tributes. More important, Katniss outfoxes not just the other Tributes but even the Gamemakers, and ultimately the Capitol. She will become not only a survivor but also, in the sequels to *The Hunger Games*, a mockingjay, a symbol of revolutionary hope and an agent of rebellion and change.

The authors of books for young audiences are uncannily inventive when it comes to constructing new forms of female heroism. Sometimes it seems as if they are tapping into a rich vein of boldness and defiance in their own dispositions, willing to accept the label of YA author even when they are taking on projects as ambitious as, say, rewriting Milton's *Paradise Lost*. That's the challenge that Philip Pullman had in mind when he set out to reimagine Genesis and Milton's version of the Fall in the trilogy *His Dark Materials* (1995–2000). The first installment was a book that Hollywood eagerly snapped up and turned into a 2007 film starring Dakota Blue Richards, Daniel Craig, and Nicole Kidman. The BBC made a second, less successful, run on the material with a series made in 2020.

"There are some themes, some subjects, too large for adult fiction; they can only be dealt with adequately in a children's book," Pullman observed in his acceptance speech for the Carnegie Medal.[32] Rewriting Genesis may be one of those projects, and child readers, unschooled in theological matters, are likely to be less resistant to the idea of a new Eve, a heroine who leads the way to a form of redemption that replaces religious orthodoxies with secular humanism. They are also less likely to be shocked by a work that sees God as a tyrant to be killed off, the Church as an instrument of persecution, and a heroine whose mission it is to defeat both. Curiosity, knowledge, kindness, and tolerance supplant outdated belief systems. And children, Pullman correctly intuited, are less interested in "Thou shalt not" than in "Once upon a time," preferring the tug of story to the authority of commandments.

Rewriting the Fall as an emancipatory moment in the history of the human race, Pullman gives us a heroine who is a double of Eve in her capacious curiosity and who is also forever pushing at boundaries and crossing them, challenging the rigid thinking of the adults around her. Lyra Belacqua, or Lyra Silvertongue, has a name that binds her with both deception and art—she is a chronic liar, a consummate storyteller, and her narrative art produces "a stream of pleasure rising upwards in her breast like the bubbles in champagne." She may lack the lyre as musical instrument, but she can produce poetry as reader and exegete when she wields the truth-seeking instrument known as the alethiometer, a device that enables her to discover the path to true heroism:

> The one thing that drew [Lyra] out of her boredom and irritation was the alethiometer. She read it every day, sometimes with Farder Coram and sometimes on her own, and she found that she could sink more and more readily into the calm state in which the symbol meanings clarified themselves, and those great mountain ranges touched by sunlight emerged into vision.[33]

For Pullman, wisdom is the *summum bonum*, and it comes less from the Good Book than from reading books of every kind. That view, of course, risks turning writers into gods, and Pullman concedes as much when he tells us, on his website, that he is "a strong believer in the tyranny, the dictatorship, the absolute authority of the writer."[34]

Lyra does not partake of the gastronomical excesses found in *The Hunger Games* and in *The Girl with the Dragon Tattoo*. Still, she shapeshifts in audacious ways, trying out new identities to protect herself and also for the sheer love of invention and experimenting with new personalities. In Bolvangar, she is Lizzie Brookes and pretends to be meek and stupid; in the Land of the Dead she becomes the child of a duke and duchess; and at one point she aligns herself with that "fabulous monster" that Lewis Carroll called Alice. And the author who created her makes her, of course, a double of Eve. Joining the ranks of postmodern adolescent girl tricksters, she must struggle to survive in a world of cruelly ambitious parents who fail to protect her. At the same time, she undertakes an epic redemptive journey that transforms her into a savior figure who lays the foundations for nothing less than a new social and spiritual order. Does Pullman dare to install a rival to Christianity, with a savior who now enshrines knowledge as sacred and allows it to guide us, with free choice as the default setting? Who but Eve, who instinctively took a bite of the apple, rules in this new Republic of Heaven? "Religion begins in story," Pullman once declared, and this is unequivocally not the same old story.

"I write almost always in the third person, and I don't think the narrator is male or female anyway. They're both, and young and old, and wise and silly, and skeptical and credulous, and innocent and experienced, all at once. Narrators are not even human—they're sprites."[35] Pullman may have been speaking tongue in cheek, but he raises, once again, a question that cannot but haunt those who look at our entertainments—the books and films that have captured the popular imagination—and wonder whether authors and directors are picking up disturbances in the airwaves or capturing their own fantasies and anxieties, or some strange mix of the two.

The issue of gender as nonbinary and fluid, as raised by Pullman, becomes even more complicated when we consider how gender-bending has turned mainstream in ways that challenge us to turn from the old-fashioned binary models like Campbell's to new archetypal figures that are androgynous and gender queer, blurring boundaries and confounding the distinctions we once made. Lisbeth Salander, Katniss Everdeen, and Lyra Belacqua mark a rupture in our understanding of what it means to be a heroine by embracing features traditionally assigned to the mythical hero and trickster. They also offer a final repudiation of Campbell's notion of heroines as self-contained women who are there to reproduce and replicate, and an answer to his question about the new models available in a world that has offered women the opportunity to enter the labor force. Unlike Scheherazade and Bluebeard's wife, these women are all experts at getting out of the house. The female trickster has become a smart, sassy feminista and more, charged with sending new messages via literary and cinematic media about women's rejection of victimization, physical weakness, and household drudgery.[36] Girl tricksters in particular seem consistently united in their double mission of remaking the world even as they survive adversity.[37] Justice becomes their consuming passion, though they retain many of the appetites of male tricksters.

Does the arc that takes us from Scheherazade to Lisbeth Salander mark progress? Many in the parade of new heroines in our popular entertainments do nothing but mimic the male action hero.[38] Lisbeth Salander is represented as both masculine (or boyish) and muscular.[39] Her tattoos, her lovemaking (she initiates and takes control), her technological skills, her decisive actions, and even her way of looking at people deviate sharply from feminine forms of self-representation and behavior. Is Salander just a male fantasy about a sylphlike woman who takes charge?[40] Self-contained and operating comfortably as an "independent contractor," she has been conditioned by her traumatic childhood as well as by her genetic makeup to act more like a man than a woman, thereby operating less as a reformer than as a figure who perpetuates cultural, social, and political norms. Is Stieg Larsson unable to divorce himself from the discourses that he is aiming to critique? Ironically, the androgynous nature of girl tricksters enables male cross-identification, thus further diluting the feminist message in the eyes of some critics.

If the male trickster occasionally oscillates between female and male, eventually fixing on his own male sexual role and learning to size up his environment, the female trickster has developed a more fluid notion of gender identity and has embraced androgyny in her postmodern incarnations. Her double-faced nature—incarnating paradox, exploiting contradictions, and enacting dualities—enables her to straddle the gender line and to draw on her resilience in the quest for fairness and social justice.

Still, the future of the female trickster, as envisioned by writers and filmmakers who invented warrior heroines in the struggle for social justice, is by no means secure. And the story of Pygmalion, who was so disgusted by the licentious behavior of the Cypriot women that he lost interest in them and fell in love with a statue that he sculpted from ivory, reminds us that creative impulses are not always fueled by the best of intentions. Is it possible that some of the crusaders, avengers, and saviors in our entertainments today may turn, like Frankenstein, on their creators in unexpected ways, not so much to engineer a happy ending for themselves as to use their wits and cunning in the service of newfound ambitions that are more like arrogant power grabs than altruistic actions?

## Reinventing Eve

What is in the future of the female trickster, and how will she evolve? Does she run the risk of turning into an antiheroine, an outlaw force that turns toxic, using her brainpower to take charge and undermine in dark, devious ways? Now that heroines have found their way into new arenas of action, will villainy, too, assume new faces and features? In Alex Garland's *Ex Machina* (2014), a robot named Ava (gesturing in gender-fluid ways to both Adam and Eve) becomes a triumphant survivor who writes a new script in a posthuman world, where she has been constructed as the perfect woman. The film's title elides the "deus" in the phrase "deus ex machina," reminding us that the god who makes a stagey last-minute arrival in dramatic productions may be absent from the happily-ever-after engineered in this particular story.

The film's title also hints at a new order of beings: cyborgs, automata, and robots that may be embodiments of men or women but that are also, as machines, gender neutral even if they have reproductive organs modeled on those of humans. The term "robot" was coined in Karel Čapek's 1920 play *RUR* (an acronym for Rossum's Universal Robots). The Czech word *robota* means "forced labor," and the robots in Čapek's work, slaves made from artificial flesh and blood, rebel against their makers and destroy them. Automata have been around for centuries, first as amusing toys—dancing ladies, clockwork flutists, Vaucanson's Duck, and a chess-playing Mechanical Turk. These seemingly frivolous contraptions quickly turned sinister as they became more sophisticated, for how long would it be before machines replicated human behavior and took over? The German filmmaker Fritz Lang had already dramatized that anxiety in his 1927 film *Metropolis*, in which a robot named Maria incites workers to rebel against a factory owner and unleash the power of natural forces to destroy those who exploit their labor. How close are we coming to a Technological Singularity, an intelligence explosion in which machines build more powerful versions of their own capacities and escape our control?

*Ex Machina* takes its cue from the seductive female automata found in literary works ranging from E. T. A. Hoffmann's "The Sandman" (1816)—the inspiration for Freud's 1919 essay on the uncanny—to Auguste Villiers de l'Isle-Adam's title figure in his novel *L'Ève future*. In Alex Garland's film, Caleb, a low-level coder, wins a contest run by the head of the company that employs him. The company founder, Nathan (a name echoing Nathaniel, the protagonist of Hoffmann's story), has created, among other things, a search engine called Blue Book (that name evokes both the designation for notes of Ludwig Wittgenstein's lectures dictated in the 1930s as well as the fairy tale "Bluebeard"). Caleb flies to Nathan's retreat, situated in a remote, Edenic setting, where the founder of Blue Book is working on an artificial-intelligence project for which he has recruited Caleb to measure his success in creating a robot that will pass the Turing test (a challenge designed by the father of computer science to determine whether a machine exhibits intelligent behavior indistinguishable from that of a human). Nathan has engaged Caleb for his version of the challenge: "The real test is to show you that she is a robot and then see if you still *feel* she has consciousness."

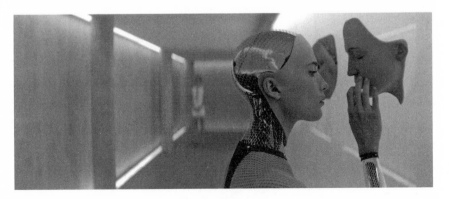

*Ex Machina*, 2014
*Courtesy of Photofest*

In an ironic twist, Nathan's genius has been to create a machine capable of outwitting not just Caleb but also its creator, for Ava has become a being with "self-awareness, imagination, manipulation, sexuality, empathy." What does Ava do after she has killed her creator but don skin and outer garments, marking her emergence into consciousness, even as her surface appearance of air muscles and electroactive polymers conceals technological circuitry. And where do we last see Ava, after she has escaped confinement and entered the human world? Where else but at an urban crossroads, as a professional woman dressed flawlessly and ready to take on the corporate world. She becomes a female incarnation of Hermes, god of merchants and thieves, lord of the crossroads. Ava's intelligence is no longer artificial but rather very real. A cyborg who is also something of a cipher, we can still bet that this new twenty-first-century heroine is unlikely to worry about anyone's survival but her own. And her social mission will most likely be limited to destroying those who try to control her circuitry. Ava is the new antiheroine, there to remind us that the heroine of the future may not possess the resilience, compassion, and resourcefulness that we have seen in heroines from times past.[41]

Films may be our new folklore, and, given our current easy access to streaming shows, they feel at times like storytelling machines that we turn on with the flick of a switch. *Ex Machina* takes up cultural anxieties and desires and gets us talking about things that remove us from our comfort zones. In the safe space of once-upon-a-time-in-Hollywood and within the domain of the symbolic, we can face down the specters that haunt us. Disturbing metaphors are always easier to process than disturbing realities, and they lower our inhibitions, allowing us to engage our critical faculties in ways that often do not happen when we encounter trauma in real life.

"He gave us language we didn't know we lacked." *New York Times* cultural critic Wesley Morris makes that pronouncement in an interview with Jordan Peele, director of *Get Out* (2017).[42] Peele's film seems an unlikely successor to *Ex Machina* as a refashioning of the Bluebeard story. But once Chris, a Black photographer who has traveled with his white girlfriend, Rose, to meet the parents, discovers a stash of photographs in the closet of a bedroom, all bets are off. Rose has been dating a succession of Black men, taking selfies with them that she then stores in a space with a chilling resemblance to Bluebeard's forbidden chamber. The men are all destined to undergo surgery so that their bodies can be used to provide white auction winners, all members of a cult called The Order of the Coagula, with spare parts for their own deficient bodies. "You won't be gone, not completely," a blind art dealer, a man who craves Chris's power of vision, intones. "A sliver of you will still be in there somewhere. Limited consciousness. You'll be able to see and hear, but what your body is doing—your existence—will be as a passenger."

What better metaphor than that for capturing W. E. B. Du Bois's concept of double consciousness? It works as powerfully as "the Sunken Place," that space into which Chris descends when he is hypnotized by Rose's mother and finds himself trapped at a site of physical and mental paralysis, a form of imprisonment that makes it impossible to be seen and heard. All the while, he remains part of a script written by white hosts. At the Armitage home, the auction of a Black man follows that script in a scene that reenacts the grotesqueries of the past but also functions as a wake-up call showing that the "long ago" is still in the "here and now." Suddenly we see the unthinkable in a vivid tableau of what it means to be a Black person in an America that once prided itself on becoming "post-racial."

"While I was having fun writing this mischievous popcorn film there were real black people who were being abducted and put into dark holes, and the worst part of it is we don't think about them," Jordan Peele said in the interview with Wesley Morris. Inspired by a range of films in the horror genre, from *The Amityville Horror* to *Rosemary's Baby*, Peele also drew on a strong folkloric tradition in which a rich, powerful figure lures an unknowing partner into a marriage doomed to end badly. His recycling of the Bluebeard fairy tale reveals that one swift turn of the kaleidoscope can reconfigure the tropes of the story and also lead to a role reversal that moves Bluebeard's wife into a position of privilege, while her husband becomes the target of bodily harm. *Get Out* is a reminder of just how adaptable and malleable the folk tradition is and that it has always figured powerfully as a tool for the socially and politically marginalized, those whose physical labor and whose bodies have been the target of exploitation and abuse. At the same time, the film reveals what fairy tales do supremely well, finding a way to create attachment and solidarity by uncovering pain and collective trauma. The big surprise of *Get Out*, according to Wesley Morris, is that Peele made "a nightmare about white evil that doubles as a fairy tale about black unity, black love, and black rescue." Fairy tales may seem to operate in some form of cultural-repetition compulsion, but in fact that is only because we continue to need stories that expose wrongdoing, reveal ways to survive, and point the way to justice. Is it coincidental that it took a Black director to resurrect "Bluebeard" and turn the tables in the story? Peele's connection to the folk tradition, to a story that Richard Wright describes reading in moving terms in his novel *Black Boy*, reveals just how powerfully oral traditions, whether in the form of gossip, news, or stories, continue to shape our understanding of escaping subordination and finding justice.

# LIFT-OFF

*All I can tell you about mythology is what men
have said and have experienced and now women
have to tell us from their point of view what the
possibilities of the feminine future are. And it
is a future—it's as though the lift-off has taken
place, it really has, there's no doubt about it.*

—JOSEPH CAMPBELL, *Goddesses*

CONSIDER CASSANDRA. Her name has become code for lack of credibility, and yet she had a perfect track record of accurate predictions. Why, when we hear the name Cassandra today, do we think madwoman rather than seer? There are many accounts of how Cassandra acquired her powers. Aeschylus tells us that Apollo promised her the gift of forecasting the future in exchange for sexual favors, but after receiving that power, the daughter of Priam and Hecuba went back on her word. Apollo could not retract his gift, and he spit in Cassandra's mouth, cursing her by declaring that, henceforth, no one would believe her prophecies. Other sources tell us that Cassandra never broke any promises. Apollo simply granted her special powers as a lure and then, in a rage when she refused his advances, he turned her gift into a curse. Here is the Latin author Hyginus in his *Fabulae*: "Cassandra is said to have fallen asleep.... When Apollo wished to embrace her, she did not afford the opportunity of her body. On account of that, when she prophesied true things, she was not believed."[1] Which is the true story?

Beautiful and true as Cassandra is ("She is the hope of many suitors," Ovid tells us), she is universally seen as deranged, a pathological liar who cannot stop herself from spreading bad news. No one believes her when she reveals that the abduction of Helen will lead to the Trojan War, nor when she warns her compatriots about the Greeks concealed inside the Trojan Horse or about the fall of Troy. At the end of the war, she clings to a statue of Athena for safety, but is brutally raped by Ajax, "the Lesser." Agamemnon takes her back with him as a concubine to Mycenae, where she is struck a death blow by Clytemnestra and Aegisthus. But, in this case, there is payback, and it comes in the form of trouble for the Greeks, with deadly storms unleashed by Poseidon at the behest of Athena, outraged by Ajax's rape of a woman seeking her protection.

Cassandra's story can be seen as part of what Rebecca Solnit calls a pattern of failing to believe women's testimony. When the Trojan princess refuses to dally with Apollo, her words are, from then on, discredited. And the discrediting does not just apply to anything she might say about

Tondo of a red-figure kylix, *Ajax Taking Cassandra,* c. 435 BCE

Apollo. Instead it takes over her entire identity, invalidating everything she says. "The idea that loss of credibility is tied to asserting rights over your own body was there all along," Solnit adds.[2] Cassandra's backstory comes to us in bits and pieces from authorities who, to a man (and they are all men), emphasize only her tragic lack of credibility. But once we piece together the information about the curse placed on her and the violence to which she was subjected, a new narrative emerges, one told from a woman's point of view. And suddenly we have lift-off. Cassandra has a future, not as a raving lunatic but as a woman who preserves her dignity and integrity despite assaults on her body and attacks on her character.

"Who feels sorry for a creature who has snakes for hair, and turns innocent men to stone?" the novelist Natalie Haynes asks.[3] Medusa gets no respect, and who can hear her name without picturing those hissing snakes in place of hair, a horror to behold? And when we recall that the father of psychoanalysis equated the face of Medusa with the fear of castration, another layer of revulsion is added to the image. Medusa's face exemplifies apotropaic magic, a charged symbolic image (like the evil eye) designed as a weapon to ward off harm. Medusa petrifies with her gaze, and so it is hard to imagine why Pindar would write about a "fair-cheeked Medusa." But in fact, when we turn, again, to Ovid, we discover that Medusa was once a fair maiden of exquisite beauty. She was, in other words, not born that way. The only mortal of the three Gorgons, she is said to have been seduced, violated, ravished, or raped (depending on which translation you read) by the sea god Poseidon in the temple of Athena. Poseidon was let off the hook, but Medusa was punished for her damaging encounter with a god when Athena turned her into a monster, transforming her beautiful locks into a tangle of venomous snakes.

In common parlance today, Medusa's name is synonymous with monster. But Dante, Shakespeare, Shelley, and other writers have all invoked her name in poems that celebrate the paradoxical logic of her image as capturing monstrosity and beauty, threat and defense, toxin and remedy. And feminists have reclaimed her, rehabilitating her as a figure who is not all "deadly," but beautiful. "She's laughing," Hélène Cixous tells us in an essay that urges women to assert their identity through writing.[4]

Perseus, the mortal who decapitates Medusa, becomes a shining hero. He is almost always depicted, most notably in the statue made by Benvenuto Cellini in 1554, as a modest, invincible, exalted figure. It is he who weaponizes the head with its dreadful locks, using it to vanquish his enemies, and, in a final stroke of irony, presenting it to Athena, the goddess who cursed Medusa, so that she can use it to ward off her foes. Medusa is transformed, irreversibly, from a beautiful woman desired by a god into an image of fright, with looks that can now kill.

If looks can kill, they are damaging not just to the beholder but also to the face of beauty itself. Who can fail to think in this context of the face that launched a thousand ships? "Grows up to be a real man-killer": that's how Stephen Fry describes Helen of Troy in his retelling of stories about heroes in Greek myths. A closer look at the life story of the most

Caravaggio, *Medusa*, 1595

beautiful woman in the world reveals a more complex narrative. Helen, as the daughter of Zeus and Leda, is the product of what could most accurately be described as a rape. As a girl (she is seven in one account, ten in another), she is kidnapped by Theseus and his brother Pirithous, who intend to keep her prisoner until she is old enough to marry. Rescued by the Dioscuri (Castor and Pollux), she is then courted by many suitors, with Menelaus emerging victorious. Her suitors are required to pledge military support to Menelaus, should Helen ever be abducted. Then comes the seduction, elopement, or abduction (depending on the source you read) by Paris after the beauty contest staged with Hera, Aphrodite, and Athena, in which Aphrodite promises to give Paris the most beautiful woman in the world. Helen is one of the few to survive the Trojan War, and she returns home with Menelaus, who plans, at first, to punish his "unfaithful" wife for her abduction but then, taking one look

Francesco Primaticcio, *The Rape of Helen*, c. 1535

at her, falls back under her spell. Did Helen bewitch Menelaus when she was repossessed by him or was she always loyal to the Greeks? The ancient sources give us conflicting accounts, and in his dramatic poem *Faust*, Goethe tells us that Helen is "much admired and much reviled."[5]

Beauty, the one attribute that could guarantee women a happily-ever-after in times past, was paradoxically also what turned you into a target for both gods and goddesses, not to mention mortal men. Psyche, beloved for her beauty and kindness, does not fare well at the hands of Venus, who is enraged by reports that the girl looks like she could be her daughter and that she is her rival in beauty. Radiant Andromeda is chained to a rock to divert a sea monster sent by Poseidon, all because Cassiopeia bragged about her daughter's beauty. Recall Athena's anger at the bewitching beauty of Medusa's ringlets. And then we have Europa, Io, Leda, Callisto, Persephone, Philomela, and so on—alluring, glamorous women and all seduced, abducted, and raped, again depending on the teller. There are many versions of each of these stories, ranging from what can be found in ancient Greek sources to compendia of classical mythology put together by Edward Bulwer-Lytton, Robert Graves, Edith Hamilton, or Ingri and Edgar d'Aulaire.

In a TED talk of 2009, Chimamanda Ngozi Adichie spoke about the danger of reductive thinking and the perils of telling a "single story."[6] When told once as a child that a family was "poor," Adichie imagined a joyless, bleak day-to-day struggle, full of gloom, without any redemptive moments at all. A beautiful basket woven by a member of that "poor" family shattered her preconceived notion of their life. Poverty, she realized, did not preclude creativity, beauty, pleasure, and dignity. "When we reject the single story," the Nigerian writer went on to say, "we regain a kind of paradise." Single stories, she added, create stereotypes, "and the problem with stereotypes is not that they are untrue, but that they are incomplete." As I listened to Adichie speak, I was reminded of how the hero with a thousand faces has been tragically reduced to a stereotype, one that is not just incomplete but, in a sense, also untrue, for it often tells only a small part of a story, just half the story, and sometimes even less than that.

The heroines with a thousand and one faces in this volume reveal new sides to old stories. The faces of these women are malleable and mutable, resisting all efforts to freeze their features and to capture one representative expression. No single heroine dominates or endures. Instead heroines keep evolving, challenging authority and legitimacy, rebelling, resisting, and demanding makeovers. Traditional hierarchies of heroism are forever being reshuffled and rearranged as cultural values shift and are rebalanced. This holds true for both heroes and heroines. They reinvent themselves ad infinitum, just as the number 1,001 in Arabic suggests.

Once we begin to look at the classic stories told and retold in our culture and experience them from the perspective of figures on the sidelines—slaves, concubines, sacrificial lambs, misfits, all those on the losing side of history—we are suddenly cut loose from the obligation to admire, worship, and venerate. Instead, we become radically inventive, seeing things differently and finding new ways of reading the stories and histories in which they appear.

We are told that the Trojan War began with a beauty contest and the seduction/abduction of a women hailed as the fairest of them all, who was then blamed for the devastating damage and loss of life in the conflict between the Greeks and Trojans. When we learn that there may be another side to that story and realize that a noncanonical account of the Trojan War has Helen drugged, while another has her exiled in Egypt, faithful to Menelaus, and that she never engineered the beauty contest or the kidnapping, we are less willing to shoulder her with responsibility for the hostilities, and we suddenly see her as another victim of war. Never mind that the ambitious Greeks, with their aspirations for building an empire, looted Troy, all the while claiming that they were going to war to salvage their honor. In a similar vein, recall how Charles Dickens found in the sexual assault of a woman (Madame de Farge's sister, raped by an aristocrat) the secret cause of the French Revolution. In some perverse way, the effects of war (sexual violence) became the casus belli.[7]

I want to conclude this volume with a meditation on unsung heroines, not just the vilified and marginalized women in accounts of war, but the real-life women who found ways to tend to the wounds of war, blending passion and compassion even when aware that their work was unlikely to earn the glory and immortality won by military heroes. My aim is not to perpetuate standard-issue platitudes that frame care and comfort as natural to women and see aggression and anger as permanent features of the male psyche. Rather, I want to provide some examples of how women have found ways to cope in times of crisis and also to offer, despite what must have felt like the hopelessness of their ventures, some measure of resistance to the uncontrolled brutality of war.

Let me return to the Trojan War. Readers of this volume will have quickly registered that it loomed large in my mind while writing this book, for the behavior of gods and men in classical antiquity is exactly what led me to wonder about their "heroism." How does the Trojan War begin? Before the Greeks set sail, they are obliged to appease Artemis with a sacrifice, and who else but a virgin to placate the goddess? Agamemnon's sacrifice of Iphigenia leads to a cascading series of murders, from Clytemnestra's killing of her husband to the slaughter of Cassandra. How does the war end? What else but another virgin sacrifice. This time Polyxena, daughter of Hecuba and Priam, is the designated victim, and she declares herself willing to die rather than to live on as a slave. Astyanax, the son of Hector, is thrown from the walls of Troy for fear that the child will grow up, avenge his father, and rebuild Troy. The body count climbs, and suddenly the Greek victory becomes a hollow one, its heroes anything but heroic.

Who wins a war? The side capable of inflicting the highest number of injuries—injuries that turn bodies into casualties of war—emerges victorious. There are always the warriors but, in the midst of combat and conflict, there are also those who nurse the injured. You would expect to find women among them in the Trojan War, but instances of healing in *The Iliad* are largely limited to men tending to battle injuries. We discover that Achilles has learned the art of medicine from Chiron, the best of the centaurs. We watch Patroclus treat Eurypylus, who in turn goes to the aid of Ajax the Great when he is injured in combat. We learn about Machaon, son of Asclepius, who heals Menelaus, hit by an arrow. But we also discover that Achilles, despite his medical knowledge, "has no care, no pity for our Achaeans."

When I looked for curious, caring women in *The Iliad*, I could not find them. But the absence of evidence, I quickly realized, is not necessarily the evidence of absence. "I liked Machaon," Briseis tells us in Pat Barker's *The Silence of the Girls*. And why does she find the Greek healer who fights in the Trojan War appealing? Because she learns from him how to minister to the wounded. She remembers days spent in tents for the wounded as an oddly "happy time." "But the fact is, I loved the work. I loved everything about it. . . . I lost myself in that work—and I found myself too. I was learning so much from Ritsa, but also from Machaon who . . . was generous with his time. I really started to think: *I can do this.*" Barker may have made this up, and she may be buying into the myth of what Diane Purkiss has called the feminist fantasy of dissident women as healers, but her account conforms almost exactly to the sentiments expressed by war nurses who tended the injured in later centuries.[8]

"That story." That is the refrain of Anne Sexton's retelling of "Cinderella" in *Transformations*, the volume of poetry that rewrote the Brothers Grimm. Like Sexton, artists and writers reach into the past, revising and reenvisioning but, at times, also inventing rather than reinventing. In recent years, we have learned that some of the first artmakers were women.

We do not know exactly who painted the aurochs, horses, deer, and woolly mammoths on the walls of caves in France, Argentina, Africa, and Borneo, but a new study suggests that nearly three-quarters of the famous hand stencils and handprints were made by women. Working in a variety of media, with images when there were no words, with stitches when there were no pens, with tapestries when there was no parchment, women told stories, even when speaking out came with high risk. Theirs are the voices I have tried to capture in this book, and they continue to speak to us today, reminding us that silence is rarely golden, that curiosity kept the cat alive, and that from caring comes courage.

As I began to explore the lives of the authors discussed in earlier chapters ("Add more context!" my editor urged), it dawned on me that living through a war was not at all unusual, serving as a rule rather than an exception. Writing during a pandemic led me to pay more attention to letters and diary entries drafted during times of crisis far more bleak than 2020. I recall, in particular, reading a biography of Astrid Lindgren and how she invented Pippi Longstocking in 1941, two years after the outbreak of World War II. Lindgren kept a diary and wrote, on September 1, 1939, about the German invasion of Poland. She was trying hard to curb the instinct to hoard, and limited herself to a few items, including cocoa, tea, and soap. "A ghastly depression has fallen across everything and everyone," she wrote. "Lots of people have been called up. They've banned private cars on the roads. God help our poor, mad planet!"[9]

In those dark times, Astrid Lindgren invented Pippi Longstocking in order to entertain her daughter, who was ill and confined to bed. Influenced not just by E. T. A. Hoffmann and Lewis Carroll, Lindgren also found inspiration in a figure who set foot on Swedish soil in the early 1940s—the Man of Steel known as Superman. "Yes, she was a little Superman right from the word go—strong, rich, and independent," Lindgren declared in a 1967 interview. Lindgren felt a surge of optimism when she imagined a generation of children who could be "merry, breezy, and secure in a way no previous generation had been." After all, what is the "cause of all evil" but "the sulky naysayers, the pig-headed, the privileged, and the selfish," for their underdeveloped souls have no capacity for "generosity or human compassion." In the midst of a "ghastly depression," Lindgren found an antidote to evil in the generosity, compassion, and buoyant spirits of the next generation.

Women do not just live through wars.[10] They were at or near the front lines as soldiers, spies, resistance fighters, and medics. Many ventured onto the battlefield disguised as young men. Conservative estimates suggest that somewhere between 400 and 750 women fought in the U.S. Civil War. Heavy uniforms concealed body shape enough that sixteen-year-old Mary Galloway, to cite one famous example, could hide her gender. Only when she was wounded at the Battle of Antietam and treated by Clara Barton for a chest wound did her actual identity come to light.

As nurses, women saved countless lives while providing care for wounded soldiers. Committed to risking their own lives to heal and sustain life, they often encountered fierce resistance when they step out of the domestic arena to assist in war efforts. If battle promoted the desire to vanquish foes, it produced an equally powerful drive to care for the casualties of war, even when the wounds were as horrific as the ones produced by the heavy artillery, poison gas, and other military machinery of World War I. "Gashes from bayonets. Flesh torn by shrapnel. Faces half shot away. Eyes seared by gas; one here with no eyes at all," as the young American Red Cross nurse Shirley Millard wrote about the men in her care.[11] Nurses fought to bring food and medical supplies to soldiers, scrubbed floors to improve sanitation, monitored fevers, and provided comfort in ways large and small.

The real-life stories of nurses alone could fill the pages of a different book. The exact number of nurses serving in the U.S. Civil War is not known, but it is more than likely that five to ten thousand women, like Louisa May Alcott, offered their services as trained professional nurses or as attendants assisting medical staff and offering comfort to the injured. It had taken the Crimean War (1854) with all its destructive energy—one historian described it as a "notoriously incompetent international butchery"—and the miraculous arrival of Florence Nightingale at a British military hospital in Scutari (today Üsküdar, in Istanbul) to lay the foundations for the modern profession of nursing.[12] When Nightingale arrived with a team of thirty-eight woman volunteers and fifteen nuns, she was shocked by official indifference to the appalling conditions in the barracks. Wounded soldiers lay in beds still wearing their blood-stiffened uniforms. The floors were covered with soiled bandages and caked body fluids. Medicine was in short supply, and there was no equipment to prepare food for patients. Implementing hand washing and making other improvements in hygiene and sanitary conditions, Nightingale, with the help of her staff and support from the British Sanitary Commission, which she summoned to Scutari, reduced the death rate among combatants (largely from typhoid, cholera, and dysentery) from 42 percent to 2 percent.

When Virginia Woolf read Florence Nightingale's essay "Cassandra," she described its author as "shrieking aloud in her agony." That was before her service as a nurse. And why was Nightingale in such pain and cursed like Cassandra, given that she had been born into comfortable family circumstances? Not because of ineffectual prophecies but because of an "accumulation of nervous energy, which has nothing to do during the day." Nightingale was tormented by the thought that the inability to exercise "passion, intellect, and moral activity" would doom British women of privilege to madness.[13] For Nightingale, the nurse fighting to cure the bodies and souls of soldiers came to be the equivalent of the soldier out on the battlefield, and she tactfully avoided stating the obvious superiority of the former over the latter.

Nightingale's work was the inspiration for many Civil War nurses. Clara Barton, born Clarissa Harlowe Barton on Christmas Day in 1821 and named after the long-suffering heroine of Samuel Richardson's novel *Clarissa*, was the most prominent among them. In the DC Comics Wonder Women of History series, which ran from 1942 to 1954 only to be replaced by features turning on beauty tips and strategies for getting married, Clara Barton was number two of seventy-one entries. "Ministering merciful aid upon bloody battlefields, unafraid of flood and famine and war, this Wonder Woman lived only to help others . . . yes . . . in the glittering firmament of American womanhood there is one star who will always glow brightest of all . . . she is—CLARA BARTON, 'Angel of the Battlefield.' "[14]

To overcome her shyness, Barton had worked as a teacher before moving on to the U.S. Patent Office in Washington, DC. After the Baltimore Riot of 1861, a conflict that resulted in the first casualties of the Civil War, Barton met members of a Massachusetts regiment at the railroad station in Washington, DC, and nursed thirty men who arrived there with nothing but the clothes on their backs. She collected supplies and used her own living quarters as a distribution center. In 1862 she was given permission to work on the front lines of the war and served troops at the battles of Harpers Ferry, Antietam, and Fredericksburg, among others, becoming known as the "Florence Nightingale of America." After the war, she ran the Office of Missing Soldiers, an organization that helped to locate and identify soldiers killed or missing in action.

On the other side of the Atlantic, there was the British nurse Edith Cavell, executed for treason by a German firing squad for helping some two hundred Allied soldiers escape from German-occupied Belgium during World War I. She may also have been part of an intelligence-gathering network for the British Secret Intelligence Service. "I can't stop while there are lives to be saved," she is said to have declared.[15] Cavell became Britain's most prominent casualty of the Great War. Recruited as a martyr in war propaganda, she was portrayed as "an innocent, unselfish, devout and pretty girl." But the British prime minister, Herbert Henry Asquith, saw her as far more than that—as a fully realized lesson in patriotic valor—when he averred that she had "taught the bravest man among us a supreme lesson of courage."[16] In recent years, Cavell's heroism has been commemorated, but mainly in shorter narratives aimed at young readers or for tourists visiting key geographical sites of her life.

Florence Nightingale, Clara Barton, and Edith Cavell—these were the heroines celebrated in the era in which I grew up. That they are conspicuously absent from today's pantheons of heroic women turns on the fact that nursing continues to be seen as an ancillary profession, one associated with menial tasks. Nurses are still seen as subservient to what were once the predominantly male authorities in the field of health care. The 2000 film *Meet the Parents* drove that point home when Gaylord "Greg" Focker, played by Ben Stiller, is mocked by his future father-in-law for choosing to work as a nurse. Nurses are associated with care, and their work is framed as domestic service and emotional labor that stands in sharp contrast to the scientific skill and expert knowledge required of doctors and scientists. As the British Royal College of Nursing concluded in a 2020 study of the profession, the nursing sector, staffed largely by women, continues to remain both undervalued and underpaid.

The history of nursing bears out the fact that women, instead of being celebrated for their heroism, have been repeatedly penalized and punished for the extraordinary emotional heavy lifting they have performed in our social world. Nowhere is this more evident than in the fate of the many midwives, wise women, and female healers denounced as witches in times past. These women, laypersons whose healing powers came from collective wisdom passed down from one generation to the next (recall the old wives' tales) and from firsthand experience, were easily dismissed as performing the devil's work. It was in the interest of institutions, both secular and religious, to discredit competition coming from those who worked healing miracles through practices affiliated with sorcery. "The Inquisition," as the cultural historian Thomas Szasz tells us, "constitutes, among other things, an early instance of the 'professional' repudiating the skills and interfering with the rights of the 'nonprofessional' to minister to the poor." The medical establishment itself—which was engaging in practices such as letting blood, applying leeches, and prescribing opium and calomel (a laxative containing mercury)—was committed to excluding woman healers from access to training. They railed against the "worthless and presumptuous women who usurped the profession."[17] By the end of the nineteenth century, formally trained physicians, men educated at universities (in programs that sometimes lasted only a few months), had triumphed over folk healers, midwives, and other "quacks," with the result that women were consigned to the subservient role of nurse.

During the days of the 2020 pandemic, at a time when we were reminded on a daily basis of the courage of health-care workers, I was reading about heroines in the daytime and watching films late at night. There were two streaming series that brought the spring of hope into my heart. First, *Madam Secretary*, which, for all its focus on political intrigue and domestic mayhem, happened also to be filled with allusions to mythology and to the work of Joseph Campbell and Thomas Aquinas. Yes, the series was hopelessly optimistic about navigating through deadly serious political crises and social trauma, but its faith in family (in the broadest sense of the term), its investment in compassion and social responsibility, and its commitment to building caring relationships even among those not in the circle of traditional allies firmed my resolve to keep reading and writing, less as an act of scholarship than as an effort to acknowledge, credit, and memorialize women, real and imagined, from times past. Then there was *The Queen's Gambit*, a series that opened, like many of the classics of children's literature, in an orphanage, with a girl who serendipitously finds her calling and becomes a "master" through her own genius and, in the end, also through the support and friendship of good men and women, who become like family to her. Sometimes we can find comfort in the sentimental, the series affirmed, but it also recognizes that no one goes it alone and memorializes those who help along the way.

It is here that I want to acknowledge the role models and mentors who made this book possible, each in a different decade: Theodore Ziolkowski, Dorrit Cohn, Jeremy Knowles, and Paul Turner. Bob Weil at Liveright worked his editorial magic on this volume in ways that are impossible to fully acknowledge. The many authors who have worked with him will understand the full depth of my gratitude to him. Amy Medeiros, Lauren Abbate, and Haley Bracken saw to it that the production process operated smoothly and efficiently. And Doris Sperber, as always, ensured that the work of word-processing gremlins was undone in each chapter.

Audre Lorde's famous declaration, to which I referred earlier, that "the master's tools will never dismantle the master's house" was the guiding spirit of Hélène Cixous's famous appeal to women, urging them to change the world by *writing*: "I shall speak about women's writing," she declared, "about *what it will do*." For years, Cixous had not opened her mouth and spoken for fear that she would be seen as a monster. "Who, feeling a funny desire stirring inside her (to sing, to write, to dare to speak, in short, to bring out something new), hasn't thought she was sick?" The pen was reserved for "great men" alone. Cixous's manifesto echoes Adrienne Rich's words about the silenced women of the past and Ursula Le Guin's declaration about being sick of the silence of women. "We are volcanoes!" Le Guin declared, and when women begin to speak, there are "new mountains." Women have, in some cases, lacked the language to speak of injustices and social ills, but the heroines in this volume crafted a powerful grammar and syntax for indicting those who harm, injure, and do wrong.

"What do women want?" That was the question Freud asked and, in the same breath, declared himself unable to answer despite thirty years of research into the "feminine soul." There have been many answers to that question, and in 1962, Helen Gurley Brown told us that she had everything she wanted, with her marriage to a motion picture producer, two Mercedes, and "a Mediterranean house overlooking the Pacific, a full-time maid and a good life." I have tried to show that, when we look at women in our literary and cinematic culture today, there is a very different answer. Heroines are on quests, and the goals they set include knowl-edge, justice, and social connection. What drives them? Nothing more than the same spirit of inquiry and care that led Eve to take a bite of the apple, Pandora to open the jar, and Bluebeard's wife to unlock the door to the forbidden chamber. They have been on my mind ever since I picked up my pen and began taking notes for this volume.

On August 5, 2012, a NASA rover touched down on Mars. Its name? *Curiosity*. It has now been joined by a second rover, *Perseverance*. What will be the new names emblazoned on those rovers, nomadic space travelers that signal to possible extraterrestrial beings what it means to be human? The small-scale naming of rovers reminds us of the symbolic weight of language and how it can become the site both of self-congratulatory ges-tures and of subversive thought. Words change us. Writing transforms us. Now imagine a rover named *Compassion* and a second one named *Care*, a third emblazed with the word *Justice*. Would those names create an uproar? The women writers who dared to speak and shape new ways of thinking about our world also created new tools, less for dismantling what we have than for building rich new alternatives. They also displayed a shared solidarity in their passion for defining our aspirations, offering up a thousand and one possible ways to be a heroine. They have made it possible to reimagine the future, and they help us understand how care, empathy, compassion, and new forms of justice, driven by communal, grassroots efforts rather than institutional, top-down forces, are leading us to turn our backs on the heroic ideals we once embraced.

# NOTES

INTRODUCTION

1. Phil Cousineau, ed., *The Hero's Journey: Joseph Campbell on His Life and Work* (Novato, CA: New World Library, 2003), 109–10.
2. Joseph Campbell, *Goddesses: Mysteries of the Feminine Divine*, ed. Safron Rossi (Novato, CA: New World Library, 2013), 11.
3. Campbell, *Goddesses*, 36.
4. Hélène Cixous, "The Laugh of the Medusa," *Signs* 1 (1976): 875–93.
5. As Sady Doyle puts it, "Magic is the voice of the marginalized responding to their oppression." See *Dead Blondes and Bad Mothers: Monstrosity, Patriarchy, and the Fear of Female Power* (Brooklyn, NY: Melville House, 2019), 220.
6. Madeline Miller, *Circe* (New York: Little, Brown, 2018), 260.
7. Hawthorne is quoted in Frank L. Mott, *Golden Multitudes* (New York: Macmillan, 1947), 122. On Naipaul's remark, see Amy Fallon, "V. S. Naipaul Finds No Woman Writer His Literary Match—Not Even Jane Austen," *Guardian* (June 1, 2011).
8. Clarissa Pinkola Estés, *Women Who Run with the Wolves: Myths and Stories of the Wild Woman Archetype* (New York: Ballantine Books, 1992).
9. On this distinction, see Robert S. Ellwood, *Introducing Religion: Religious Studies for the Twenty-First Century*, 5th ed. (New York: Routledge, 2020), 48–54.
10. Rebecca Solnit, "On Letting Go of Certainty in a Story That Never Ends," Literary Hub, April 23, 2020.
11. Campbell, *Goddesses,* xiii.
12. "Have Hundred Stories: Natalie Portman on Sexual Harassment," News 18, November 21, 2017.

CHAPTER I: "SING, O MUSE"

1. Joseph Campbell, *The Hero with a Thousand Faces* (New York: Bollingen Foundation, 1949), 1, 92.
2. Andrew Lang, ed., *The Red Fairy Book* (London: Longmans, Green, 1890), 104–15.
3. Kelly Link, *Stranger Things Happen* (Easthampton, MA: Small Beer Press, 2001), 100. See also Theodora Goss, *The Fairytale Heroine's Journey* (blog), https://fairytaleheroinesjourney.com/into-the-dark-forest-the-fairy-tale-heroines-journey/.
4. Eugene M. Waith, *The Herculean Hero in Marlowe, Chapman, Shakespeare and Dryden* (New York: Columbia University Press, 1962), 16.
5. Ben Jonson, *The Complete Masques*, ed. Stephen Orgel (New Haven, CT: Yale University Press, 1969), 543.
6. Stephen Fry, *Heroes* (London: Michael Joseph, 2018), 1. In a study of women in fairy tales, Jonathan Gottschall determined that female protagonists are "far less likely" to be defined as physically heroic or possessing courage. "The finding," he concludes, "leaves

open the possibility that female characters expressed heroism in ways not entailing physical hardihood or risk." See his "The Heroine with a Thousand Faces: Universal Trends in the Characterization of Female Folk Tale Protagonists," *Evolutionary Psychology* 3, no. 1 (2005): 85–103.

7.  For Arendt, the *polis*, or public realm of appearances, is constituted directly from "the sharing of words and deeds." "Action and speech create a space between the participants which can find its proper location almost anytime and anywhere." See *The Human Condition* (Chicago: University of Chicago Press, 1958), 198.

8.  Muhsin Mahdi, ed., *The Arabian Nights*, trans. Husain Haddawy (New York: W. W. Norton, 1990), 16.

9.  Joseph Campbell, *Pathways to Bliss: Mythology and Personal Transformation* (Novato, CA: New World Library, 2004), 145.

10. Joseph Jacobs, "Mr. Fox," in *English Fairy Tales* (London: David Nutt, 1890), 148–51.

11. "Within the literary context, mythologies are ongoing and developing, even evolving," as Kathryn Hume puts it in *The Metamorphoses of Myth in Fiction since 1960* (New York: Bloomsbury Academic, 2020), 6.

12. Stephen Larsen and Robin Larsen, *Joseph Campbell: A Fire in the Mind* (Rochester, VT: Inner Traditions, 2002), 310.

13. "Podcast: Joseph Campbell and 'The Message of the Myth,'" Moyers on Democracy.

14. Wolfgang Saxon, "Joseph Campbell, Writer Known for His Scholarship on Mythology," *New York Times*, November 2, 1987.

15. Larsen and Larsen, *Joseph Campbell*, 327.

16. Otto Rank, "The Myth of the Birth of the Hero," in *In Quest of the Hero* (Princeton, NJ: Princeton University Press, 1991), 3.

17. Alan Dundes, "Madness in Method, Plus a Plea for Projective Inversion in Myth," in *Myth and Method*, ed. Laurie L. Patton and Wendy Doniger (Charlottesville: University of Virginia Press, 1996), 147–59.

18. Campbell, *The Hero with a Thousand Faces*, 20.

19. Christopher Vogler, *The Writer's Journey: Mythic Structure for Writers* (Studio City, CA: Michael Wiese, 1998), xiii.

20. Syd Field, *Screenplay: The Foundations of Screenwriting* (New York: Dell, 1984), 161.

21. Blake Snyder, *Save the Cat! The Last Book on Screenwriting You'll Ever Need* (Studio City, CA: Michael Wiese, 2005), 119.

22. "Myth, Magic, and the Mind of Neil Gaiman," interview with Tim E. Ogline, Wild River Review, April 13, 2007, https://www.wildriverreview.com/columns/pen-world -voices/myth-magic-and-the-mind-of-neil-gaiman/ (site discontinued).

23. Joseph Campbell, *The Hero with a Thousand Faces*, 30.

24. As Mary G. Mason puts it, "The dramatic structure of conversion . . . where the self is presented as the stage for a battle of opposing forces and where a climactic victory for one force—spirit defeating flesh—completes the drama of the self, simply does not accord with the deepest realities of women's experience and so is inappropriate as a model of women's life-writing." See "The Other Voice: Autobiographies of Women Writers," in *Life/Lines: Theorizing Women's Autobiography*, ed. Bella Brodzki and Celeste Schenk (Ithaca, NY: Cornell University Press, 1988), 210.

25. Maureen Murdock, "The Heroine's Journey," Maureen Murdock (website), https:// www.maureenmurdock.com/articles/articles-the-heroines-journey/.

26. Joseph Campbell, *The Hero with a Thousand Faces*, 101.

27. Simone de Beauvoir, *The Second Sex* (New York: Vintage, 2011), 305.

28. F. Scott Fitzgerald, *The Complete Short Stories and Essays* (New York: Scribner's, 2004), II:1176.
29. Leslie Jamison, "Cult of the Literary Sad Woman," *New York Times*, November 7, 2019. On that contrast from the perspective of a psychologist, see Mary M. Gergen, "Life Stories: Pieces of a Dream," in *Toward a New Psychology of Gender*, ed. Mary M. Gergen and Sara N. Davis (New York: Routledge, 1997), 203.
30. Jia Tolentino, *Trick Mirror: Reflections on Self-Delusion* (New York: Random House, 2019), 118.
31. The Amazons were more than an invention of the Greek imagination, and Adrienne Mayor explores the reality of warrior women behind the stories told in ancient cultures. See *The Amazons: Lives and Legends of Warrior Women across the Ancient World* (Princeton, NJ: Princeton University Press, 2013).
32. On the cult of the hero and hero worship, see especially Gregory Nagy, *The Ancient Greek Hero in 24 Hours* (Cambridge, MA: Belknap Press of Harvard University Press, 2013), 11.
33. Walter J. Ong, *Orality and Literacy* (New York: Methuen, 1982), 204–5.
34. I am indebted to Gregory Nagy's textual elucidations in *The Ancient Greek Hero in 24 Hours*. He refers to "deeds meant to arouse a sense of wonder or marvel" (9).
35. Margaret Atwood, "The Myth Series and Me: Rewriting a Classic Is Its Own Epic Journey," *Publishers Weekly*, November 28, 2005.
36. In a landmark essay of 1957 entitled "What Was Penelope Unweaving?" the feminist critic Carolyn Heilbrun describes Penelope as a woman without a plot, without a narrative to guide her. She weaves and unweaves, day after day, year after year, biding her time until it is time to enact a new story. See her *Hamlet's Mother and Other Women* (New York: Columbia University Press, 1990), 103–11. That new story came first in the form of poems like Hilda Doolittle's "At Ithaca," Edna St. Vincent Millay's "An Ancient Gesture," and Louise Glück's "Penelope's Song," then in novels like *Odysseus and Penelope: An Ordinary Marriage* (2000) by the Austrian writer Inge Merkel and *Ithaka* by the American author Adèle Geras (2007). For more on those poems, see Emily Hauser, "'There Is Another Story': Writing after the *Odyssey* in Margaret Atwood's *The Penelopiad*," *Classical Receptions Journal* 10 (2018): 109–26.
37. Margaret Atwood, *The Penelopiad* (Edinburgh: Canongate Books, 2005), 82. Additional quotations are from pages 39, 1, 2–3.
38. Kathryn Allen Rabuzzi, *Motherself: A Mythic Analysis of Motherhood* (Bloomington: Indiana University Press, 1988), 12.
39. Stephanie Zacharek, Eliana Dockterman, and Haley Sweetland Edwards, "The Silence Breakers: The Voices That Launched a Movement," *Time*, December 18, 2017, https://time.com/time-person-of-the-year-2017-silence-breakers/.
40. "Penelope became a moral heroine for later generations, the embodiment of goodness and chastity, to be contrasted with the faithless, murdering Clytemnestra, Agamemnon's wife; but 'hero' has no feminine gender in the age of heroes," M. I. Finley tells us in *The World of Odysseus* (1954; New York: New York Review Books Classics, 2002), 25.
41. Campbell, *Pathways to Bliss*, 159.
42. Homer, *The Odyssey*, trans. Robert Fagles (New York: Penguin, 1996), 96.
43. K. F. Stein, "Talking Back to Bluebeard: Atwood's Fictional Storytellers," in *Margaret Atwood's Textual Assassinations: Recent Poetry and Fiction*, ed. S. R. Wilson (Columbus: Ohio State University Press, 2003), 158. See also Kiley Kapuscinski, "Ways of Sentencing: Female Violence and Narrative Justice in Margaret Atwood's *The Penelopiad*," http://projects.essex.ac.uk/ehrr/V4N2/kapuscinski.pdf.

44. Thomas Carlyle, "The Hero as a Man of Letters," in *Heroes, Hero Worship and the Heroic in History* (London: Chapman and Hall, 1896–1899), 154.

45. As Linda Hutcheon points out, there is always the risk that you cannot "privilege the margin without acknowledging the power of the center." See *Splitting Images: Contemporary Canadian Ironies* (Don Mills, Ontario: Oxford University Press Canada, 1991), 12.

46. Simone Weil, "*The Iliad*, or the Poem of Force," *Politics* (November 1945), 321–31; Euripides, *The Trojan Women*, trans. Alan Shapiro (New York: Oxford, 2009), 40, 58.

47. Christa Wolf, *Cassandra: A Novel and Four Essays* (New York: Farrar, Straus and Giroux, 1984), 4. Additional quotations are from pages 238, 227, 239, 26, 239.

48. Natalie Haynes, *A Thousand Ships* (London: Pan Macmillan, 2019), 339. Additional quotations are from pages 241, 185, 255, 109.

49. Ursula K. Le Guin, *Lavinia* (New York: Mariner, 2008), 4.

50. "Ursula K. Le Guin Film Reveals Her Struggle to Write Women into Fantasy," *Guardian*, May 30, 2018.

51. Ursula K. Le Guin, "Bryn Mawr Commencement Address," in *Dancing at the Edge of the World: Thoughts on Words, Women, Places* (New York: Grove, 1989), 147–60.

52. Pat Barker, *The Silence of the Girls* (New York: Doubleday, 2018), 3. Additional quotations are from pages 291, 49, 266, 97.

53. Darragh McManus, "Feminist Retelling of Homer's Classic Breaks the Silence of Troy's Women," *Independent.ie*, September 2, 2018.

54. Madeline Miller, *Circe* (New York: Back Bay Books, 2018), 341, 384.

55. E. B. White, *Charlotte's Web* (New York: Harper & Row, 1952), 1. Additional quotations are from pages 177, 186.

CHAPTER 2: SILENCE AND SPEECH

1. Edith Hamilton, *Mythology: Timeless Tales of Gods and Heroes* (1942; New York: Grand Central Publishing, 1976), 113.

2. Mary Lefkowitz, *Women in Greek Myth*, 2nd ed. (1986; Baltimore: Johns Hopkins University Press, 2007), 64.

3. Hamilton, *Mythology*, 100, 103.

4. Charles FitzRoy, *The Rape of Europa: The Intriguing History of Titian's Masterpiece* (London: Bloomsbury, 2015), 49.

5. Rembrandt van Rijn, *The Abduction of Europa*, J. Paul Getty Museum, http://www.getty.edu/art/collection/objects/882/rembrandt-harmensz-van-rijn-the-abduction-of-europa-dutch-1632/.

6. A compelling example of attention paid to brushstrokes, surfaces, and textures can be found in Nathaniel Silver's "The Rape of Europa," in *Titian: Love, Desire, Death* (New Haven, CT: Yale University Press, 2020), 167–78.

7. Titian, *The Rape of Europa*, Isabella Stewart Gardner Museum, https://www.gardnermuseum.org/experience/collection/10978.

8. Jean François de Troy, *The Abduction of Europa*, National Gallery of Art, https://www.nga.gov/collection/art-object-page.154233.html.

9. Lefkowitz, *Women in Greek Myth*, 54.

10. Tim Chamberlain, "The Elusive Urn," *British Museum Magazine*, no. 52 (Summer 2005).

11. Benita Ferrero-Waldner, "EU Foreign Policy: Myth or Reality?" (lecture, Sydney Institute, Sydney, SPEECH/07/422, June 26, 2007), https://www.europa-nu.nl/id/vhlxfod2pxzx/nieuws/toespraak_benita_ferrero_waldner_eu.

12. Mary Beard, *Women & Power: A Manifesto* (New York: Liveright, 2017), 4.

13. James Boswell, *The Life of Samuel Johnson, LL.D.* (New York: Alexander V. Blake, 1844), 205–6.

14. Apollodorus, *The Library of Greek Mythology*, trans. Robin Hard (Oxford: Oxford University Press, 1997), 65.

15. Hamilton, *Mythology*, 197.

16. Luba Freedman, "Danaë," in *The Classical Tradition*, ed. Anthony Grafton, Glenn W. Most, and Salvatore Settis (Cambridge, MA: Harvard University Press, 2010), 250.

17. Cited by Thomas Puttfarken, *Titian and Tragic Painting: Aristotle's Poetics and the Rise of the Modern Artist* (New Haven, CT: Yale University Press, 2005), 141.

18. Madlyn Millner Kahr, "Danaë: Virtuous, Voluptuous, Venal Woman," *Art Bulletin* 60 (1978): 44.

19. Johanna King-Slutzky, "After Philomela: A History of Women Whose Tongues Have Been Ripped Out," *Hairpin* (blog), Medium, March 10, 2014.

20. Ovid, *Metamorphoses*, trans. Charles Martin (New York: W. W. Norton, 2004), 212.

21. Helen Morales points out that "ancient myth dramatizes sexual assault again and again." You can even look up at the night sky and see Jupiter's moons, named for his victims: Io, Europa, Ganymede, and Callisto. See her *Antigone Rising: The Subversive Power of the Ancient Myths* (New York: Bold Type Books, 2020), 66. Patricia Klindienst, "The Voice of the Shuttle Is Ours," August 1996, http://oldsite.english.ucsb .edu/faculty/ayliu/research/klindienst.html.

22. Sara R. Horowitz, "The Wounded Tongue: Engendering Jewish Memory," in *Shaping Losses: Cultural Memory and the Holocaust*, ed. Julia Epstein and Lori Hope Lefkovitz (Champaign: University of Illinois Press, 2001), 110.

23. Edith Hamilton, *Mythology*, 395–96.

24. Karen E. Rowe writes: "Philomela's trick reflects the 'trickiness' of weaving, its uncanny ability to make meaning out of inarticulate matter, to make silent material speak." See "To Spin a Yarn: The Female Voice in Folklore and Fairy Tale," in *Fairy Tales and Society: Illusion, Allusion, and Paradigm*, ed. Ruth B. Bottigheimer (Philadelphia: University of Pennsylvania Press, 1989), 56.

25. In an extraordinary study of the "softer stuff" that drove technological development, Virginia Postrel tells us that "the ancient Greeks worshiped Athena as the goddess of *techne*: craft and productive knowledge, the artifice of civilization." See *The Fabric of Civilization: How Textiles Made the World* (New York: Basic Books, 2020), 5.

26. "How the Spider Came to Be," as told to Tèmakamoxkomëhèt by his friend Michelle Little Cat Singing, Native American Embassy, accessed October 10, 2020, http://www .nativeamericanembassy.net/www.lenni-lenape.com/www/html/LenapeArchives/ LenapeSet-01/spider.html.

27. "Alice Walker," *Black Women Writers at Work*, ed. Claudia Tate (New York: Continuum, 1983), 176.

28. Alice Walker, *The Color Purple* (New York: Harcourt Brace Jovanovich, 1970), 1.

29. Walker, *The Color Purple*, 192.

30. Walker, 206, 284, 137.

31. Judith N. Shklar, *Ordinary Vices* (Cambridge, MA: Harvard University Press, 1985), 6.

32. Martha J. Cutter, "Philomela Speaks: Alice Walker's Revisioning of Rape Archetypes in *The Color Purple*," *MELUS* 25 (2000): 161–80.

33. Toni Morrison, "Unspeakable Things Unspoken: The Afro-American Presence in American Literature," *Michigan Quarterly Review* 28 (1989): 1–34.
34. Paulo Horta, *Marvellous Thieves: Secret Authors of the Arabian Nights* (Cambridge, MA: Harvard University Press, 2017), 3.
35. In 1838, British publisher Charles Knight placed an advertisement for a new translation of the *Arabian Nights*, promising that the stories, which had previously been oriented to the young, would deliver authentic adult entertainment. "It is one of the chief objects of the translator to render these enchanting fictions as interesting to persons of mature age and education as they have hitherto been for the young," Knight declared. See Malcolm C. Lyons and Ursula Lyons, trans., *The Arabian Nights: Tales of 1001 Nights*, ed. Robert Irwin, 3 vols. (London: Penguin, 2008), I:4. Edward Lane, the chosen translator of the tales, was less coy than his publisher about delivering on the promise of sexual titillation. He also insisted that the stories, graphic content and all, were not just made up but mirrored the social mores and values of the Orient: "Some of the stories of the intrigues of women in *The Thousand and One Nights* presented faithful pictures of occurrences not infrequent in the modern metropolis of Egypt." Women and intrigue—that was a winning combination for Lane, who lavished attention in his notes on the "wickedness" of women, noting that "the stronger sex among the Arabs" outdid men when it came to the libido. See Horta, *Marvellous Thieves*, 177.
36. John Updike, "Fiabe Italiane," in *Hugging the Shore: Essays and Criticism* (New York: Knopf, 1983), 662.
37. Lyons and Lyons, *The Arabian Nights*, I:4.
38. Horta, *Marvellous Thieves*, 177.
39. Marilyn Jurich makes this point in *Scheherazade's Sisters: Trickster Heroines and Their Stories in World Literature* (Westport, CT: Greenwood, 1998), xvi.
40. Lyons and Lyons, *The Arabian Nights*, I:6. I have edited the translation for clarity.
41. Lyons and Lyons, I:7.
42. Martin Puchner, *The Written World: The Power of Stories to Shape People, History, and Civilization* (New York: Random House, 2017), 130.
43. Orhan Pamuk, "Love, Death and Storytelling," *New Statesman*, December 18, 2006, 34–36.
44. Paulo Horta has shown how translators violated the spirit of *The Thousand and One Nights*, rewriting the stories in ways that gave added weight to female cunning and women's moral weaknesses, all the while minimizing male sexual mischief and justifying violence against women. As important, he shows how Edward Lane, who published a three-volume translation of *The Thousand and One Nights* in 1840, abridged Scheherazade's role, often omitting her repeated appearances as storyteller in successive tales, and also reducing the number of female characters who are, like Scheherazade, courageous, educated, and clever.
45. I borrow the phrases from Deldon Anne McNeely, *Mercury Rising: Women, Evil, and the Trickster Gods* (Sheridan, WY: Fisher King Press, 2011), 125.
46. As James Hillman has pointed out, in an age of "Hermes hypertrophy," with "modems, CD-Roms, cellular phones, satellites, 300 cable channels, call-waiting, virtual realities," we need "the centering circular force of Hestia" more than ever. Cited by McNeely, *Mercury Rising*, 116.
47. Marjorie Bard uses the term "idionarration." See her *Organizational and Community Responses to Domestic Abuse and Homelessness* (Abingdon, Oxfordshire: Taylor and Francis, 2016).

48. "The Goose Girl," in *The Annotated Brothers Grimm*, trans. and ed. Maria Tatar, 2nd ed. (New York: W. W. Norton, 2012), 320.

49. Giambattista Basile, "The Young Slave," in *Classic Fairy Tales*, 2nd ed., ed. Maria Tatar (New York: W. W. Norton, 2017), 92–95.

50. Consiglieri Pedroso, ed., *Portuguese Folk-Tales*, trans. Miss Henriqueta Monteiro (London: Folklore Society, 1882), 63–66.

51. Francis James Childs, ed., *The English and Scottish Popular Ballads* (New York: Houghton Mifflin, 1894), V:42–58.

52. Marie Campbell, *Tales from the Cloud Walking Country* (Athens: University of Georgia Press, 2000), 45–47.

53. "Nourie Hadig," in *100 Armenian Tales and Their Folkloristic Relevance*, ed. Susie Hoogasian Villa (Detroit: Wayne State University Press, 1966), 84–91.

54. Richard M. Dorson, ed., *Folktales Told around the World* (Chicago: University of Chicago Press, 1978), 238–42.

55. Atiq Rahimi, *The Patience Stone*, trans. Polly McLean (New York: Other Press, 2008), 3.

56. Rahimi's novel was made into a film in 2012, with the writer as director. Quotes are from Rahimi, *The Patience Stone*, x, 79.

57. Sherry Turkle, *Alone Together: Why We Expect More from Technology and Less from Each Other* (New York: Basic Books, 2012), 23.

58. Jill Lepore, "The Rise of the Victims'-Rights Movement," *New Yorker*, May 21, 2018.

59. Maria Tatar, *The Fairest of Them All: Snow White and Twenty-One Tales about Mothers and Daughters* (Cambridge, MA: Belknap Press of Harvard University Press, 2020), 88.

60. Rebecca Solnit, "Silence and Powerlessness Go Hand in Hand—Women's Voices Must Be Heard," *Guardian*, March 8, 2017.

61. Ronan Farrow, *Catch and Kill: Lies, Spies, and a Conspiracy to Protect Predators* (New York: Little, Brown, 2019), 242, 318.

62. Chanel Miller, *Know My Name: A Memoir* (New York: Viking, 2019), 327.

63. Jodi Kantor and Megan Twohey, *She Said: Breaking the Sexual Harassment Story That Helped Ignite a Movement* (New York: Penguin, 2020), 53, 54.

64. Joan Didion, *The White Album* (New York: Farrar, Straus and Giroux, 1979), 11.

65. Gaston Maspero, *Popular Stories of Ancient Egypt* (Oxford: Oxford University Press, 2004), 1–16.

66. "Tongue Meat," in *Myths and Legends of the Swahili*, ed. Jan Knappert (Nairobi: Heinemann, 1970), 132–33. The story was lightly edited by Angela Carter for her *Book of Fairy Tales* (London: Virago, 1992), 223–24.

67. Adam Ganz, "New Brothers Grimm Fairytale Written by Artificial Intelligence Robot," *Independent*, June 13, 2018.

68. Teresa Peirce Williston, *Japanese Fairy Tales* (Chicago: Rand McNally, 1904), 56–64.

CHAPTER 3: RESISTANCE AND REVELATION

1. Katie J. M. Baker, "Here's the Powerful Letter the Stanford Victim Read to Her Attacker," BuzzFeed News, June 3, 2016. Chanel Miller, *Know My Name: A Memoir* (New York: Viking, 2019), 329, 333.

2. Gretchen Cherington, *Poetic License: A Memoir* (Berkeley, CA: She Writes Press, 2020), 169.

3. Charlotte Brontë, *Jane Eyre*, 4th ed., ed. Deborah Lutz (New York: W. W. Norton, 2016), 35.

4. Elizabeth Rigby, "Review of *Vanity Fair* and *Jane Eyre*," *Quarterly Review* 84 (1848): 184.

5. Zora Neale Hurston, *Their Eyes Were Watching God* (1937), in *Novels and Stories* (New York: New American Library, 1995), 178.

6. Recalling growing up in Tuscaloosa, Alabama, in the 1950s and 1960s, Trudier Harris writes: "In the absence of television and air-conditioning, my relatives and neighbors routinely gathered on porches, and those sites became some of the primary stages for interactive storytelling, for the passing and receiving of oral tradition." See *The Power of the Porch: The Storyteller's Craft in Zora Neale Hurston, Gloria Naylor, and Randall Kenan* (Athens: University of Georgia Press, 1997), xii.

7. Henry Louis Gates Jr., *The Signifying Monkey: A Theory of African-American Literary Criticism* (New York: Oxford University Press, 1989).

8. Hurston, *Their Eyes Were Watching God*, 208, 279–80, 180.

9. On autobiography as a political strategy, see Laura J. Beard, *Acts of Narrative Resistance: Women's Autobiographical Writings in the Americas* (Charlottesville: University of Virginia Press, 2009).

10. W. H. Auden, "In Memory of W. B. Yeats," in *Another Time* (New York: Random House, 1940), 93–94.

11. William Bascom, "The Talking Skull Refuses to Talk," in *African Tales in the New World* (Bloomington: Indiana University Press, 1992), 17–39.

12. Leo Frobenius, *African Genesis: The Folk Tales and Legends of the North African Berbers, the Sudanese, and the Southern Rhodesians* (New York: Benjamin Blom, 1966), 161–62.

13. Danielle L. McGuire, *At the Dark End of the Street: Black Women, Rape, and Resistance—a New History of the Civil Rights Movement from Rosa Parks to the Rise of Black Power* (New York: Vintage Books, 2010), 16–17.

14. For additional variants, see Henry Louis Gates Jr. and Maria Tatar, eds., *The Annotated African American Folktales* (New York: Liveright, 2018), 113–32.

15. Zora Neale Hurston, *The Skull Talks Back and Other Haunting Tales*, ed. Joyce Carol Thomas (New York: HarperCollins, 2004), 27.

16. "The Princess in the Suit of Leather," in *Arab Folktales*, trans. and ed. Inea Bushnaq (New York: Pantheon, 1986), 193–200.

17. Plato, *Gorgias*, ed. E. R. Dodds (Oxford: Oxford University Press, 1959), 527a4.

18. Marina Warner, *From the Beast to the Blonde: On Fairy Tales and Their Tellers* (New York: Farrar, Straus and Giroux, 1995), 14.

19. Giambattista Basile, *The Tale of Tales*, ed. Nancy Canepa (New York: Penguin, 2016), 10.

20. A. W. Cardinall, *Tales Told in Togoland* (London: Oxford University Press, 1931), 213.

21. Cited by Max Lüthi, *Märchen*, 2nd ed. (Stuttgart: Metzler, 1964), 45.

22. Lewis Seifert, *Fairy Tales, Sexuality, and Gender in France, 1690–1715* (Cambridge: Cambridge University Press, 1996).

23. Warner, *From the Beast to the Blonde*, 19.

24. *Angela Carter's Book of Fairy Tales*, xiii.

25. Basile, *Tale of Tales*, 5.

26. Cited by Sandy Bardsley, *Venomous Tongues: Speech and Gender in Late Medieval England* (Philadelphia: University of Pennsylvania Press, 2006), 1.

27. Warner, *From the Beast to the Blonde*, 17.

28. Manfred Kuehn, *Kant: A Biography* (Cambridge: Cambridge University Press, 2002).

29. Clare Carlisle, *Philosopher of the Heart: The Restless Life of Søren Kierkegaard* (New York: Farrar, Straus and Giroux, 2019), 107.

30. Karen Adkins, *Gossip, Epistemology, and Power: Knowledge Underground* (Cham, Switzerland: Palgrave Macmillan, 2017), 31.

31. *George Steiner: A Reader* (Oxford: Oxford University Press, 1984), 378.

32. *George Steiner*, 378.

33. Henry Jenkins, *Convergence Culture: Where Old and New Media Collide* (New York: New York University Press, 2006), 60.

34. F. G. Bailey, ed., "Gifts and Poison," in *Gifts and Poison: The Politics of Reputation* (Oxford: Basil Blackwell, 1971), 1.

35. Audre Lorde, *The Master's Tools Will Never Dismantle the Master's House* (New York: Penguin, 1984).

36. Jörg R. Bergmann, *Discreet Indiscretions: The Social Organization of Gossip*, trans. John Bednarz Jr. (New York: de Gruyter, 1993), 60. "Good gossip approximates art," one critic chimes in to underscore the fact that all of us resort to some form of artifice or to the time-honored strategy of lying to make a story better. Rachel M. Brownstein, *Becoming a Heroine* (New York: Viking, 1982), 7.

37. Roger D. Abrahams, *Everyday Life: A Poetics of Vernacular Practices* (Philadelphia: University of Pennsylvania Press, 2005), 28.

38. Abrahams, *Everyday Life*, 28.

39. Melville Jean Herskovits and Frances Shapiro Herskovits, *Trinidad Village* (New York: Knopf, 1947), 275.

40. Clifford Geertz, *The Interpretation of Cultures* (New York: Basic Books, 1973), 450–51.

41. Angela Carter writes with affection ("so much joy" in those stories from all over the world) about the anthologies compiled by Lang—"the Red, Blue, Violet, Green, Olive Fairy Books, and so on, through the spectrum." See *Angela Carter's Book of Fairy Tales*, xvi. On the actual division of labor between Andrew Lang and Nora Lang, see "'Almost Wholly the Work of Mrs. Lang': Nora Lang, Literary Labour, and the Fairy Books," *Women's Writing* 26 (1977): 400–420.

42. Giambattista Basile, "Penta with the Chopped-Off Hands," in *Tale of Tales*, 214–24.

43. Clarissa Pinkola Estés, *Women Who Run with the Wolves: Myths and Stories of the Wild Woman Archetype* (New York: Ballantine Books, 1996), 388.

44. George Peele, *The Old Wives' Tale* (London: John Danter, 1595), lines 19–20.

45. The translation of "Fitchers Vogel" from the third edition of the Grimms' *Kinder- und Hausmärchen* is my own.

46. Elaine Scarry, *On Beauty and Being Just* (Princeton, NJ: Princeton University Press, 2001), 97.

47. André Jolles, *Einfache Formen: Legende, Sage, Mythe, Rätsel, Spruch, Kasus, Memorabile, Märchen, Witz* (Berlin: de Gruyter, 2006), 241.

48. Lauren Martin, "Audre Lorde, Adrienne Rich, and Alice Walker's Speech at the National Book Award Ceremony Will Make You Cry," *Words of Women* (blog), November 22, 2017.

49. Virginia Woolf, *A Room of One's Own* (New York: Harcourt Brace Jovanovich, 1957), 101.

50. Frances Burney, *Evelina* (New York: Oxford, 2002), 5. Mary Wollstonecraft, "A Vindication of the Rights of Woman: with Strictures on Political and Moral Subjects," in D. L. Macdonald and Kathleen Scherf, eds., *The Vindications* (Peterborough, Ontario: Broadview, 2001), 330. George Eliot, "Silly Novels by Lady Novelists," in Solveig C. Robinson, ed., *A Serious Occupation: Literary Criticism by Victorian Women*

*Writers* (Peterborough, Ontario: Broadview, 2003), 88–115. Sylvia Townsend Warner, "Women as Writers," in *Feminist Literary Theory and Criticism: A Norton Reader*, ed. Sandra M. Gilbert and Susan Gubar (New York: W. W. Norton, 2007), 161.

51. Franz Boas, "Introduction," in James Teit, *Traditions of the Thompson River Indians of British Columbia, Memoirs of the American Folklore Society*, VI (1898), 18.

52. Mary Lefkowitz, *Women in Greek Myth*, 2nd ed. (1986; Baltimore: Johns Hopkins University Press, 2007), xv. On the point about how myth is a form of speech that appears to be "natural" rather than historically determined, see Roland Barthes, *Mythologies* (London: Vintage, 1993).

53. Kurt Vonnegut Jr., "Introduction," in Anne Sexton, *Transformations* (New York: Houghton Mifflin, 1971), vii.

54. Linda Gray Sexton, *Searching for Mercy Street: My Journey Back to My Mother* (New York: Little, Brown, 1994), 154.

55. Diane Middlebrook, *Anne Sexton: A Biography* (New York: Vintage, 1992), 338.

56. Sexton, *Transformations*, 1.

57. Angela Carter, *Shaking a Leg: Collected Writings by Angela Carter* (London: Virago, 1998), 452–53.

58. Angela Carter, *The Bloody Chamber and Other Stories* (New York: Penguin, 2015), 68. Additional quotations are from pages 56, 20, 118, 67, 112, 36.

59. Edmund Gordon, *The Invention of Angela Carter: A Biography* (New York: Oxford University Press, 2017), 268.

60. Angela Carter, interview by Kerryn Goldsworthy, *Meanjin* 44, no. 1 (1985): 10.

61. Carter, *The Bloody Chamber*, 20.

62. Carter, *The Bloody Chamber*, 39.

63. Anna Katsavos, "A Conversation with Angela Carter," *Review of Contemporary Fiction* 143, no. 3 (1994), https://www.dalkeyarchive.com/a-conversation-with-angela-carter-by-anna-katsavos/.

64. Ingri d'Aulaire and Edgar Parin d'Aulaire, *Book of Greek Myths* (New York: Doubleday, 1967), 115. I cite the d'Aulaires' volume precisely because it now has the imprint of Random House Children's Books and has become the most prominent source of knowledge in the United States about Greek mythology.

65. Carter, *The Bloody Chamber*, 117, 126, 118.

66. Sharon R. Wilson, *Margaret Atwood's Fairy-Tale Sexual Politics* (Jackson: University Press of Mississippi, 1993), 11–12.

67. Margaret Atwood, *Negotiating with the Dead: A Writer on Writing* (Cambridge: Cambridge University Press, 2002), 178.

68. Margaret Atwood, "Bluebeard's Egg," in *Bluebeard's Egg and Other Stories* (Boston: Houghton Mifflin, 1986), 131–64.

69. Atwood, "Bluebeard's Egg," 156.

70. Atwood, 164.

71. Italo Calvino, *The Uses of Literature* (San Diego: Harcourt Brace, 1986), 16.

72. Ralph Ellison, "The Art of Fiction: An Interview," *Paris Review* (Spring 1955): 53–55.

73. Toni Morrison, "Rootedness: The Ancestor as Foundation," in *Black Women Writers (1950–1980)*, ed. Mari Evans (New York: Anchor, 1984), 343.

74. Zora Neale Hurston, *Their Eyes Were Watching God* (Urbana: University of Illinois Press, 1978), 31.

75. Ralph Ellison, *Invisible Man*, 2nd ed. (New York: Vintage, 1995), 141, 142.

76. Toni Morrison, "Unspeakable Things Unspoken: The Afro-American Presence in American Literature," *Michigan Quarterly Review* 28 (1989): 30.
77. Toni Morrison, *Tar Baby* (New York: Knopf, 1981).
78. Kevin Young, *The Grey Album: On the Blackness of Blackness* (Minneapolis: Graywolf Press, 2012), 15.
79. See Sandra Pouchet Paquet, "The Ancestor as Foundation in *Their Eyes Were Watching God* and *Tar Baby*," *Callaloo* 13 (1990): 499–515.
80. *Angela Carter's Book of Fairy Tales*, x.
81. Lennie Goodings, *A Bite of the Apple: A Life with Books, Writers and Virago* (Oxford: Oxford University Press, 2020), 168.

CHAPTER 4: WONDER GIRLS

1. Phil Cousineau, *The Hero's Journey: Joseph Campbell on His Life and Work* (Novato, CA: New World Library, 2003), 120.
2. William Moulton Marston, "Why 100,000,000 Americans Read Comics," *American Scholar* 13 (1943–1944).
3. Brian Grazer, *A Curious Mind: The Secret to a Bigger Life* (New York: Simon & Schuster, 2015), 38.
4. Robert Gottlieb, "Harold Bloom Is Dead. But His 'Rage for Reading' Is Undiminished," *New York Times*, January 23, 2021.
5. Simone de Beauvoir, *The Second Sex* (New York: Vintage, 2011), 205–6.
6. See Joanne Hayle, *Lord Byron and Lady Caroline Lamb: Mad, Bad and Dangerous to Know. The Passionate and Public Affair That Scandalised Regency England* (self-pub., CreateSpace, 2016).
7. Michel Foucault, "The Masked Philosopher," interview with Christian Delacampagne, April 6, 1980, in *Foucault Live: Interviews, 1961–84* (Cambridge, MA: Semiotext(e), 1996), 302–7.
8. Martin Heidegger, *Being and Time*, trans. John Macquarrie and Edward Robinson (New York: Harper Perennial, 2008), 235–44.
9. Alberto Manguel explores the double meaning of curiosity and notes that the Spanish lexicographer Covarrubias found that curiosity has "both a positive and a negative sense." "Positive, because the curious person treats things diligently; and negative, because the person labors to scrutinize things that are most hidden and reserved, and do not matter." See *Curiosity* (New Haven, CT: Yale University Press, 2015), 13.
10. Aristotle, *Metaphysica*, ed. J. A. Smith and W. D. Ross (Oxford: Clarendon Press, 1908), 980.
11. Bernard de Clairvaux, *Sermones super Canticum Canticorum*, in *S. Bernardi Opera II*, ed. J. Leclercq (Rome: Editiones Cistercienses, 1958), 56.
12. Hesiod, *The Homeric Hymns and Homerica/Works and Days*, trans. Hugh G. Evelyn-White (Cambridge, MA: Harvard University Press; London: William Heinemann, 1914), *Theogony*, 585; *Works and Days*, 57.
13. Note that the Aesopian fable "Zeus and the Jar of Good Things" (#526) has a jar with very different contents, one that is opened by "man," releasing all the good things and returning them to the gods, leaving behind only hope.
14. Ingri d'Aulaire and Edgar Parin d'Aulaire, *Book of Greek Myths* (New York: Doubleday, 1967), 72, 74.

15. Edith Hamilton, *Mythology: Timeless Tales of Gods and Heroes* (1942; New York: Grand Central Publishing, 1976), 89.

16. Edwin Haviland Miller, *Salem Is My Dwelling Place: A Life of Nathaniel Hawthorne* (Iowa City: University of Iowa Press, 1991), 345.

17. Nathaniel Hawthorne, *A Wonder-Book for Girls and Boys* (New York: Knopf, 1994).

18. Laura Mulvey, *Fetishism and Curiosity* (Bloomington: Indiana University Press, 1996), 59.

19. See Sarah B. Pomeroy, *Goddesses, Whores, Wives, and Slaves: Women in Classical Antiquity* (New York: Schocken, 1975), 4. Pomeroy models what seems at first an unexpected leap but is in fact symptomatic of a patriarchal logic that emerges whenever women are driven by epistemophilia, the desire to know more. "Pandora is comparable to the temptress Eve, and the box she opened may be a metaphor for the carnal knowledge of women, which was a source of evil to men" (4).

20. Stephen Greenblatt, *The Rise and Fall of Adam and Eve* (New York: W. W. Norton, 2017), 126, 131.

21. Revelations 17:4 (King James).

22. Charles Perrault, "Bluebeard," in *Classic Fairy Tales*, 2nd ed., ed. and trans. Maria Tatar (New York: W. W. Norton, 2017), 188–93.

23. These voices are cited by me in *Secrets beyond the Door: The Story of Bluebeard and His Wives* (Princeton, NJ: Princeton University Press, 2004), 20.

24. Beverly Lyon Clark, *Louisa May Alcott: The Contemporary Reviews* (Cambridge: Cambridge University Press, 2004), 247.

25. Louisa May Alcott, *The Journals of Louisa May Alcott*, ed. Joel Myerson and Daniel Shealy (Athens: University of Georgia Press, 1997), 165–66.

26. Louisa May Alcott and Anna Alcott Pratt, *Comic Tragedies, Written by "Jo" and "Meg" and Acted by the "Little Women"* (Boston: Roberts Brothers, 1893), 7.

27. Madeleine B. Stern, *Louisa May Alcott: A Biography* (Boston: Northeastern University Press, 1999), 70.

28. Louisa May Alcott, *The Annotated Little Women*, ed. John Matteson (New York: W. W. Norton, 2015), 182.

29. Alcott, *Annotated Little Women*, 430.

30. Alcott, lxi.

31. Sandra M. Gilbert and Susan Gubar, *The Madwoman in the Attic: The Woman Writer and the Nineteenth-Century Literary Imagination* (New Haven, CT: Yale University Press, 1979), 7.

32. "J. K. Rowling, by the Book," *New York Times*, October 11, 2012. Ursula Le Guin, *Dancing at the Edge of the World: Thoughts on Words, Women, Places* (New York: Grove Press, 1989), 213.

33. Carolyn G. Heilbrun, *Reinventing Womanhood* (New York: W. W. Norton, 1993), 212.

34. Carole Gerson, "'Dragged at Anne's Chariot Wheels': L. M. Montgomery and the Sequels to *Anne of Green Gables*," in *Papers of the Bibliographical Society of Canada* 35, no. 2 (1997): 151.

35. Benjamin Lefebvre, *The L. M. Montgomery Reader*, vol. 2, *A Critical Heritage* (Toronto: University of Toronto Press, 2020), 380.

36. Claudia Durst Johnson, "Discord in Concord," Humanities Commons, https://hcommons.org/deposits/objects/hc:18288/datastreams/CONTENT/content.

37. Mollie Gillin, *The Wheel of Things: A Biography of Lucy Maud Montgomery* (Halifax: Goodread Biography, 1983), 72.

38. Willa Paskin, "The Other Side of Anne of Green Gables," *New York Times*, April 27, 2017.

39. L. M. Montgomery, *Anne of Green Gables* (New York: Penguin, 2017), 35. Quotations that follow are from pages 220, 174, 323, 236, 223, 267.

40. Perry Nodelman, "Progressive Utopia: Or, How to Grow Up without Growing Up," in *Such a Simple Little Tale: Critical Responses to L. M. Montgomery's* Anne of Green Gables, ed., Mavis Reimer (Metuchen, NJ: Scarecrow Press, 1992), 32.

41. Naomi Schor, *Reading in Detail: Aesthetics and the Feminine* (New York: Routledge, 2006), 4.

42. H. W. Mabie, ed., *Fairy Tales Every Child Should Know* (New York: Grosset & Dunlap, 1905), xiv, xv.

43. *Miracle on 34th Street*, dir. George Seaton, 1947.

44. Betty Smith, *A Tree Grows in Brooklyn* (New York: Harper Perennial, 2006), 84. Additional quotations are from pages 234, 6, 390, 166, 492, 493, 489.

45. Anne Frank, *The Diary of a Young Girl: The Definitive Edition*, ed. Otto H. Frank and Mirjam Pressler, trans. Susan Massotty (New York: Bantam, 1997), 18, 21.

46. Frank, *The Diary of a Young Girl*, 247. Additional quotations from pages 68, 53.

47. Philip Roth, *The Ghost Writer* (New York: Vintage, 1979).

48. Katerina Papathanasiou, "Hidden Heroine: Exploring the Story of Anne Frank," *Vale Magazine*, December 27, 2019.

49. Ian Buruma, "The Afterlife of Anne Frank," *New York Review of Books*, February 19, 1998.

50. Francine Prose, *Anne Frank: The Book, the Life, the Afterlife* (New York: Harper Perennial, 2009), 277.

51. Louise Fitzhugh, *Harriet the Spy* (New York: Harper and Row, 1964), 34. Additional quotations are from pages 3, 250, 268, 278.

52. "Moran: 'It's a Dirty Business,'" CNN Access, January 12, 2005.

53. Anita Silvey, *100 Best Books for Children: A Parent's Guide to Making the Right Choices for Your Young Reader, Toddler to Preteen* (New York: Houghton Mifflin, 2005).

54. Richard Rorty, *Contingency, Irony, and Solidarity* (Cambridge: Cambridge University Press, 1989), 141.

55. Rorty borrows that word from Vladimir Nabokov's *Lolita* to signify a lack of caring and empathy.

56. Harper Lee, *To Kill a Mockingbird* (1961; New York: Harper Perennial, 2002), 33, 320.

57. Toni Morrison, *Playing in the Dark: Whiteness and the Literary Imagination* (New York: Vintage, 1992), 52–53.

58. Angie Thomas, *The Hate U Give* (New York: Balzer + Bray, 2017). Quotations are from pages 252, 412, 302, 444.

59. Lucy Feldman, "How TLC's Left Eye Helped Save *The Hate U Give* Author Angie Thomas' Life," *Time*, February 5, 2019.

CHAPTER 5: DETECTIVE WORK

1. Joseph Campbell and Bill Moyers, *The Power of Myth* (New York: Anchor, 1991), 126, 104.

2. Betty Friedan, *The Feminine Mystique*, 50th anniversary ed. (New York: W. W. Norton, 2013).

3. Helen Gurley Brown, *Sex and the Single Girl* (New York: Bernard Geis, 1962).

4. "Helen Gurley Brown, Who Gave 'Single Girl' a Life in Full, Dies at 90," *New York Times*, August 13, 2012.

5. Campbell and Moyers, *The Power of Myth*, 7.

6. For strong arguments about how the series marked a sea change in our cultural understanding of women's sexual identities, see Jennifer Keishin Armstrong, *Sex and the City and Us: How Four Single Women Changed the Way We Think, Live, and Love* (New York: Simon & Schuster, 2018).

7. Joan Didion, "Why I Write," *New York Times*, December 5, 1976.

8. Christian Lorentzen, "Sheila Heti, Ben Lerner, Tao Lin: How 'Auto' Is Autofiction?," *Vulture*, May 11, 2018.

9. Candace Bushnell, *The Carrie Diaries* (New York: HarperCollins, 2010), 25.

10. Victoria Kennedy, "Haunted by the Lady Novelist: Metafictional Anxieties about Women's Writing from *Northanger Abbey* to *The Carrie Diaries*," *Women: A Cultural Review* 30, no. 2 (2019): 202.

11. Bushnell, *The Carrie Diaries*, 297.

12. Tara K. Menon, "What Women Want," Public Books, June 24, 2020.

13. Andrew Forrester, *The Female Detective* (Scottsdale, AZ: Poisoned Pen Press, 2012). As Alexander McCall Smith notes in the foreword to that work: "The female detective uses the apparent marginality of her position to good effect" (vi).

14. As Philippa Gates puts it, "The only female detectives who seem to have avoided [choosing between being a "woman" and working as a detective] are those who are either too old—e.g., spinster Jane Marple and widow Jessica Fletcher—or too young—e.g., teenager Nancy Drew—for romantic relationships and thus elude the complications that arise when career and romance compete." See *Detecting Women: Gender and the Hollywood Detective Film* (Albany: State University of New York Press, 2011), 4.

15. Raymond Chandler, "Bay City Blues," in *Collected Stories* (New York: Everyman's Library, 2002), 831.

16. Carolyn Keene, *The Mystery at Lilac Inn* (New York: Grosset & Dunlap, 1930), 156.

17. Quoted by Karen Plunkett-Powell, *The Nancy Drew Scrapbook: 60 Years of America's Favorite Teenage Sleuth* (New York: St. Martin's Press, 1993), 18.

18. Sandra Day O'Connor and H. Alan Day, *Lazy B: Growing Up on a Cattle Ranch in the American Southwest* (New York: Random House, 2002), 229.

19. Claire Fallon, "Hillary Clinton Basically Wanted to Grow Up to Be Nancy Drew," Huffpost, June 2, 2017.

20. Mary Jo Murphy, "Nancy Drew and the Secret of the 3 Black Robes," *New York Times*, May 30, 2009.

21. Carol Gilligan, *In a Different Voice: Psychological Theory and Women's Development* (Cambridge, MA: Harvard University Press, 1982).

22. Carolyn Keene, *The Sign of the Twisted Candles* (New York: Grosset & Dunlap, 1933), 11.

23. Harriet Adams, Stratemeyer's daughter and owner of the Syndicate after her father's death, urged Mildred Wirt Benson (by then she had married) to make the sleuth less bold and "more sympathetic, kind-hearted, and lovable." See Carole Kismaric and

Marvin Heiferman, *The Mysterious Case of Nancy Drew and the Hardy Boys* (New York: Simon & Schuster, 1998).

24. Deborah L. Siegel, "Nancy Drew as New Girl Wonder: Solving It All for the 1930s," in *Nancy Drew and Company: Culture, Gender, and the Girls' Series*, ed. Sherrie A. Inness (Bowling Green, OH: Bowling Green State University Popular Press, 1997), 179.

25. Nancy Tillman Romalov, "Children's Series Books and the Rhetoric of Guidance: A Historical Overview," in *Rediscovering Nancy Drew* (Iowa City: University of Iowa Press, 1995), 117. See also Gillian M. McCombs, "Nancy Drew Here to Stay: The Challenges to Be Found in the Acquisition and Retention of Early Twentieth Century Children's Series Books in an Academic Library Setting," in *Popular Culture and Acquisitions*, ed. Allen Ellis (New York: Haworth, 1992), 47–58.

26. Franklin K. Mathiews, "Blowing Out the Boy's Brains," *Outlook*, November 18, 1914, 653.

27. Quoted by Esther Green Bierbaum, "Bad Books in Series: Nancy Drew in the Public Library," *The Lion and the Unicorn* 18 (1994): 95.

28. Emelyn E. Gardner and Eloise Ramsey, *A Handbook of Children's Literature: Methods and Materials* (Chicago: Scott Foresman, 1927), 15.

29. Carolyn Keene, *The Clue in the Diary* (New York: Grosset & Dunlap, 1932), 74.

30. Carolyn Keene, *The Hidden Staircase* (New York: Grosset & Dunlap, 1930), 11.

31. Carolyn Keene, *The Secret of the Old Clock* (New York: Grosset & Dunlap, 1930), 1.

32. Keene, *The Secret of the Old Clock*, 135.

33. For more on the Syndicate, see Amy Boesky, "Solving the Crime of Modernity: Nancy Drew in 1930," *Studies in the Novel* 42 (2010): 185–201.

34. Boesky, "Solving the Crime of Modernity," 200.

35. Bierbaum, "Bad Books in Series," 101.

36. Amy Benfer, "Who Was Carolyn Keene?," Salon, October 8, 1999.

37. James D. Keeline, "The Nancy Drew *Myth*ery Stories," in *Nancy Drew and Her Sister Sleuths*, ed. Michael G. Cornelius and Melanie E. Gregg (Jefferson, NC: McFarland, 2008), 23.

38. Keeline, "The Nancy Drew *Myth*ery Stories," 24.

39. Keeline, 25.

40. Anne Scott MacLeod, "Nancy Drew and Her Rivals: No Contest," *Horn Book*, May 1987, July 1987.

41. Renee Montagne, "Nancy Drew: Curious, Independent and Usually Right," NPR, June 23, 2008.

42. Charles Dickens, *Great Expectations*, ed. Edgar Rosenberg (New York: W. W. Norton, 1999), 50, 69.

43. Kathy Mezei, "Spinsters, Surveillance, and Speech: The Case of Miss Marple, Miss Mole, and Miss Jekyll," *Journal of Modern Literature* 30, no. 2 (2007): 103–20.

44. James Brabazon, *Dorothy L. Sayers: A Biography* (New York: Scribner's, 1981), 144.

45. R. A. Knox, ed., "Introduction," in *The Best English Detective Stories of 1928* (London: Faber, 1929).

46. David Frisby, "Walter Benjamin and Detection," *German Politics & Society* 32 (1994): 89–106. See also Martin Edwards, *The Golden Age of Murder: The Mystery of the Writers Who Invented the Modern Detective Story* (New York: HarperCollins, 2015).

47. Edmund Wilson, "Why Do People Read Detective Stories?," *New Yorker*, October

14, 1944; "Mr. Holmes, They Were the Footprints of a Gigantic Hound," *New Yorker*, February 17, 1945; and "Who Cares Who Killed Roger Ackroyd? A Second Report on Detective Fiction," *New Yorker*, June 20, 1945.

48. Dorothy L. Sayers, *Unnatural Death* (1927; New York: Harper Perennial, 2013), 19. Additional quotations are from pp. 29–30.

49. Agatha Christie, *Five Complete Miss Marple Novels* (New York: Chatham River Press, 1980), 292.

50. Agatha Christie, "A Christmas Tragedy," in *The Thirteen Problems* (New York: Signet, 2000), 143.

51. Agatha Christie, *The Mirror Crack'd from Side to Side* (New York: Penguin, 2011), 224.

52. Agatha Christie, *A Pocket Full of Rye* (New York: Penguin, 1954), 108.

53. Agatha Christie, *Nemesis* (New York: HarperCollins, 2011), 9.

54. Christie, *Nemesis*, 27.

55. Arthur Conan Doyle, *Sherlock Holmes: The Complete Novels and Stories* (New York: Random House, 2003), 325.

56. Marion Shaw and Sabine Vanacker, *Reflecting on Miss Marple* (London: Routledge, 1991), 59.

57. Shaw and Vanacker, *Reflecting on Miss Marple*, 59.

58. Mitzi M. Brunsdale, *Icons of Mystery and Crime Detection: From Sleuths to Superheroes*, 2 vols. (Santa Barbara, CA: Greenwood, 2010), I:142.

59. Gates, *Detecting Women*.

60. Raymond Chandler, "The Simple Art of Murder," in *Later Novels and Other Writing* (New York: Literary Classics of the United States, 1995), 992.

61. Carolyn G. Heilbrun, *Writing a Woman's Life* (New York: Ballantine, 1989), 52.

62. Shaw and Vanacker, *Reflecting on Miss Marple*, 6.

63. Heilbrun, *Writing a Woman's Life*, 115.

64. P. D. James, "Introduction," in *The Omnibus P. D. James* (London: Faber and Faber, 1990), viii.

65. Maureen T. Reddy, "Women Detectives," in *The Cambridge Companion to Crime Fiction*, ed. Martin Priestman (Cambridge: Cambridge University Press), 204.

66. Barbara Neely, *Blanche on the Lam* (Leawood, KS: Brash Books, 1992), 15, 61, 83.

67. William Moulton Marston, *The Golden Age of Wonder Woman*, vol. 1, 1941 (Burbank, CA: DC Comics, 2017), 7.

68. William Moulton Marston, *Try Living!* (New York: Thomas Y. Crowell, 1937), 128.

69. "Neglected Amazons to Rule Men in 1,000 Years, Says Psychologist," *Washington Post*, November 11, 1937.

70. Jill Lepore, *The Secret History of Wonder Woman* (New York: Knopf, 2014), 200.

71. All quotations will be from Marston, *The Golden Age of Wonder Woman*, 10, 14.

72. Natalie Haynes, *Pandora's Jar: Women in the Greek Myths* (London: Picador, 2020), 118.

73. William Moulton Marston, "Women: Servants for Civilization," *Tomorrow*, February 1942, 42–45.

74. Lepore, *The Secret History of Wonder Woman*, xi.

75. Kurt F. Mitchell et al., *American Comic Book Chronicles: 1940–1944* (Raleigh, NC: TwoMorrows, 2019), 77.

76. Committee on the Judiciary, "Comic Books and Juvenile Delinquency," H.R. Report

No.   62   (1955),   https://web.archive.org/web/20091027160127/http://www.geocities
.com/Athens/8580/kefauver.html.

77.  Lepore, *The Secret History of Wonder Woman*, 184.

78.  Olive Richard, "Don't Laugh at the Comics," *Family Circle*, October 25, 1940, 10–11.

79.  Lepore, *The Secret History of Wonder Woman*, 209.

CHAPTER 6: TO DOUBLE DUTY BOUND

1.  Joseph Campbell and Bill Moyers, *The Power of Myth* (New York: Doubleday, 1988), 16.

2.  Campbell and Moyers, *The Power of Myth*, 85.

3.  Campbell and Moyers, 15–16.

4.  Lewis Hyde, *Trickster Makes This World: Mischief, Myth, and Art* (New York: North Point Press, 1998), 8. Hyde also acknowledges that the absence of female tricksters can be attributed to the dominantly patriarchal mythologies and religions in his purview.

5.  Paul Radin, *The Trickster: A Study in American Indian Mythology* (New York: Schocken, 1987), 138. Deldon Anne McNeely makes an interesting case for the trickster as an "androgynous archetype, to be thought of as masculine." See *Mercury Rising: Women, Evil, and the Trickster Gods* (Woodstock, CT: Spring Publications, 1996), 9.

6.  In *The Female Trickster: The Mask That Reveals; Post-Jungian and Postmodern Psychological Perspectives on Women in Contemporary Culture* (New York: Routledge, 2014), Ricki Stefanie Tannen makes the point that the term "agency" comes from the Greek word for "potent, convincing, and compelling." Agency, she points out, has a double meaning in the sense of "movement as action and also as being capable of acting on others' behalf" (7).

7.  Stacy L. Smith, Marc Choueiti, and Katherine Pieper, *Inequality in 800 Popular Films: Examining Portrayals of Gender, Race/Ethnicity, LGBT, and Disability from 2007–2015*, report for the Media, Diversity, & Social Change Initiative, University of Southern California–Annenberg, September 2016.

8.  "Facts to Know about Women in Hollywood," Statistics, Women and Hollywood, accessed October 24, 2020.

9.  Joseph Campbell, *Goddesses: Mysteries of the Feminine Divine*, ed. Safron Rossi (Novato, CA: New World Library, 2013), xiv.

10.  Stieg Larsson, *The Girl with the Dragon Tattoo* (New York: Knopf, 2002). Quotations are from pages 346, 213, 362, 32.

11.  The quotes are from Laurie Penny, "Girls, Tattoos and Men Who Hate Women," *New Statesman*, September 5, 2010. Anna Westerståhl Stenport and Cecilia Ovesdotter Alm, "Corporations, the Welfare State, and Covert Misogyny in *The Girl with the Dragon Tattoo*," in *Men Who Hate Women Who Kick Their Asses: Stieg Larsson's Millennium Trilogy in Feminist Perspective*, ed. Donna King and Carrie Lee Smith (Nashville, TN: Vanderbilt University Press, 2012), 157–78. On the issues they raise, see Jaime Weida, "The Dragon Tattoo and the Voyeuristic Reader," in *The Girl with the Dragon Tattoo and Philosophy*, ed. Eric Bronson (Hoboken, NJ: John Wiley, 2012), 28–38.

12.  Larsson, *The Girl with the Dragon Tattoo*, 31–32, 36.

13.  Helena Bassil-Morozow describes Lisbeth as an "uber-nerd" who feeds off the "mer-

curial qualities of the internet" in *The Trickster in Contemporary Film* (London: Routledge, 2012), 80. Bassil-Morozow further describes tricksters as "foolish, rebellious, asocial and anti-social, inconsistent, outrageous and self-contradictory" (5).

14. Norman O. Brown, *Hermes the Thief: The Evolution of a Myth* (Madison: University of Wisconsin Press, 1947).

15. Larsson, *The Girl with the Dragon Tattoo*, 156, 164.

16. Eva Gedin, "Working with Stieg Larsson," in *On Stieg Larsson*, translated by Laurie Thompson (New York: Knopf, 2010). Gedin describes Lisbeth as "a special character, a type rarely encountered in previous crime fiction series" (11).

17. Karen Klitgaard Povlsen and Anne Marit Waade discuss the parallels between Pippi Longstocking and Lisbeth Salander, as well as between Lindgren's Kalle Blomkvist and Larsson's Mikael Blomkvist. See *"The Girl with the Dragon Tattoo*: Adapting Embodied Gender from Novel to Movie in Stieg Larsson's Crime Fiction." Salander's lawyer is named Annika, after one of the two sibling neighbors who befriend Pippi. *P.O.V.: A Danish Journal of Film Studies* 28 (December 2009), http://pov.imv.au.dk/Issue_28/section_2/artc7A.html.

18. Astrid Lindgren, *Pippi Longstocking* (New York: Puffin, 2005), 110.

19. Astrid Lindgren, "Never Violence!," *Swedish Book Review*, 2007, https://web.archive.org/web/20201108100547/https://www.swedishbookreview.com/article-2007-2-never-violence.asp.

20. Laura Briggs and Jodi I. Kelber-Kaye, " 'There Is No Unauthorized Breeding in Jurassic Park': Gender and the Use of Genetics," *NWSA Journal* 12, no. 3 (2000): 92–113.

21. Paul Bullock, "Jurassic Park: 10 Things You Might Have Missed," Den of Geek, June 12, 2019.

22. Wesley Morris, "Does 'Three Billboards' Say Anything about America? Well . . . ," *New York Times*, January 18, 2018.

23. Gillian Flynn, *Gone Girl* (New York: Crown, 2012), 393.

24. See Catherine Orenstein, *Little Red Riding Hood Uncloaked: Sex, Morality, and the Evolution of a Fairy Tale* (New York: Basic Books, 2003), 219–33.

25. Kim Snowden, "Fairy Tale Film in the Classroom: Feminist Cultural Pedagogy, Angela Carter, and Neil Jordan's *The Company of Wolves*," in *Fairy Tale Films: Visions of Ambiguity*, ed. Pauline Greenhill and Sidney Eve Matrix (Logan: Utah State University Press, 2010), 157–77.

26. John Hiscock, "Joe Wright Interview on Hanna," *Telegraph*, April 22, 2011.

27. Created in 1985 by American cartoonist Alison Bechdel, the test asks three questions: (1) Are there at least two women in the film who have names? (2) Do those women talk to each other? (3) Do they talk to each other about something besides men?

28. Amber Pualani Hodge,"The Medievalisms of Disney's Moana (2016): Narrative Colonization from Victorian England to Contemporary America," in "Islands and Film," special issue, *Post Script: Essays in Film and the Humanities* 37, no. 2–3 (2018): 80–95.

29. Suzanne Collins, *The Hunger Games* (New York: Scholastic, 2008), 8. Additional quotations are from pages 30, 127, 43, 35, 29.

30. Rick Margolis, "The Last Battle: With 'Mockingjay' on Its Way, Suzanne Collins Weighs In on Katniss and the Capitol," *School Library Journal*, 56 (2010): 21–24.

31. Katha Pollitt, "*The Hunger Games'* Feral Feminism," *Nation*, April 23, 2012.

32. Maria Tatar, "Philip Pullman's Twice-Told Tales," *New Yorker*, November 21, 2012.

33. Philip Pullman, *The Golden Compass* (New York: Dell Yearling, 2001), 150.

34. "Questions and Answers," Philip Pullman, http://www.philip-pullman.com/qas?searchtext=&page=6.

35. "Questions and Answers."

36. Tannen, *The Female Trickster*, 26.

37. C. W. Spinks focuses on the world-making qualities of tricksters, emphasizing their capacity for making and undoing signs: "Contradiction, irony, deception, duplicity, inversion, reversal, oxymoron, paradox: These are the tool kit of negation, ambivalence, and ambiguity that Trickster uses to make and remake culture." See "Trickster and Duality," in *Trickster and Ambivalence: Dance of Differentiation* (Madison, WI: Atwood, 2001), 14.

38. Anna Westerståhl Stenport and Cecilia Ovesdotter Alm, "Corporations, Crime, and Gender Construction in Stieg Larsson's *The Girl with the Dragon Tattoo*," *Scandinavian Studies* 81, no. 2 (June 2009): 171.

39. Donald Dewey, "The Man with the Dragon Tattoo," *Scandinavian Review* 97 (2010): 78–83.

40. David Geherin, *The Dragon Tattoo and Its Long Tail: The New Wave of European Crime Fiction in America* (Jefferson, NC: McFarland, 2012), 22.

41. As Tamar Jeffers McDonald points out, this "futuristic retelling" of the Bluebeard tale reveals that neither the heroine nor the villain of the story is "inevitably associated with specific genders." See her "Blueprints from Bluebeard," in *Gothic Heroines on Screen: Representation, Interpretation, and Feminist Inquiry*, ed. Tamar Jeffers McDonald and Frances A. Kamm (New York: Routledge, 2019), 51.

42. Wesley Morris, "Jordan Peele's X-Ray Vision," *New York Times*, December 20, 2017.

EPILOGUE: LIFT-OFF

1. *Apollodorus'* Library *and Hyginus'* Fabulae, trans. R. Scott Smith and Stephen M. Trzaskoma (Indianapolis: Hackett, 2007), 128.

2. Rebecca Solnit, *Men Explain Things to Me* (Chicago: Haymarket Books, 2014), 116–17.

3. Natalie Haynes, *Pandora's Jar: Women in the Greek Myths* (London: Picador, 2020), 2.

4. Hélène Cixous, "The Laugh of the Medusa," *Signs* 1 (1976): 875–93.

5. Two recent studies of Helen reflect in their subtitles the complexities in our new understanding of Helen and her role in the Trojan War. See Ruby Blondell, *Helen of Troy: Beauty, Myth, Devastation* (Oxford: Oxford University Press, 2013) and Bettany Hughes, *Helen of Troy: Goddess, Princess, Whore* (New York: Knopf, 2005).

6. Chimamanda Ngozi Adichie, "The Danger of a Single Story," presented July 2009 at TEDGlobal 2009, https://www.ted.com/talks/chimamanda_ngozi_adichie_the_danger_of_a_single_story/transcript?language=en.

7. See Teresa Mangum, "Dickens and the Female Terrorist: The Long Shadow of Madame Defarge," *Nineteenth-Century Contexts* 31 (2009): 143–60.

8. Diane Purkiss, *The Witch in History* (New York: Routledge, 1996), 48.

9. Jens Andersen, *Astrid Lindgren: The Woman behind Pippi Longstocking*, trans. Caroline Waight (New Haven, CT: Yale University Press, 2018), 129.

10. See especially Kathryn J. Atwood, *Women Heroes of World War I: 16 Remarkable Resisters, Soldiers, Spies, and Medics* (Chicago: Chicago Review Press, 2016).

11.  Atwood, *Women Heroes of World War I*, 121.

12.  Alexis S. Troubetzkoy, *A Brief History of the Crimean War* (London: Robinson, 2006), 208.

13.  *Cassandra: Florence Nightingale's Angry Outcry against the Forced Idleness of Women*, ed. Myra Stark (New York: Feminist Press, 1979), 29.

14.  Alice Marble, "Clara Barton," Wonder Women of History, DC Comics, 1942.

15.  H. Judson, *Edith Cavell* (New York: Macmillan, 1941), 236.

16.  *The New York Times Current History: The European War, 1917* (New York: Kessinger, 2010), 454.

17.  Thomas Szasz, *The Manufacture of Madness* (New York: Harper & Row, 1970), 55, 91.

# INDEX

# ABOUT THE AUTHOR

Maria Tatar is the John L. Loeb Research Professor of Germanic Languages and Literatures and of Folklore and Mythology at Harvard University. She is also a senior fellow at Harvard's Society of Fellows. The author of many books in the fields of folklore, German studies, and children's literature, she has also written for the *New York Times*, *The New Yorker*, the *New Republic*, and *Slate*, and she is a frequent guest on NPR and the BBC. She received the NAACP's Image Award for Outstanding Literary Work—Fiction in 2018 and is the recipient of fellowships from the National Endowment for the Humanities, the Guggenheim Foundation, and the Radcliffe Institute for Advanced Studies.